PENGUIN BUSINESS

CONVERSATIONS WITH THE CAREER DOCTOR

Saundarya Rajesh is an award-winning social entrepreneur, a sought-after DEI (diversity, equity and inclusion) strategist and a torchbearer for women in workplaces. As the founder–president of Avtar, India's top DEI consulting firm, she is a trusted adviser for hundreds of organizations and has facilitated the creation of inclusive workplaces for nearly 10 lakh women. One of the earliest proponents of gender diversity in the workplace at a time when women's careers were viewed as unnecessary, Saundarya firmly believes that women's workforce participation can promote national economic prosperity. A pioneer of the idea of second career paths for women and the concept of career intentionality, an innovative success tool for women, she has made it possible for thousands of women to re-enter the workplace after a break and flourish in it.

Saundarya has demystified DEI for a remarkable range of audiences including women, policymakers, CEOs, HR leaders and DEI enthusiasts, through her training sessions and speeches across various platforms. Her stellar contribution in the space of women's workforce participation has won her several awards including the Ministry of Women and Child Development's #100 Women Achiever Award (2016), NITI Aayog's Women Transforming India Award (2016) and the Chevening Global Changemaker Award (2019).

Her first book, *The 99 Day Diversity Challenge* (2018), is a unique and practical DEI guide for business leaders that continues to be a bestseller.

ADVANCE PRAISE FOR THE BOOK

'I believe that if we ever are to become a developed country, the one thing we will need to increase is women's participation in the workforce, and there is no one that I know who has done as much towards this cause as Saundarya, and no one better qualified than her to write a hands-on guidebook for women to flourish in their careers, which is what *Conversations with the Career Doctor* is. This book provides sound advice and practical tools for Indian women to smoothly manage family and work and is written in a simple and emphatic manner. You can open this book on any page and find something meaningful that will stay with you'—Aditya Mittal, chief human resources officer (CHRO), Citi (South Asia)

'With practical tips and strategic tools like "intentional career pathing" to help women with the professional problems they face, *Conversations with the Career Doctor* is relevant, much needed, and is the friend and adviser we all need! Having taken a career break myself, I only wish I had something like this to support me when I re-entered the workforce. A must-add to any Indian woman's book collection, irrespective of whether she is working or not'—Aparna Rao, country head and board member, Cargill Business Services India

'*Conversations with the Career Doctor* is an eye-opening read! As a leader, I witness the multifaceted challenges that women encounter in their quest for a successful career. This book offers invaluable insights to women on how they can confront various difficulties and move forward in their professional paths. A must-read not only for women but also any business leader committed to diversity and inclusion, and keen on driving innovation and staying ahead in today's global market'—Bharat Gala, chief executive officer, Global Technology Centre, AtkinsRéalis

'Saundarya's writing is as insightful, incisive, crisp and as in your face as her talking. Her deep understanding of working women and their multiple challenges comes so much alive as she hits the ground running with Ambuja's story in her first chapter. The book not only inspires but also comes with many to-do things that are concrete steps for improving women's situation significantly'—C.K. Venkataraman, managing director, Titan

'*Conversations with the Career Doctor* is a testament to Saundarya's dedication to empowering women. Saundarya dips into her rich experience and shares powerful narratives that reveal the intricate challenges women face in the workplace and at home, and through true stories and practical wisdom, she crafts a clear road map for women to overcome obstacles and thrive in their careers. This book is the superhero suit that every woman needs, and I recommend it to all women aspiring to pursue a thriving career'—Dhanya Rajeswaran, global vice president and country managing director (India), Fluence

'Saundarya Rajesh draws attention to the ground realities that deter women from realizing their dreams and takes us through the journey of the Indian woman professional in her inimitable style, which is peppered with relatable situations and subtle humour. She makes it real by sharing her own experiences, which brings a lot of authenticity and conviction to the book. Among the various valuable life hacks that she shares, tips for women to overcome guilt and leverage power are the icing on the cake! Engaging, exhorting, empowering and inspiring, Conversations with the Career Doctor is a book you don't want to miss, and you will thank yourself immensely for reading it'—Geetha Ramamoorthi, managing director, KBR India

'Real-life stories and examples are brought to life beautifully in this book, and sometimes you wonder if it is yourself that you are reading about. This is a must-read for all women, in whatever career stage they may be in—women in leadership or women just trying to understand the road ahead for them—and everyone in between. The challenges that women face are analysed in a very comprehensive fashion, which I found extremely valuable. I am sure every woman will find her own mantra to "thrive" as she reads this compelling book'—Irani Srivastava Roy, CHRO, Signify (India subcontinent)

'Conversations with the Career Doctor is a very easy and illustrative read and an amazing book for women who, unfortunately, are still largely trapped in a biased work setting. It is also a great read for men who need to be agents of change. Saundarya has done justice to the pioneering work of her organization in the field of women's workforce participation. Sometimes, it is hard to capture all the nuances of your groundbreaking work in a book, but Saundarya manages it beautifully, offering deep insights to readers through her organization's research, personal experiences and interviews with other women. The in-depth examination of various topics is really striking—a classic example of this is the chapter on guilt. Kudos to her, and here's wishing her continued success in her crusade to boost women's financial independence'—Pavan Kumar Mocherla, executive vice president, Becton Dickinson (Greater Asia)

'Ensuring women thrive and win at work is important—not just for women but for our workplaces and our society too. As any woman will tell you, it's not easy. Saundarya's Conversations with the Career Doctor is a book that every career woman will find useful—many will wish that it was written earlier. It's got everything a woman always wanted to know about managing her career but did not know whom to ask. I am sending a copy to my newborn granddaughter's mother right away!'—Prakash Iyer, author and former CEO, Kimberly-Clark

'Saundarya has distilled more than two decades of her work at Avtar and Project Puthri, and her deep understanding of women at work in this easy-to-read treatise that is a tapestry of touching anecdotes of struggles of working women. With practical and easy-to-follow tips to overcome these challenges, based on sound theories and concepts, this book is a must-read for women at any stage of their career but equally valuable for men (husbands, managers, CEOs and board members) to get a perspective they never would otherwise have. I am convinced that this book will help millions of women to thrive and win at work'—Raman Ramachandran, director and dean, K.J. Somaiya Institute of Management

'Since 2000, Saundarya Rajesh has worked tirelessly to build women's careers through various initiatives—for example, by building career intentionality in them, helping them navigate guilt, assisting them in getting back into the workforce and so on. And now, she shares her extensive expertise and experience in her new book, *Conversations with the Career Doctor*, which is a comprehensive manual for women. As someone who has partnered with Saundarya, it has been a privilege to have been a part of her journey and it is a pleasure to see it laid out so elegantly in this new book of hers!'—Sandhya Vasudevan, distinguished professor, independent director, strategic adviser to start-ups, and former managing director, Thomson Reuters India and Deutsche Bank

'*Conversations with the Career Doctor* is a thoughtfully crafted, lucid guide for women professionals seeking success, growth and fulfilment in their careers. Saundarya's storytelling weaves a captivating narrative, highlighting the boundless potential within every Indian woman. Her stories resonate beyond the professional sphere, offering relatable experiences for those balancing work and home responsibilities, managing family guilt, and trying to align career goals with personal values. Readers are sure to find multiple stories that resonate deeply and take away valuable nuggets. This book is a true resource for women navigating their professional and personal paths, providing both inspiration and practical guidance'— Sheenam Ohrie, managing director, Broadridge Financial Solutions (India)

'Saundarya has been involved in facilitating women's career growth for years now. In our society, where problems and biases are deep-rooted, it is not always easy to maintain your dedication to your mission, but Saundarya has been the light for Indian women even in the darkest moments. She brings her wealth of knowledge in the space of women's workforce participation to this amazing book, *Conversations with the Career Doctor*, which is an A–Z guide for women to flourish at work and the beacon of hope that we all need'—Sonal Jain, global CHRO, EPL Limited

'*Conversations with the Career Doctor* is a wonderful read with such relatable stories but at the same time packed with very helpful tips. I am sure women reading this book will experience a sense of reassurance and optimism when they realize that the challenges they face are not unique and that these challenges can be overcome by following a few simple steps. The practical tips to secure support at home and work, manage home and family smoothly, handle workplace bias and more, which form the crux of the book, will be valuable. Kudos to Saundarya, who has shared her extensive expertise in the book'—Swati Rustagi, board member, National Human Resource Development Network (NHRDN)

'Saundarya eloquently navigates the complex landscape of women's lives in India, shedding light on the everyday challenges they face at work and in society. She debunks myths surrounding women's careers and meticulously explores topics such as women's mental well-being at work, challenges navigating the intricate balance between home and work, gender bias at work and complexities of superwoman syndrome in this groundbreaking book, which I believe is a beacon of empowerment for women. *Conversations with the Career Doctor* is also a must-read for anyone committed to fostering diversity and inclusion in the workplace'— Thirukkumaran Nagarajan, vice president, HR head, IBM (India/South Asia)

CONVERSATIONS WITH THE
CAREER DOCTOR

Women Thriving and Winning at Work

SAUNDARYA RAJESH

**PENGUIN
BUSINESS**

An imprint of Penguin Random House

PENGUIN BUSINESS

Penguin Business is an imprint of the Penguin Random House group of companies
whose addresses can be found at global.penguinrandomhouse.com

Published by Penguin Random House India Pvt. Ltd
4th Floor, Capital Tower 1, MG Road,
Gurugram 122 002, Haryana, India

First published in Penguin Business by Penguin Random House India 2024

10 9 8 7 6 5 4 3 2 1

The views and opinions expressed in this book are the author's own and the
facts are as reported by her which have been verified to the extent possible,
and the publishers are not in any way liable for the same.

ISBN 9780143466918

Typeset in Adobe Garamond Pro by Manipal Technologies Limited, Manipal

www.penguin.co.in

This book is dedicated to you—the amazing Indian woman. Whether you are working, earning, steering through a break, trying to ace an interview, hoping to create an identity or simply a happy moment, making a profound statement or just making it through the day, do remember: you are awesome! This is for you to find that job, thrive at it and win the gorgeous game of life!

Contents

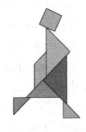

Introduction

The Bus Ride to Gender Inclusion!

We were a bus full of hundred women—actually, two buses with fifty in each bus—from every part of the country. It was a beautiful melee of saris, lehengas, Patiala suits, pantsuits and jeans—a colourful and vibrant microcosm of India's women population, of varying ages, hues and mother tongues, depicting our country's gorgeous diversity. We were a noisy, loud and excited bunch—laughing, joking, recounting memories and each thrilled to be on that bus. We were happy for ourselves and for each other. No one could have guessed that we had all met just a few minutes ago. Or that our journey was only a couple of kilometres long. That chilly January morning in Delhi will forever be etched in our memories. We were headed to a destination that we were in complete awe of. We were the #100 Women Achievers, selected by the Government of India's Ministry for Women and Child Development for our work in the space of empowering other women in 2016. We were going for lunch with none other than the (late) Hon'ble President of India, Pranab Mukherjee. Yes, we were en route to Rashtrapati Bhavan.

While that bus journey began at 11 a.m. on 22 January 2016, my own journey of being an observer and later a repairer of women's careers began two decades before that, sometime in June 1996. I sat before an interview panel of academicians who were about to carve an entirely unexpected future for me. It was a large, dimly lit room of the principal of a college in Chennai, where my curriculum vitae (CV) was perused by four highly respected doyens of education. They were trying to decide if the eager, young yet serious twenty-eight-year-old woman, keen on proving her credentials for a job in which she had no experience, would actually fit into their start-up team. It was then, as an MBA and MA (English Literature) graduate with three years of work experience followed by three years of a career break, that I began the journey of understanding the complex medley that is the identity of an Indian woman professional (IWP).

Teaching was not my first choice, but it was the only one that I believed—at that time—would offer me a good assortment of all the happy chemicals needed to lead a purposeful life. I was an IWP myself, just attempting, at that time, to re-enter a career. But I realized that companies did not want to give women careers; they just wanted to give them jobs. Careers are long-term prospects where both the professional and the employer have to commit to a partnership, much like a marriage. It involves accepting the other person, warts and all, for the long haul. Jobs, on the other hand, don't call for that kind of commitment on either side.

Perhaps they were right; women are probably better off pursuing just jobs. Given the loaded inequities in the ecosystem, which is charged with social, familial and economic biases, perhaps women just need to stay employed, make money, achieve financial security and keep moving. Especially since the whole set-up seemed to be focused on making the woman irrelevant in the scheme of things. She could be educated, taught values and shown how to do things, but somehow her place in the overall fabric was vitiated. She could be urban or rural; live in Mumbai, Chennai or Ranchi; be a banker, doctor, teacher, consultant or manager; be married or unmarried; have no children or three children. No matter her situation or circumstances, she, the IWP, the hero of this book, always seemed to be working with weights around her ankles.

India ranks among the lower countries when it comes to women's participation in the workforce, as per research by ILO[1] and other reputed organizations.[2] Despite considerable progress towards gender equality in the last few decades, study after study shows that Indian women still don't have it easy—both at work and at home. The United Nations International Children's Emergency Fund (UNICEF) reports that girls spend 40 per cent more time on household chores than boys.[3] Data from the World Bank and ILO reveals that the female labour force participation rate for 2022 was just about 24 per cent in our country.[4] And when women do not work formally, everyone ends up losing something. The government loses a significant income generator. Corporations lose great talent. And the Indian woman loses both her identity and her economic self-sufficiency.

Research conducted by Avtar over the years indicates that every industry presents its own set of challenges for women.

- Women in the information technology and IT-enabled services (IT–ITeS) sector rarely have the opportunity to fully deploy their skills because of inherent gender bias.
- When it comes to women in the banking, financial services and insurance (BFSI) sector, upskilling or flexible working

are not encouraged, both of which are critical for women to thrive in the workplace.

- Women in the telecom and fast-moving consumer goods (FMCG) sectors travel in rough conditions to remote corners of the country where hygiene and safety are grave concerns. The ultra-competitive and unsupportive work environment is a big hurdle too.

- When it comes to manufacturing, since there are so few women in influential roles, flexibility is not even on the radar for these companies. And with no role models, mentors or sponsors, women in manufacturing are left to wrestle with a host of challenges on their own.

- The consulting domain, which is highly competitive and fast-paced, causes rapid burnout in women because engaging in high-revenue client projects often makes work–life integration unfeasible.

Clearly, no industry is devoid of challenges for women, but we must acknowledge that along with these external blights, women self-sabotage their careers too. There are many ways we do this. For instance, I find that a lot of women are addicted to perfection; they always want their work to be exemplary and this pursuit of faultlessness can result in high stress, create a fear of failure and, more significantly, make them inflexible and less creative, certainly not a characteristic that bodes well for success.

Another common problem that women face is our inability to manage our emotions well. We realized this during our in-depth 2015 Viewport study on the career intentionality of men and women, where we explored extensively the various reasons for the success and non-fulfilment of career pursuits of men and women.[5] The study which also included many focused group discussions

(FGDs) showed us that women often engage in catastrophizing—that is, we imagine that a situation is much worse than it is. For example, I've come across women who fear that a change in leadership is going to ruin their career; I've seen women obsessively fret over a single minor work-related mistake and I've met women who've quit their jobs after a single failure. Many women fully surrender to self-doubt and believe that luck and others' goodwill have gotten them to where they are—imposter syndrome affects most women at some point in their careers. And when things go wrong, many women tend to hold on to a victim narrative, blaming others and lacking agency.

Along with these internal struggles with emotional self-regulation, women also tend to be less proactive when it comes to engaging with external partners for support. For instance, most women quit their careers because of shaky support systems at home. A woman finds it hard to ask for help or outsource childcare to others.

When it comes to networking, women network far less than men and prefer networking only upstream, while men network across ranks, which has multiple benefits, including access to fresh perspectives and allies who can possibly advocate for your development in the future. However, because of a weak grasp of how the work world works, women do not optimize these channels of support.

In essence, women score lower on career intentionality compared to men and hardly ever reflect on their future career trajectory. All of this results in India having a paltry 24 per cent women's workforce participation. Why is this a bigger problem than it appears? Let's do some quick math. Given India's population of 1.4 billion, of which 49 per cent are women, we are talking about approximately 686 million women, of which 35 per cent live in urban and semi-urban towns and cities. This is about 250 million women, 62 per cent of whom fall into the working-age category. That is 150 million women, of whom a mere 24 per cent actually pursue economically productive careers. (I am not counting household, unpaid work, even if it is quantified and an economic value assigned, given that this notional money does not make the woman a taxpayer or potential taxpayer.) As such, a mere 27 million women out of a population of 1.4 billion are urban, working and earning members of society. And the gloomier truth is that while women joining the workforce is low, Indian women quit in even larger ratios.

And that was true for me, too. I, myself, dropped out of the workforce in favour of home and childcare. All I had were three short years of a very fulfilling career for which I was selected from my B-school campus by Citibank, one of the most cherished employers at the time. When I received my offer letter from Citi, I was giddy with happiness—for a freshly minted MBA, the money was unheard of! The job was fantastic too: cool, cutting-edge work, introducing credit cards, managing merchant services and handling global interchange processes that involved selling, communicating and influencing. What's more, it was performed from the swanky sixth-floor office of Chennai's Shakti Towers, with thick carpets into whose abundant fibres you could actually lose a pen, and glassed walls that showed the River Cooum prettily flowing nearby after filtering out the unpleasant odour.

But outside, without the identity of a paying job and the money and security that came with it, I understood the meaning of being a secondary citizen—one who was relegated to that place due to a variety of different historical and geopolitical reasons. I began looking for a job in a company that was progressive and flexible, one that respected what I had done before the break and offered me an opportunity to recreate myself. Such a company, I understood, was mythical at that time. Over the next few years, three to be exact, I continued my search while adding a second post-graduate degree in English Literature (which was my first love!) and also clearing the University Grant Commission's (UGC) National Eligibility Test for a lectureship in English.

That brought me face-to-face with the interview panel in 1996 at MOP Vaishnav College for Women in Chennai. I had applied for the job of a lecturer in English, but Jayshree Suresh, dean of the business administration department and assistant principal, looked at my resume and appointed me as guest faculty for sales and marketing, with the additional responsibility of grooming and preparing the young girls to get placed. That decision by Jayshree ma'am ensured that serendipitously, even as I was part of the problem of poor percentage of women's employment (having dropped out of a well-paying job myself), I became part of the solution.

Over the next three decades, I started Avtar and worked with several thousand women—training them, helping them upskill and counselling them—leading to over 1,00,000 women re-entering the workplace (until 2021). Our training programmes, diagnostics, diversity audits, corporate goodness sessions and mind-shaping conversations with tens of thousands of leaders have resulted in a remarkable increase in women's representation within the companies we advise, with numbers jumping by over 4,00,000. My team at Avtar—senior leaders Umasanker Kandaswamy, Karthik Ekambaram, Priya Dayabaran, Roy Vijay, Eswar Bala, Anand Vishwanathan, Anju G. Parvathy, Anumitha Sharma, Devi Anindya, Divya Ramesh, Janani Sampath, Lakshmi Vijaykumar, Latha Narasimhan, Mohammed Imran, Murugeshwari, Nandini Murali, Rashmi Ravindran, Shankari

Nandi, Sridevi Bharadwaj, Sumona Chetia, Swetha Lakshmi, Usha Pillai and Veena Mukund—and the entire team of over 120 of us who believe in the potential of women and other underrepresented talents in the Indian workplace, have created one of the most comprehensive social efforts that ensure that every individual, notwithstanding their identity, can take their place in the Indian corporate arena.

A few years ago, I was in a discussion with a large multinational company's leadership team. The CEO (of German origin) was fascinated with our work and by how much a small, understated company like Avtar, with unlimited determination, could achieve. The senior team consisted of many doctors with backgrounds in scientific research and medical care who were part of the discussion. As they asked more and more questions about our work and the very pragmatic solutions that we had created, the CEO suddenly mentioned, 'We have many doctors here, but you are the Career Doctor! You have healed many careers, especially those of women and ensured their good health!'

The name 'Career Doctor' stuck and became a focal point for our work. That generous compliment brought to mind the countless women who have been part of Avtar's journey—my journey. Each of these women—early career, mid-career, matured leaders, from various parts of India and around the world, women who have created amazing lives for themselves, women who have faced adversity of many kinds, with challenges that one can only imagine, women who have fought battles of different hues and tenors, who have shaped their careers like a phoenix from burnt embers—they are the true career doctors. They have healed their thoughts and approaches, corrected their habits and practices and also transformed people around them. They have taken what has been given to them—a motley set of backgrounds, skills, beliefs and life events—and shaped inspiring lives. Much like the brilliant Tangram woman who adorns the cover page of this book, the Indian woman professional works with those random parts of her identity and brings them to a whole. She ungroups and regroups each time, is different at different stages in her life, and different at different points of time in her day. She is at once a working executive, a mother, a partner, a household manager, a leader and a rebel. She is today a carefree spirit, swaying to the music of unheard songs and tomorrow a savant, seeking spiritual progress. Even as the Tangram's array of vibrant colours come together to form diverse identities, our Indian women too, emerging from varied backgrounds, with varied lived experiences and dealing with varied challenges, align in their exceptional ability to empathize, adapt, collaborate, persevere, bounce back and win. They may not all be well-known, famous or headline creators—they are simple, unsung women who are puzzles for those who don't take the effort to understand them. They form the fulcrum of India's women in the workforce. They are our inspiring career doctors.

This book is an unabashed ode to some incredible women who have traversed my life. As I share twenty-six stories (no particular explanation for why it is twenty-six, except that many of us at Avtar share that date of birth!) of how the IWP has cracked many career problems (and even life challenges), I realize that her resolutions are not just managed at work—they are managed in her mind, with a sense of intentionality to emerge successful at every crossroad.

I invite you to join the journey of the many women, as well as men, who have shared their solutions in the pages of this book. They are the real career doctors and in their stories, you may recognize your own and become a career doctor for yourself and others in your life.

Note: Throughout this book, there are hundreds of women whose stories find a place. They are women whom we have worked with, counselled and placed in jobs. Some stories and identities are the fusion of more than one woman. In order to maintain their confidentiality, I have chosen to use fictitious first names. Also featured in this book are women whose identities have been retained and shared as is, with their consent and willingness. And for them, I have used both first name and last name.

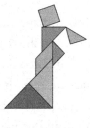

1

Women's Careers—Is That Even a Thing?

Ambuja is darting around the kitchen, chopping, mixing and juicing. She is cooking in a rush, simultaneously making breakfast, lunch and snacks for the five members of her family. Masala chai is brewing in a large pan, to be ladled out to people as and when they ask for it. She remembers that the washing machine needs to be switched on if the washed clothes are to be hung out to dry in the next thirty minutes and she runs to the service area. Her son, Sonu, is playing in the yard and Ambuja's eyes dart to the clock—it is almost 8 a.m. and she must get him ready for school. The school van will shortly arrive and if Sonu is late, the van driver (and the other parents) will give her an earful in person *and* on the Mommy WhatsApp group. Her parents-in-law are sitting on the veranda, their calmness in striking contrast to Ambu's frenzy. They are variously reading a newspaper and stringing some flowers.

She is particularly in a hurry today because she plans to attend a job interview. After a five-year break, Ambu, who used to be a programmer for a leading IT product company, is planning to return to work. Securing the acceptance of all her family members, she has spruced up her CV, spoken to a few former colleagues to understand the latest trends and applied to several job postings. One company has responded and she is thrilled to stand a chance. She has planned her outfit, requested the local auto*wallah* to pick her up at 9 a.m. and also arranged for her friend to manage Sonu after school. She's almost done preparing lunch, as she woke up at 5 a.m. to ensure that there would be no compromise with regard to her family's lunch during her absence. She is now filling a thermos with tea for her father-in-law's mid-morning cup and the fruits are washed and cut for her mother-in-law.

'Is my breakfast ready?' asks Dev, her husband, as he peeps into the kitchen, his eyes sweeping over the maze of vessels, semi-cooked dishes and vegetable peels overflowing the counters. He has promised to clean up the kitchen after she leaves and seems to be assessing the extent of the work. 'One second,' says Ambu, as she piles the poha she has made onto a plate and begins chopping onions to layer over them. She could have avoided the onions today, but then poha itself was considered a 'lazy' breakfast and if she cut corners even with this, she would have an argument to tackle. As she hands over the plate, she hears Sonu wailing. She rushes out to find that Sonu has hurt his elbow on the corner of the table and, in the process, spilled his glass of milk onto his uniform. There is no time to chastise him today, she tells herself, and she runs to the cupboard to fetch another pair of clothes. Hearing the commotion, her father-in-law walks in and begins calming Sonu.

As Dev emerges in his dish-washing apron with a pan and scrubber in his hand and fusses around Sonu, Ambu's mother-in-law leaves the half-finished string of flowers and proceeds to assist in getting the little boy into the new uniform. As she starts feeding him, Ambu's father-in-law also joins him at the breakfast table. Ambu begins serving him the poha, along with a mint chutney and pickle. The school van has arrived. The driver honks and then honks again, impatiently, registering the added minutes. Ambu sweeps up Sonu along with his bag and hands him into the extended arms of the van conductor, who shuts the door with an extra loud thud. Ambu then recognizes the rumble of hunger in her own stomach and realizes that she has not had anything to eat or drink since she woke up. Quickly having a few spoonfuls of the poha, which she downs with a glass of buttermilk, Ambu hurries to the bedroom to change when she overhears snatches of a conversation. 'Such unwanted stress on the whole family.' 'What is the need for her to work? Isn't Dev earning enough already? It is not as if we are poor.' 'We all rushed around and finished things today but is this what we have to do every day?' 'I thought after Sonu's birth, she would become a housewife.' 'Educating girls these days is a challenge—they become obsessed with their careers.' 'I am unable to understand this concept of a career for women. Who is putting these thoughts in her head? This poor fellow has to wash dishes now.' 'In our days, women would be the pillar of the family, helping everyone—today, everything is upside down, everyone has to help her.' 'Women's careers—is that even a thing?'

Ambu sits down on the bed, her heart heavy with sadness. 'Women's careers—is that even a thing?' she reflects.

I refer to this situation as the 'entoptic phenomenon' of women's issues. Have you noticed tiny, squiggly, floating substances when you look at the blue sky or bright light? The visual experience resulting from the interaction of light with your retina causes the floating spots and is termed the entoptic phenomenon. Those images are created internally; they are not external objects. They exist only for you. And what I see is different from what you see. Even if you and I stood in the exact same position and looked at the light from the very same angle, the way light is processed within my retina is different from how you see it. My squiggly figures are different from yours. In the exact same way, the problems that a woman like Ambu—educated, well-informed, possessing the relevant skills, yet unable to carve a space for herself—perceives in her career are entoptic and unique to her. India's history, societal views, family values, the woman's own experience, the point of time in India's history and the economic development that she finds herself in—all of these determine the entoptic career she witnesses. You or I will not be able to see the same thing. Her career is indeed a 'thing' and this book attempts to see how her career ailments can be resolved.

Since the advent of liberalization and privatization in the early 1990s, India has witnessed sweeping changes in its demographic composition. From being an agrarian economy, India slowly metamorphosed into an IT-led services economy, fuelled by the enormous increase in engineering, management and computer science institutions, which produced a massive number of skilled workers, both men and women. During the following decades, from 1990 to 2023, we saw many transformations in India that are typical of a developing economy—the number of metropolitan cities exploded, urban infrastructure became enhanced, and the Indian consumer became empowered to buy the best of global products while companies from around the world entered India to set up shop.

Hand-in-hand with this rapid economic growth, we also observed many other sociological changes, such as women's fertility rates decreasing (an important barometer of development), the education of boys and girls at primary level becoming equal and the number of women who completed tertiary education more than tripling.

So, we must credit our governments at various levels for showing keen interest in empowering women. Several schemes have been introduced to strengthen their capacity to thrive in society. On the financial and education fronts, we have scholarships and special savings schemes for girls and women. To enable meaningful participation of women in governance, we have the reservation of seats in panchayats, municipalities, legislative assemblies and the Parliament, along with political empowerment campaigns aimed especially at encouraging rural women to actively participate in politics. The country has placed high emphasis on women's health and safety too, providing them with protective tools such as a national emergency helpline number, mobile safety apps, special cybercrime prevention cells, panic buttons in public transport and multiple health schemes. Clearly, India has not shied away from boosting women's agency, health and safety. Rural women, in particular, have received significant attention, and rightly so!

But the bizarre conundrum is that, despite all these gains, the Indian woman professional (IWP)—a woman like you, me or Ambu, the white-collar woman who works in the metros, Tier 1, Tier 2 and Tier 3 cities—still seems mired in a complex web of various influences that seem to get more and more convoluted.

This is because a working woman's career has not been a top priority for anyone over the years. Bear in mind that the IWP is not a small cohort. Avtar's work in the space of women's workforce participation shows that despite there being hundreds of thousands of women in urban India who seek employment, there is a dearth of efforts, first to get women to be a part of the workforce and secondly, to provide a supportive environment to the minuscule number of women who are already there. Hence, even the mere handful of women who do work are left with no option but to exit or go on an extended hiatus when they become mothers.

While certain measures, such as the six-month maternity leave, have certainly helped women to an extent, they have also created problems. Several companies, micro and small enterprises in particular, hesitate to hire women because they simply cannot afford to hire a person and not use her services for six months. At best, these small-scale companies hire women as contract workers; hence, they do not receive any benefits, including provident fund (PF), gratuity, insurance or pension. This unfair compensation hits not just women but the nation too—the working woman's contribution to the national gross domestic product (GDP) remains terribly low in our country. It stands at just around 17 per cent, which is less than half the global average.[1]

As stated earlier, the IWPs are less likely to pursue satisfying careers and more inclined to be in rather unexciting jobs. Is this a major issue? Let's look at the fundamental difference between a 'career' and a 'job'—a career refers to the long-term work that you do, work that you typically find fulfilling, covering multiple roles that you may take up within the same field over an extended stretch of time, while a job refers to short-term work that you take up and that may or may not align with your goals and aspirations. While it is ideal to pursue a career as compared to shifting through a series of unrelated jobs, we must realize that many of us—both men and women—sometimes find ourselves accepting job offers solely for financial reasons or to avoid too long a gap in our resume and that's okay. But the problem is that women find themselves in this less-than-ideal position way more than men. And it is further accentuated when it comes to the IWP as compared to women in the developed world because of the prevailing sociocultural norms and economic factors.

Jobs or careers aside, one of the questions I am often asked is if there is a 'business case' for women to be employed. Recently, during a conversation I had with leaders in a large automotive manufacturing company, a variety of views were openly discussed. A male, mid-level manager mentioned that it would be a great strain on the family if a woman chose to work. Another gentleman stated that it costs more for a family to have a working woman than the income she brought home (like the British purportedly said of the Mahatma, that it costs more to keep him poor). A senior woman leader (she was the only one at the table) stated that women's employment is more of a political thing that organizations espouse since they want to be 'seen' as doing the right thing. Yet another person mentioned that horizontal reservation (reservation for women, children, persons with disabilities, transgender et al.) and vertical reservation (reservation for backward castes and communities) are affirmative actions that fall solely within the government's realm and are not the concern of profit-driven businesses.

All the above views are debatable and reservation, in particular, is a touchy topic. In private enterprise, where the objective is profit, reservation has not found success, and for good reason. Even companies that have attempted targets for representation of women or other minorities in the workplace have realized that a number focus can at best be a secondary goal to developing the quality of talent via skilling. Organizations require skilled people who are best suited for the role. 'Fitness to purpose' is always the norm and if a quota system is imposed to fulfil promises, they are reduced to just that—an empty promise that loses steam fast. It also acts as a double-edged sword that makes even deserving candidates feel uncomfortable and unsure about themselves. Whenever women are hired, promoted or given a plum assignment in a company that has a stated diversity target, they are perceived as feeble options, unworthy of the role, unless their personal brand is a powerful one. Even in the case of a well-qualified, competent woman who joins a company that speaks about reservation or diversity targets, her work is not taken seriously and she becomes a quarry for jibes and put-downs.

While reservation may not be the best option to promote gender diversity in commercial settings, there are other ways to do so. For instance, by providing women with special enablers such as flexibility, remote work options and sponsorship programmes. We must understand that providing women with these special privileges does not amount to inequality or discrimination against men. If both men and women are provided with the exact same resources, wouldn't we be ignoring the historical oppression that women have experienced and the privilege that men have enjoyed for years? It is imperative that we go beyond gender equality and look at gender equity—that is, providing women with customized resources based on their needs. Over time, gender equity will lead to gender equality, which is our ultimate goal.

Hence the question: What kind of support do women like Ambu need? And while external support factors are critical, is there a way for women to support themselves? These are pivotal questions that we must find answers to, because yes, women's careers, especially the career of the IWP, are 'a thing'. And it needs our mental space and attention.

So, what is the Career Doctor's advice to Ambu? Women like Ambu are likely to face three main challenges. Let's examine these challenges along with tips to tackle each of them.

Top Three Challenges	Quick Tips
1. Dealing with guilt and doubts about your decision to work	• The first step in initiating your career journey is to understand that women deserve to have fulfilling careers as much as men. You need not sacrifice your career to help your spouse progress smoothly in his professional path. When you have a solid career, it helps your children, your family and your country. • Let go of that guilt, though this is easier said than done—we will explore this point in more depth later in the book.

Top Three Challenges	Quick Tips
2. Difficulty managing work and home responsibilities	• Do not hesitate to hire external help for childcare and household chores if your family is unable to provide that support. • Delegate work to others, both at home and at work. • Leverage technology to the fullest to make things easier for yourself—be it at home or in the workplace.
3. Unsupportive employer who views flexibility, remote work options and other enablers as unnecessary and unproductive	• Speak up about your challenges, your need for flexibility and sponsorship and the necessity for family-friendly policies. Advocate for change. • Understand that women need special enablers and that demanding these special privileges does not amount to inequality.

Note that the tips shared above are just brief pointers. How to approach and implement each of these suggestions is discussed at length in various sections of the book.

Now that we have established that women's careers are indeed a thing, let's engage deeply with what you, the IWP, can do to build a fulfilling career for yourself and how you can leverage everyone's support in advancing your career. Let's dive in!

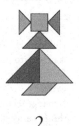

2

Identity of the Indian
Woman Professional (IWP)

I look at the young girl, resolute and determined, sitting at the very edge of the chair opposite my table. She is a first-generation graduate from one of the smaller towns near Chennai and has excellent scores in her school board exams. She is twenty-two, about 5 feet 3 inches tall, with her hair oiled and plaited and is wearing a well-pressed salwar-kameez set. It is June 2001, barely six months since I started Avtar and we are in my cabin in the small office on Lloyd's Road, one of Chennai's arterial roads. Our neighbours are a large wedding hall and the national headquarters of a political party, both vying with each other to provide a wide range of enhancements to our acoustic experience. At that precise moment, we are listening to the crescendo of the *nadhaswaram*, which usually accompanies a high point in Hindu wedding rituals and I raise my voice to be heard over it.

'This role is for engineers, Sushmita,' I explain, 'of the mechanical variety.' Sushmita is a BTech computer science graduate with a 3.75 CGPA and among the scores of engineers whose offer letters (with salary packages of about Rs 15,000 per month, which was serious money for freshers at the time) from a top IT company were rescinded on account of the dotcom bust of late 1999–early 2000. After having waited for almost six months for word from the company regarding a fresh joining date, Sushmita, like countless other engineers, has decided that her dream of cashing in on the IT wave has been aborted early and has decided to look for other options. Sushmita and her friends have been scouring newspapers every day (those were the days before Naukri and Monster became popular) for opportunities and knocking on doors, cold-calling for jobs. For women like Sushmita, who are newly entering the workforce, this is a blow to gender equality. For a newly formed company like Avtar, whose focus is to increase the ratio of women in the Indian workplace, this is one more impediment to surmount.

Given her excellent grades and fluent English skills, the placement officer at Sushmita's college has offered her a teaching assistant role at the college at a salary of Rs 6000 per month. She has been seriously considering this, given that her batchmates are joining companies completely unrelated to their core education, in sub-optimal jobs, in petrol pumps, retail outlets and in recruitment, at half the salary she has been promised for the teaching role. Seeing the walk-in ad in *The Hindu* for a turnkey project for a container shipping terminal, asking for engineers, Sushmita has done just that—she has walked in wanting to try her luck.

'Ma'am, the engineering subjects are common in the first two years of all BTech programmes,' she earnestly replies when I point out to her that I am looking for candidates with a background in mechanical engineering. 'I read the job description (JD), ma'am, it is an rubber-tired gantry (RTG) crane operator's role', she says, and then goes on to repeat, like a child reciting multiplication tables, 'Rubber tyre gantry cranes are large machines for loading and unloading containers in the yard. The operator sits in a cabin and his function is to transfer the containers within the blocks, rows, tiers or any other type of stacking.' I catch the pronoun and point out to her that the JD she just mentioned was for a *male* candidate. I explain once again, pointing to the newspaper advertisement that I have open on the table in front of me, that the call was for male engineers, given that the job is not a desk-bound one and is for a logistics company where the heavy lifting is not metaphoric. I find it strange that I am actually telling a woman that she can't apply for a job advertised by a client of Avtar when I have set up Avtar with the express purpose of finding jobs for women. I wonder why we did not push back when the client mentioned a gender specification. Then I remember—it has been about four months since we generated sufficient revenue to be able to pay salaries and if we don't successfully complete this assignment, I will have to make another trip to Puducherry, my hometown, to ask my father for working capital the second time around.

'Madam, I understand. But all I want is one chance. You will not regret it,' she says. I am running out of excuses and then I realize that Sushmita should probably not have been shortlisted in the first place and even made it to my table. The process we follow is that the initial interviews are conducted by teammates Lakshmi, Satish and Priya, the second round by Umasanker, and the final interview by me. I push the intercom to dial Umasanker's extension. In the tiny six feet by five feet room, I try to scrunch myself as much as possible away from the table to try to reduce the possibility of Sushmita overhearing my conversation with Umasanker. 'Did we not tell her that this is for male candidates?' I demand, in a harsh whisper. 'Yes, we did and I also undersold the job, mentioning that it was a tough, on-ground one. But she is the topper in the entrance test for this role,' he replies, adding, 'She convinced all of us of her capability from a qualification and attitude perspective.'

As I put down the phone, Sushmita looks expectantly into my eyes. I decide to take a different route. 'This job requires working in shifts, including night shifts,' I state. 'I am fine with that, ma'am,' she responds immediately. 'Plus, you may have to stay in a hostel, given that you can't commute from home,' I counter. 'My friends have helped me identify a paying-guest (PG) accommodation near the port area, ma'am. My dad will come with me to finalize once I get the job,' she responds in a flash. 'Your earlier IT job offer was Rs 15,000; this job will only pay around Rs 12,000,' I say, using the last weapon in my arsenal. 'Ma'am, it is double the salary I will be paid as a teaching assistant!' she replies with a smile. At this point, I am resolved that it would be easier for me to convince our Australian client about hiring a candidate who clearly doesn't fit the specifications of 'a well-built, male candidate with mechanical engineering qualifications' that are not mentioned in the written JD but have been shared confidentially during our briefing discussion. Her excellent scores and great communication skills will make up for her lack of the 'right gender', I conclude. As Sushmita proudly takes the interview call letter, I realize that I have met a career-primary woman professional—one that accounts for about a small percentage of India's working women.

Avtar's research on Indian women (and the tons of conversations we have had with them) shows that they align into three segments—career primary, career-and-home and home primary. A career-primary woman is someone who prioritizes professional growth over most other concerns and may even decline to take on traditional family responsibilities. She may take very short or no breaks in her career. A career-and-home woman is dedicated to both her career and her home responsibilities. She may take a short to medium break from professional work to attend to familial duties. A home-primary woman is someone who prioritizes her caregiving role, may take extended breaks in her career and may or may not return to the workforce. A woman who has never engaged in paid work also belongs to this category. The National Family Health Survey (NFHS-5) reveals that only 32 per cent of married women in India between the ages of fifteen and forty-nine are employed.[1] This means that 68 per cent of women in this age group belong to the home-primary segment.

There is an assumption that only men are typically career-primary and the above study supports this viewpoint, but if you run a simple Google search on 'workers', you will find that historically, quite a few women have prioritized work outside of the home. They have been working in agricultural fields, preparing items and goods at home and selling them, executing tasks on the shop floor in factories, and running their small businesses. In the Vedic period and the recorded history of Hinduism, Buddhism and Jainism, women have been warriors, educators and scholars. Women's leadership in history is well known with inspiring tales about Razia Sultan, Rani Padmini, Rani Lakshmi Bai and Ahilyabai Holkar.

The history of women's careers has evolved dramatically in the last fifty years. Since the late nineteenth century, women have become a vital component in every field—we have joyfully received news of the first teacher, doctor, engineer, entrepreneur, IAS, IPS, MP and so on, stepping in and making a mark. With several glass ceilings broken across fields like the Armed Forces and in industries considered only the forte of men, women's careers have reached a point where there are choices aplenty. Yet many barriers have remained. With more avenues opening for women, new hurdles have been added to their journeys as they attempt to secure fulfilling careers.

A few years ago, Anand Mahindra shared an image on Twitter (now X), which showed a man and a woman set for a sprint towards their career goals. For the man, it is a straight path, while for the woman, there are a set of unique and insurmountable hurdles (both on the domestic and professional front) on her journey to her destination. The post went viral. It also trained the spotlight on the tough choices women are forced to make. Many women try hard to either circumvent the hurdles or do away with them completely—these women, we refer to as career-primary. Sushmita, who addresses each barrier that comes in the way of her obtaining the job and decides that she must pursue a career by involving her family and friends in the journey is a typical example of a career-primary woman professional.

As a woman, you can pursue a career with vigour, defeating all odds or choose to focus on family or strike a balance between both. You can choose to be a career-primary woman who doesn't give up on her career ambitions and dreams. This is the career-intentional woman who plans and advances in her career, trouncing hurdles and choosing to stay firmly on the career path. Career-primary women may or may not want to find a partner, marry them or 'settle down' (as described in the Indian context). Amrita, whom I have known as a child, is a classic example of this category. Studious and driven, Amrita loved being referred to as a 'nerd'. After school, she studied at a premier engineering college and pursued an MBA in finance from an equally reputed institution. Amrita didn't marry until she was thirty-four. In 2022, she decided to tie the knot with Ranjit, whom she believed supported her dreams. When I met her at her wedding, I told her that her parents looked both happy and relieved. She laughed at my remark, adding, 'They completely understood that I would never start a life with a guy who expects me to be home all day, but that didn't stop them from worrying about the ticking clock.'

While there are women like Sushmita and Amrita, there are also numerous women like Jacqueline (Jacky to friends), a neighbour of mine in Puducherry. Jacky's story is also very familiar to all of us. She worked for a brief while in an ad agency but quit her job as soon as she got engaged. As someone who loved drawing analogies, she would tell me, 'I prefer the sound of a grinder all day to facing the grind of a job.' Soon after marriage, Jacky moved to France, accompanying her spouse, who was based in Paris. Jacky soon had two kids, a boy and a girl, with a gap of three years between them. As her children grow up, Jacky regrets nothing and is happy she has been able to give undivided attention to both kids. This is the home-primary woman we have all known from our circles or our mothers' or grandmothers'. They choose the familial responsibilities of caregiving, and this could be a choice or a compulsion of the circumstances.

Amid the Amritas and the Jackys are the Sonams. Sonam, a friend of my aunt, was born in the 1950s and completed her school education in a small town deep within Punjab. Soon after, she moved to Chandigarh to work and support her family. Sonam, who had learned shorthand and typewriting in her town as a seventeen-year-old, was determined to build a career using that skill and managed to find a data entry job after some struggle. After marriage, she found a supporter in her husband, who was keen for her to continue her job. Sonam raised three children— two sons and a daughter—with the support of her husband and the family in an era when maternity benefits were unheard of. Her story of tremendous growth despite not having a college degree and having childcare responsibilities is nothing short of remarkable. She recently retired after forty years of service as an accomplished, respected leader and a veritable role model for her children. Sonam is a career-and-home woman who divides her time between her work and family. This is a choice and, again, these women can be career-intentional as well. The career-and-home women may need multiple enablers to continue uninterrupted on their career paths.

So what kind of career model is the most popular? Remember that women are judged for their choices, come what may. If you are a woman successful in your career, you will be blamed for neglecting your family. If you decide not to work, again, you are judged for idling away time and wasting your education. It does seem like the identity of the IWP is always under scrutiny. Know that it is easy for people to judge. Only you know what your personal circumstances are and what led you to decide what kind of personal and professional life you want.

Here are some key factors that you must consider while deciding on a career scenario for yourself:

- Does your spouse or partner understand and support your career ambitions? Can he be your ally and support system that you can lean on? If yes, to what degree?
- Can your family step in and cover for you when you need help with childcare, allowing you to give your career the attention it needs? And to what extent?
- Does your organization support your various life stages through its policies and programmes? These will include their maternity policy, childcare benefits and programmes, flexibility options, career advancement programmes, sponsorship programmes and mentorship.

Coming up with clear answers to the above questions will help you decide whether a career-primary option or a career-and-home option will work for you.

And what about those who choose the home-primary option? Is it wrong to not have a career? Avtar's white paper titled 'Significance of Careers to Indian Women Professionals: A Socio-Economic Study' published in 2014 found that social pressure to work was non-existent for women, whether married or unmarried, employed full-time or part-time.[2] Only 4 per cent of the women surveyed stated that satisfying social pressure inspired them to pursue careers. The white paper states that the average Indian mindset does not require women to work, reinforcing the stereotype that women's primary responsibilities are the 3 Cs (cooking, cleaning and caring). That brings us to the question: is it okay for women to not pursue a career?

There is no right or wrong in this, but it is important for a woman to make an informed decision. A career empowers you financially. It enables spending, saving and investing according to your priorities. As a result, you have a fair share in the decision-making related to the health and education of your children and family. And honestly, your career is not just about you. It has several implications for your family, community, company and country. Most importantly, pursuing a career, as the same white paper revealed, means achievement of intellectual satisfaction and the creation of self-identity for a woman, sometimes more significant than financial security or independence. About 82 per cent of women on a break associate careers with self-identities, showing that a career hiatus deeply affects a woman's societal identity. So, the question is not about whether it is right or wrong to not pursue a career. It is more about considering the positives of having one.

Circling back to Sushmita, our career-primary woman from 2001. Witnessing her indomitable motivation to land the job, we convinced the leaders from the Australian logistics and container shipping company to at least interview her for the RTG crane operator's role. We shared all the points of conviction that Sushmita had pitched to us as to why she would be fully suitable for the job, despite her gender. After a lot of hesitation, they finally agreed. Sushmita travelled to Mumbai for her final round, but after that, we did not know whether Sushmita actually got the offer, given that ours was a turnkey assignment, where we were paid only for the process and not based on the results of who was selected.

It's a rainy September day in 2001 when we are invited for the first official visit after the container terminal changed hands and began its new operations. Umasanker and I are walking around the freshly refurbished terminal. It is impressive, the equipment is shiny and bright and the large area is filled with newly hired people energetically running about to get the job done. Suddenly, we hear someone's voice from afar. 'Ma'am, sir!' she calls. We look around, trying to figure out who is calling out to us. 'Ma'am, look here, up! Up, ma'am, I am here!' yells Sushmita. As we raise our heads to look up into the sky, we see Sushmita waving at us from inside the console of an RTG crane. Career-primary Sushmita is on top of the world!

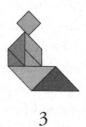

3

Pursuing a Career Is Not Selfish,
It Is Patriotism

We are on the fifth and topmost floor of the Ramada Raj Park, a humble hotel on TTK Road, one of the oldest localities in Chennai. When you open the windows, the forceful breeze from the sea, which is just a couple of kilometres away, pushes in, ruffling papers. So we keep them shut. It's a large vacant hall and we have separated it into two parts: a row of interview booths and an area cordoned off for group discussions. Lakshmi is one of the three of us (of the team of ten) who possesses a mobile phone and she is making some last-minute calls. Vijay places a bottle of water on each of the desks and then exchanges them, quite unnecessarily. Smitha nervously aligns the writing pad and pen on one of the desks as we look at our watches. It is 9.20 a.m. We have all had our packed 'event-day' breakfasts of idli, vada and coffee from Saravana Bhavan. Umasanker, a recruiter, goes over the process flow once more with Eswar and Priya—two more recruiters like Umasanker (all three presently in senior leadership roles at Avtar), ticking things off. The process is to start at 9.30 a.m. The year is 2006 and it is the humid month of July. 'We' are Team Avtar and something historic was about to happen.

Avtar was started in December 2000 as a talent strategy consulting firm with the primary goal of providing India Inc. with exceptional female talent. After five years of intense effort, we had managed a breakthrough. A large multinational bank was ready to experiment with hiring second-career women for the very first time. The phenomenon of women entering the workforce and then dropping out is quite unique to India. Though this issue is not unheard of in other countries, the overwhelming number of women quitting work is largely limited to ours. I realized this when I attended an international conference in Sri Lanka in 2019 with scholars from across the world speaking about issues faced by working women in developing economies. There were professors, academicians, people from non-profits and social scientists from Japan, Nepal, Maldives, Bangladesh, South Africa, Kazakhstan, several other Asian and African countries and, of course, the hosts, Sri Lanka. While people shared studies about lack of mentoring, the pressure of work–life integration, the biases that existed in the workplace, et al., there was just one researcher who spoke about women dropping out—me. During the Q&A after my talk, the audience expressed astonishment and even shock at the sheer magnitude of the numbers of women dropping out of careers in India and the gaping difference between the ranks of educated women and employed women.

Back to the Ramada and the project we are about to implement. We've been engaged by the bank to select 100 women for their call centre and they were happy to 'experiment' with women on career breaks. The brief is simple—women candidates with a good educational background, great team skills and communication, the ability to manage irate customers, strong operational rigour and a pleasant demeanour. Prior work experience is preferred. However, we've convinced them to also include first-time career-seeking homemakers who possess the skills required for this task. The bank agreed but also laid the condition that the quality of candidates could not be compromised even remotely and that they would all have to pass the stringent final interview by their own team. What made this assignment all the more exciting for us as a young start-up was that this was a turnkey project. If we concluded the whole programme successfully (we had already received an advance), we would complete our revenue targets for the next six months.

It is 9.25 a.m. T minus 5 and we are expecting to meet and interview at least 700 people, giving us a ratio of about 1:7 making it to the final round. Since this was the first ever such programme in India, we'd gone ahead and released a large quarter-page ad in *The Hindu*. Even as I signed the cheque for the ad release (being an unknown little firm, we had to pay in advance), I had the jitters, but I believed in my heart that this would be a success. Not stopping with an ad, we'd also dropped pamphlets in middle-class neighbourhoods and even visited apartment complexes, addressing stay-at-home moms. I also did the rounds at a few schools and spoke to the parent–teacher association (PTA) committees, urging mothers who had dropped off, to return to work. We wanted to cover about 3000 women and hoped that at least 750–800 of them would land up. That way, we would hit our ratio. We had arranged for about 100 candidates to come every hour from 9.30 a.m. to 3.30 p.m. so that we would have sufficient space and individual face time for the interviews.

It is 9.30 a.m. and we don't have a single candidate as yet. I cross-check with the team to see if we had mentioned the date and time accurately in all our communication. They confirm the same. I check a sample email with my own eyes (even though I had drafted it myself and sent a few thousand of those) just to be sure. We are getting desperate. I ask Umasanker, who front-ended with the client, if we could go back and tell them that we would somehow repay the advance or else work for them for free to compensate. The team is perspiring, despite the fans running at full speed. I say my prayers and beseech the universal energy to come to our rescue.

At that moment, the intercom buzzes. I pick it up, my hands clammy. It is from the front desk. 'Madam, you are aware we have only one lift to the fifth floor, right?' asks the receptionist from the ground floor. 'Yes, yes, I am aware,' I reply in a shaky voice. 'How can we send all these women up in one lift?' she demands. 'All these women?' I ask. 'Which women?' 'Madam, please look outside the third window in the hall; you will get a view of the road. Just see!' she says, her voice filled with irritation at my lack of understanding. All of us run to the third window. Despite our careful opening, the truant sea breeze hurtles in, disrupting papers on the nearby desk.

A glorious sight awaited us. The road was filled with women—at least 500 of them, standing in a serpentine queue, quietly and intently, but impatient to board the elevator to a second career! They had come! In a record turnout, the women landed up in response to an impassioned team that promised them a new life. As we ran down the five stairs to guide them up, tears of happiness and relief washed down our faces. Thus began the assessment of women who had taken breaks of two to eighteen years! We counted 2350 women at the end of the day, each one of whom had to be interviewed, assessed and sent for group discussion (GD) rounds. Finally, the team from the bank met over 200 women for the final and ended up hiring over 148 of them. 120 second-career women and twenty-eight first-time workers. And that was the official launch of India's first-ever career re-entry programme!

But this chapter is not about that. It is about an amazing conversation that I had with Hema, an MCom graduate and mother of two who taught neighbourhood children how to play the veena. She was among the twenty-eight first-time career-making women who got selected. (I had many heartening exchanges with the women who came that day, but this was special.) Forty-two-year-old Hema lived in a large joint family comprising parents-in-law, brothers and sisters-in-law, children of varying ages and elderly grandparents who needed care. After brilliant results in her school final (she was a topper in commerce), Hema wanted to become a banker. She completed her graduation and attempted the banking service recruitment board exam. Even as she received the happy news that she had been selected, her parents had other plans. They found a suitable match for her and convinced her to get married. Life took over.

The next two decades sped by. With her position in the family advancing to a more 'senior' role, Hema's aspiration to do something beyond her identity as a mother and caregiver egged her to start looking for jobs. When I asked her why she had applied, she replied (in Tamil): 'Desabhakti, ma'am, patriotism! My family has a sufficient income, so it is not money that makes me want to work. I want to contribute to my nation's development. I want to build my country!'

I was thrilled. This was such an incredible reason why Indian women must pursue careers. To further challenge her (and to hear for myself how this banker-in-another-dimension made her arguments), I asked, 'Doesn't the home come before the nation?'

Her response is one that I still vividly remember. 'When India was fighting for freedom from the British fifty-nine years ago, men, women and even children came out to fight,' she said. Then she elaborated on how her grandmother would quickly finish her cooking chores and join the march for Independence. 'My grandmother was fully supported by her family. Her mother-in-law felt that she was doing her duty as an Indian citizen! For something to happen on a large scale, everyone's efforts are needed, ma'am,' said Hema. It had taken Hema so long to convince her family that her contribution to the nation, even if it was delayed, was critical. She wanted to show her daughter that it was possible to do this. And she wanted to show her son that he could also encourage his future wife to do her share. 'Today, we are not fighting for freedom, but for a better quality of life for our future generations,' said Hema with great fervour.

How does the nation benefit when women work? It is fair to say that more women in the workforce pushes the entire country towards social and economic empowerment. Let's delve further into this:

- In a paper published by the World Economic Forum in 2018, the International Monetary Fund (IMF) Chief Christine Lagarde stated that India's GDP will see a 27 per cent jump if India manages to raise women's workforce participation to the same level as men.[1] According to a report by McKinsey Global Institute, if India strives towards gender parity, we could add $700 billion to our GDP by 2025.[2]
- Both research and anecdotal evidence show that gender diversity in an organization leads to new ideas, more creativity and innovation and better teamwork, thereby boosting company profits, which in turn fuels economic development. For example, a 2022 study conducted by researchers at the Kellogg School of Management and other prominent schools,

found that 'mixed-gender teams significantly outperformed same-gender teams on both novelty and impact.'[3]

- Financial independence for women enables enhanced discretionary spending, which leads to greater economic development of the nation.

- Educated and self-supporting women are veritable building blocks of societal progress. When women from economically weak backgrounds pursue careers, their children break free from a gamut of issues, including poverty, early marriage and abuse.

To sum it up, empowering women empowers the nation and disregarding women's self-sufficiency does not make economic sense. So, the next time you doubt your decision to pursue a career, remind yourself that you are not being selfish—you are being patriotic!

But if women's participation in the workforce is a win-win for everyone, why is India still grappling with abysmal women's workforce participation numbers? Well, it is a deep-rooted problem. For one, we, as a society, still believe that childcare is the primary responsibility of mothers. While conversations centred on how dads must 'help' their partners in childcare are becoming increasingly common, we are still far from understanding that dads must do more than that. The very choice of the word— help—indicates that childcare is the woman's responsibility and, if they are lucky, they will receive 'help' from their partners.

Women are reinforcers of these gender norms too. The depth of ingrained gender biases becomes evident when we learn that even marriage pushes a significant chunk of women in India to quit work. The Periodic Labour Force Survey for 2019–20 reveals that the workforce participation rate of young single women in their mid- to late-twenties is around 60 per cent in urban India, which isn't too bad. But after marriage, only one in ten women are in paid work.[4] Gender role stereotyping is indeed a grave setback for women's careers.

Another pressing challenge that keeps women at home is the lack of solid support systems—childcare options carry a hefty price tag in our country and the extended family often falls short in providing support because they expect mothers to prioritize childcare responsibilities. To compound the trouble, many organizations fail to adequately support their female employees returning from their maternity break. Without enabling work options such as remote work, flexible hours and part-time roles, women are left with no choice but to take an indefinite break.

And what becomes of these women who pause their careers in their prime years? Childcare and housework consume them. Since they are financially dependent on others, they feel obligated to shoulder an insane amount of household chores. So, they do not enlist any help from family nor do they hire external help for domestic work or babysitting. This leaves these women with very little time for anything else. Upskilling and networking are nowhere in the equation. After an extended break, when they long to get back to work, they find themselves grappling with skill gaps and feelings of isolation and self-doubt. Many organizations aggravate the situation by disapproving of career breaks, discouraging flexible work schedules and failing to provide a supportive work environment.

But trust me, a starkly different path is possible for second-career women and Avtar's work in the field of women's workforce participation clearly proves this point. Avtar has worked with over 500 organizations to help them achieve gender diversity and assist them in fostering a supportive environment for women. We have made this possible by ensuring that flexible work options, mentoring support, employee assistance programmes (EAPs) and more are available for these women. We have trained over 25,000 leaders and managers on the best practices of diversity, equity and inclusion (DEI), thus ensuring that they foster an environment of empathy and assistance for women, free of gender biases and norms. Through myavtar.com, India's first diversity portal (known earlier as Avtar I-WIN), Avtar has enabled over 1,00,000 women to pursue fulfilling careers in organizations that place diversity and inclusion above everything else. A significant chunk of these women are second-career professionals and first-time career seekers. Through Project Puthri, an initiative of the Avtar Human Capital Trust (AHCT), we reach out to thousands of underprivileged girls every year with the goal of making them career-intentional, thereby enabling them to work around traditional gender roles and approach their careers with commitment and focus.

While we are incredibly happy with what we have achieved to date, we know that we are still far from our goal. Through the course of our work, we have come to realize that just about 700 organizations in India, out of a potential 7 lakh, follow the best practices for creating a positive work culture. And we still have a long way to go before we completely denounce gender roles, expectations and stereotypes. Until every woman out there is able to dream without bounds and pursue those professional dreams fearlessly and unapologetically, Avtar's work will continue. And when a woman asks me how she can keep the passion for her career and profession alive, I simply reply, 'Desabhakti!'

4

The Three Routes to a Successful Career

It is planning time for the 2022 'Best of the Best' (BoB) Conference, Avtar's annual celebration of the best companies for diversity in India and with just two weeks to go, the conference rooms at Avtar's headquarters on East Coast Road in Chennai are abuzz. Session managers are brainstorming about a bunch of things and as I walk past these rooms, I hear peals of laughter from one particular room. The sound of happy voices draws me in. I find Priya Dayabaran, Anju G. Parvathy and Janani Sampath deep in discussion. They enjoy each other's points of view and even disagreeing is fun. They are discussing a specific BoB session for women professionals that identifies different routes that women can take to achieve career success. As I listen to their different points of view, I realize that each of them—Priya, Anju and Janani—could not be more different in the paths they have followed to attain professional success.

Our initiatives in the realm of women's labour force participation reveal that women usually follow one or a combination of these routes—the skills route, the education route and the passion route—to a successful career. Whichever field it may be—arts, entrepreneurship, science, teaching, training, banking, sales, strategy or management—successful women (and men) have had to always face adversity and break barriers. In the case of women, due to the small number of them who can stand up and be counted in the Indian workplace, their battles have been won by doggedly focusing on their education, their skills or their passion. Each of these routes has its own ambassadors and is distinctly different, especially in the way in which steps are initiated and carried out during the early career stage. Whether through honing specific skills, attaining advanced education or channelling unbridled passion, or all three, women have been able to attain success and leave an indelible mark on the professional landscape.

Priya, a first-generation graduate who began her career as a front-office executive, now leads the recruitment delivery vertical at Avtar. When I first met her in November 2000, I recognized her deep desire to rise above her circumstances and make a difference for her family. Her intentionality shone in the way in which she learned English (although her K-12 education was in Tamil) and willed herself to write without grammatical errors. Her eagerness to build new skills resulted in a prestigious project around service quality being given to her in early 2003 and with characteristic focus, Priya delivered it successfully. Her vote is for the skills route.

'As a front-office executive, I noticed that the recruiters who made more money and also received performance incentives did not have a very different educational background as compared to me', states Priya, adding, 'but they had killer skills. I realized that developing those skills made all the difference between travelling in a shared auto and having a car of my own.' Priya realized that if you are strong in relationship management, negotiation and marketing, pay great attention to detail and apply your mind diligently, you could crack a successful recruitment career. She earnestly focused on developing these skills and within months, she moved from her ops role to recruitment and rose to become a practice lead within a few short years. After having placed thousands of candidates in suitable roles, Priya believes that the skills route is a dynamic pathway to achieving success. Her approach places a strong emphasis on honing expertise in a particular area and leveraging that expertise to create an upwardly mobile career. For women, the skills route offers a versatile way to excel in various fields, regardless of traditional barriers or industry biases.

How does one implement the skills route? Here are the Career Doctor's tips:

1. **Identifying and defining your niche skills:** The first step in the skills route is to identify skills that not only match your interests but are also in demand within your chosen industry. These skills could range from technical abilities, such as coding or data analysis, to soft skills like communication, leadership or problem-solving.

2. **Continuous learning:** Skills need to be continually honed and updated to stay relevant in a rapidly evolving job market. Pursue ongoing learning through courses, workshops, online tutorials and other resources to keep your skill set up-to-date.

3. **Building expertise:** Becoming an expert in your chosen skills requires dedication and practice. Seek out opportunities to apply your skills in real-world scenarios to gain practical experience.

4. **Networking and exposure:** Networking is crucial for showcasing your skills. Attend industry events, workshops and

conferences to connect with professionals, potential clients or employers.

5. **Creating a portfolio:** Compile a portfolio showcasing your best work and projects, including case studies, client testimonials and before-and-after examples to demonstrate the impact of your skills. This portfolio acts as tangible proof of your capabilities and can be shared with potential clients or employers to demonstrate your value.

6. **Marketing yourself:** Create a professional online presence through a personal website and social media profiles. Utilize these platforms to share insights related to your skills and engage with your target audience.

Women such as Ursula Burns and Arundhati Bhattacharya are veritable examples of how the skills route has worked fabulously. Ursula Burns, who joined as an intern at Xerox in 1980, steadily rose up the ranks by virtue of her admirable leadership, communication and management skills and went on to serve as the company's CEO from 2009 to 2016, also becoming the first black woman to be a CEO of a Fortune 500 company. Anne Mulcahy, who selected Burns as her successor, said in an interview with Fast Company, 'I was impressed by Burns' skills, particularly her outspoken confidence.'[1]

Arundhati Bhattacharya, the first woman chairperson of the State Bank of India (SBI), joined the bank in 1977 as a probationary officer when she was just twenty-two, after studying English literature and rose to the top post in 2013, primarily through the skills she mastered along the way. And we all know what Oprah Winfrey managed to do, don't we? Born into poverty and with no training in talk show hosting, she became a star of television thanks to her phenomenal communication, storytelling and interviewing skills, all of which she largely refined on her own.

'The skills route empowers women to break through gender barriers,' points out Priya. 'We can thrive even in a tough economic market based on the expertise we have built.' By cultivating in-demand skills, staying adaptable and embracing continuous learning, women can carve out successful and fulfilling careers that showcase their unique talents and contributions.

Janani Sampath, who has been attentively listening to Priya, nods in agreement but is quick to state, 'I feel that the education route is an equally powerful one, if not more.' An X celebrity, Janani is a journalist-turned-digital marketing professional. As a young post-grad at journalism school and as a professional journalist, Janani has written about various issues that cut across realms of social status and geography, such as the problem of child marriages and its effect on the health and economic participation of women, domestic violence and women's mental health. After fifteen years of on-field journalism, writing about crime, politics, social issues and culture, Janani did a post-pandemic career pivot and discovered a new calling in becoming a product manager and editing the 'Diversity Digest' for Avtar—our popular blog that brings together news and perspectives from the world of DEI.

As a child, success for Janani meant topping her class and excelling in her studies. When she landed a seat at a top journalism college, it strengthened her belief that educational qualifications would always help her build a successful career. True to her belief, the solid grounding she received during her educational journey has been instrumental in helping Janani excel professionally.

The education route to success revolves around harnessing the power of knowledge and academic achievements to pave the way for a fulfilling and impactful career journey. While acknowledging that alternative career routes are available, the education route capitalizes on the advantages gained from formal education to open doors, enhance skill sets and position women for influential roles in various fields.

Formal education, especially for women, is crucial and the reasons for this are many. To begin with, formal education provides a strong foundation in theory, principles and concepts relevant to specific industries or disciplines. This knowledge equips women with a deep understanding of their chosen field, setting the stage for informed decision-making and problem-solving. It not only imparts theoretical knowledge but also helps develop practical skills through assignments, projects and hands-on experience, which are critical for succeeding in professional roles.

Acquiring degrees from reputable institutions can also enhance one's credibility and provide recognition within the industry, thereby opening doors to higher-level positions and leadership roles. And the connections that we make with peers, professors and professionals during our time in college can lead to valuable mentorship, collaboration and future job opportunities.

This route offers a structured and knowledge-driven pathway to success. By leveraging the advantages of formal education, women can gain a competitive edge, build a strong professional foundation and position themselves for meaningful contributions in their chosen fields.

Anju G. Parvathy, a national CBSE topper and a nine-pointer in BE from BITS Pilani, has always greatly valued education, but over thirteen years of professional experience have taught her that enthusiasm and passion for work can sometimes be a bigger determinant of career success than education. 'You need passion to learn new things, unlearn stuff and proceed with unflagging motivation!' states Anju, currently head of research and audits at Avtar. 'Societal benchmarks for career success for men and women can be different', she says, 'but the feeling of success is the same.' She speaks about how success can not only be defined in terms of tangible milestones, such as promotions, investments or materialistic possessions, but also by people who've been inspired by our work and those whose lives we've touched. 'And for that, it is passion that is the core dynamic,' she says with conviction.

The passion route to success involves transforming one's genuine interests and enthusiasm into a viable and fulfilling career path. This approach enables women to merge their personal passions with professional pursuits, leading to a sense of purpose, creativity and satisfaction in their work. After off-ramping from a very successful career as a scientist in the space of artificial intelligence with patents to her name, Anju decided to make a career comeback into a domain she knew little about—diversity and inclusion consulting. Her passion for making a difference in the lives and careers of thousands of women, persons with disabilities and people from the trans and queer community, resulted in her landing one of Avtar's largest projects in diversity analytics in May 2016. The project involved using intellectual, operational and people skills in proportions that Anju didn't fathom she had. As a team member who played a crucial role in setting up the Avtar and Seramount '100 Best Companies for Women in India' study in 2016, Anju's passion has seen the study scale to influence the lives of over 5 lakh women professionals year after year.

Converting a passion into a career requires careful planning, dedication and a willingness to overcome challenges, but the rewards can be truly remarkable.

Here are ways in which you can convert your passion into a career:

1. **Identifying your passion:** The first step is recognizing what truly excites and motivates you. Your passion could be

anything—from art, music or writing to sports, technology or social causes. It's essential to identify a passion that genuinely resonates with you and aligns with your values.

2. **Research and exploration:** Once you've identified your passion, conduct thorough research to understand the potential career opportunities within that field. Develop a detailed plan outlining how you will monetize your passion by exploring different niches, industries and roles to find the best fit for your passion.

3. **Skill development:** To turn your passion into a career, you'll likely need to develop relevant skills. This might involve formal education, workshops, self-study or gaining hands-on experience. Acquiring the necessary skills is crucial for establishing credibility in your chosen field.

4. **Creating value:** Successful passion-based careers often revolve around providing value to others. You should have clarity around this and determine how your passion can solve problems, fulfil needs or enhance experiences for your target audience.

5. **Building a brand:** Establish yourself as an expert in your chosen field by creating a personal brand. This includes showcasing your work, sharing insights and engaging with your audience through social media, blogs, networking events or other platforms.

6. **Resilience and adaptability:** The path to turning your passion into a career may not always be smooth. Be prepared to face challenges and setbacks and maintain a willingness to adapt and learn from your experiences.

By embarking on the passion route, individuals can turn what they love into a fulfilling career. It's a journey that requires dedication, authenticity and a willingness to learn, but the satisfaction of aligning your work with your passions can lead to a truly enriching and purposeful life. Women such as Rukmini Banerji and Prerna Singh Bindra show us the incredible potential of the passion route. Rukmini Banerji, an economist and educationist who studied at prestigious institutions such as St Stephen's, the Delhi School of Economics, Oxford University and the University of Chicago, is the CEO of Pratham Education Foundation, an innovative learning organization that caters to the less privileged children. Under her leadership, Pratham has recorded tremendous growth, come up with innovative teaching methods and done path-breaking work, such as designing the Annual Status of Education Report, an annual source of data on children's learning outcomes in India. Rukmini's passion to bridge the gap in the Indian education system shines through in every endeavour of Pratham's.

Prerna Singh Bindra, a top wildlife conservationist in our country today, has authored scores of articles, research papers and books for both children and adults on environmental issues, worked with governments and organizations at all levels to promote ecological well-being and served on the National Board for Wildlife (NBWL). The intense passion that Prerna harbours for the planet's well-being is evident in the diverse and impactful work that she does.

These women show that passion can indeed drive people towards success. But we must understand that the superiority of one route over the others in leading to success is subjective and depends on various factors, including an individual's goals, strengths, circumstances and preferences. Each route offers unique advantages and can lead to success in its own right.

Ultimately, the 'best' route depends on what an individual values most, their strengths and their long-term goals. In many cases, a combination of these routes can lead to a more well-rounded and adaptable path to success. Moreover, each individual's journey is unique and what works for one person may not be the ideal path for another. It's important to carefully evaluate one's own situation, aspirations and resources before deciding which route to pursue.

How to Identify Which Route Suits You Best

Identifying the route that suits you best—the skills route, the education route or the passion route—requires a thoughtful self-assessment and consideration of various factors. Here's a step-by-step guide to help you determine which route aligns with your goals, strengths and circumstances.

1. **Self-reflection:** Start by reflecting on your interests, values and long-term aspirations. Consider what excites you and makes you feel fulfilled and motivated. Think about the type of work environment, lifestyle and impact you want to create through your career.

2. **Assess your strengths:** Evaluate your natural strengths and talents by asking these questions: What skills come easily to you? What subjects or activities do you excel in? Recognize where your aptitudes lie, as this can guide you towards the route that leverages your strengths.

3. **Research career paths:** Research various career paths and industries related to each route. Look into the skills, education requirements and job prospects associated with each path. Consider the day-to-day responsibilities and challenges you might face in each field.

4. **Consider lifestyle and goals:** Think about the lifestyle you want to lead. Are you willing to invest a significant amount of

time and resources into formal education? Do you value the flexibility of freelancing or entrepreneurship that the skills or passion route can offer?

5. **Examine your learning preferences:** Reflect on how you prefer to learn and develop. Are you someone who thrives in a formal educational setting with structured courses and academic challenges? Or do you learn best by diving into hands-on projects and building practical skills?

6. **Evaluate risk tolerance:** Assess your risk tolerance. Are you comfortable taking calculated risks to pursue your passion or do you prefer the stability that can come from a more traditional career path with educational credentials?

7. **Seek advice and guidance:** Reach out to mentors, professionals and individuals with experience in the routes you're considering. Their insights can provide valuable perspectives and help you understand the realities of each path.

8. **Trial and experimentation:** If possible, test the waters by taking small steps along each route. Volunteer, intern or take on freelance projects to gain first-hand experience and determine what resonates with you.

9. **Combine routes:** Recognize that these routes are not mutually exclusive. You can combine elements of all three routes based on your circumstances. For instance, you might pursue formal education to develop skills related to your passion. Take, for example, filmmakers. There are numerous youngsters who get formal education in various aspects of filmmaking to acquire the necessary skills before they follow their passion for making movies.

10. **Listen to your gut:** Trust your intuition. Pay attention to the route that resonates most deeply with you when you imagine

your future. Your intuition often knows what mirrors your authentic self.

Remember that career paths can evolve over time and it's okay to reassess and adjust as you gain experience and clarity. What's most important is choosing a route that falls in line with your values, strengths and aspirations, leading to a fulfilling and successful journey.

5

Intentional Career Pathing (ICP)©

It is September 2019 and I am at the gorgeous Google office in Hyderabad, waiting in one of their conference rooms to meet Jo Keiko Terasawa. A young mother of three girls and a first-generation Japanese immigrant living in Australia, Jo was a teacher in her earlier avatar. Passionate about being a 'bridge between gaps', as she puts it, her energy is evident in her work in enabling underrepresented people to make the leap to a new future. She is part of the team that builds the inclusion and equity programme strategy for Google in the Asia–Pacific (APAC) region and she also leads the APAC Disability: IN corporate council forum as co-chair.

Jo and I have had several virtual meetings and both of us are excited to be in the same time zone and see each other in person for the first time. We have been talking about what Google and Avtar can jointly do to equip women with the skills to raise their career employability quotient and even improve their career quality. Those conversations would go on to become the foundational blocks of a profoundly meaningful and immensely popular programme called DigiPivot, which is in its fifth edition in 2024, designed to help women pivot their careers to digital marketing by upskilling them in the field.

I've observed that the best programmes—the most effective and truly impactful ones—are never the result of a key responsibility area (KRA); they are always the results of a personal cause. In Jo's case, it is deeply so. Having multifariously been a teacher, translator and interpreter, she understands what it's like to pivot to a different career. She also realizes that moving into the corporate world requires genuine recognition and acceptance and that there are enormous gaps between what we are taught at school about a career and what it really is. Hence her passion to be a 'bridge between gaps'.

Jo's commitment to making a difference and utilizing Google's vision is palpable in the energy and focus that she exhibits. When we first began shaping the DigiPivot project, which has a massive fan following among women in India Inc. today, it was among the long list of projects that Jo was working on. One meeting particularly stands out in my memory. It was 4.30 p.m. in India, conveniently in the middle of a neat working day for me, but I was concerned about Jo since it was 9.30 p.m. for her in Sydney. She assured me that it was fine and we proceeded to start the meeting. I could not see Jo's image clearly in the video and when I asked her about it, she informed me that her children were sleeping in the same room and she was speaking softly and under low light so as not to disturb them. Over the last few years, I have observed Jo to be her best, most authentic self, consistently demonstrating what we at Avtar call Career Intentionality©.

And thereby hangs another tale—the story of how we at Avtar discovered the concept of 'career intentionality' and its immense potential in creating fulfilling careers for women. It was 2015 and I was in Bengaluru, meeting a former managing director (MD) of a large tech company over coffee on MG Road. We spoke about a bunch of things, including the vicissitudes of corporate life, Vedanta, quantum physics, pickle making, et al., when a topic close to both our hearts came up—women's careers. 'Do we really know what causes women to be successful in the Indian corporate world?' she asked. 'Yes, we do have all the usual reasons—skills, family support, attitude, the right education, focus and so on— but why do some women with the same set of qualifications and life enablers succeed so wonderfully while others don't?' This question spurred one of Avtar's largest research projects on how Indian women create their careers, and led to the discovery of the concept of career intentionality.

As part of the research, we embarked on a nationwide study covering both men and women, where we examined various factors essential for a person to do well.[1] We discovered that the depth of focus and zeal in one's line of work is a critical factor for career success, what we refer to as career intentionality. There are other ways of defining career intentionality too—for example, the fire in the belly, the intrinsic urge or the intent that we must exhibit to make very strategic career progress. Every leader, gender notwithstanding, demonstrates career intentionality—not just in the corporate world. Every successful person one can think of, everyone who we might even call an overnight success, is career-intentional and has followed the tenets of ICP either by design or default.

Our study revealed that women tend to demonstrate less drive and fervour for career progress compared to their male counterparts around the mid-career stage, so we figured out that being career-intentional is more critical for women compared to men. Let's also not forget that there are a plethora of intrinsic and extrinsic factors waiting to derail women from their career paths.

Career intentionality is the nitro boost that we can use to remain steadfast and accelerate our career trajectories.

Now that we have a fair idea of the 'what' and 'why' of ICP, our next step is to understand the 'how' of it. Since ICP is a strategic approach to shaping one's career path based on personal goals, values, strengths and aspirations, it involves actively making choices and taking actions that align with one's vision for their professional journey. When I look back at the numerous career-intentional women I have met at different junctures of my life, I clearly see some common traits in all of them.

- I believe ICP begins with **self-awareness**. Women who are intentional about their careers take time to understand their values, strengths, weaknesses and passions. They reflect on their skills, interests and what truly motivates them in their work.
- These women **set clear and specific career goals**. They identify both short-term and long-term objectives and create a roadmap to achieve them. These goals could be related to job titles, responsibilities, skills to develop or industries to explore.
- Another important attribute of career-intentional women is **adaptability**. These women are open to change, embracing challenges and viewing setbacks as opportunities for growth. This mindset allows them to navigate uncertainties and seize new opportunities.
- Finally, **continuous learning** is a cornerstone of ICP. Career-intentional women invest in developing new skills and enhancing existing ones. This might involve formal education, attending workshops, online courses or seeking on-the-job training opportunities.

As we further explored the concept of career intentionality, we realized that apart from instilling the above-discussed traits in girls and women, we needed a solid framework identifying the key pillars of ICP, which every woman professional must stay attuned to throughout their career journey.

The Six Tenets of ICP

1. **Build a good relationship with your manager:** This is crucial because a great working relationship ensures that your manager is aware of your career aspirations and is more likely to involve you in the right projects, recognize your contributions, help you navigate challenges and provide genuine feedback for your growth—all of which can help fast-track your career progress. Communicating honestly, understanding your manager's objectives and expectations, demonstrating your interest and drive and being dependable can make a world of difference.

2. **Seek mentors:** A mentor is not only a guide; he or she is also your well-wisher and role model who can provide realistic strategies for attaining your objectives, introduce you to people in their wide networks, offer you a peek into how leadership works and strengthen your intent to succeed. Finding the right mentor can take time, so be ready to explore multiple avenues. Participate in industry events, reach out to pioneers in your field on LinkedIn and other professional networking sites, join mentorship programmes if your organization offers one and explore virtual mentoring too. You could also approach your ex-managers; since they are familiar with your plus points and working style, you can kick off from the get-go. When you reach out to a potential mentor, remember to

highlight what you can bring to the table too—for example, you could be up to speed on technology or have innovative ideas and fresh perspectives on how the industry can improve.

3. **Become a team player:** Team player ability is critical for career intentionality and the first step in cultivating this capability is self-awareness and recognizing how you can effectively contribute to your team. Other key actions include actively participating in meetings and offering support to your colleagues by sharing performance hacks and time-saving strategies with them. Remember, it is a continuous effort that requires sincere commitment.

4. **Network with your peers:** Developing good relationships with peers at work makes you feel more connected at work and, as a result, boosts your productivity. So set aside some time for company events, workshops, employee resource groups (ERGs) and lunch dates to bond with your peers over light-hearted conversations. The relationships that you build at these events can boost your sense of job satisfaction and help you make steady progress in your career.

5. **Develop negotiation skills:** The ability to build your case, assert your stance and broker a deal that works for everyone is necessary in many professional settings as it helps translate your career intentionality into real growth. The most crucial step in developing your negotiation skills is enhancing your communication acumen—clear and crisp communication ensures that your arguments and ideas land well with others. Skilful negotiation also involves active listening and empathy, solid research and preparation, as well as sound, analytical judgement.

6. **Master work–life integration:** This is crucial for the prevention of burnout, as a well-integrated professional

and personal life makes it possible for you to set ambitious goals and surge forward in your career path. So explore all the possible ways to blend work and family—this can be different for each of you, depending on your role and family situation. Some general suggestions: Be candid about your need for flexibility and remote working options; put technology to good use and keep your daily commute to work short if you can.

Remember, ICP cannot follow a one-size-fits-all approach for the sole reason that every woman's journey is unique. It's about making deliberate choices to align one's career with personal values, passions and aspirations.

ICP must be inculcated when one is young because the early embrace of career intentionality allows you to build a strong foundation for your professional life. This is one of the most important reasons why I started Project Puthri, India's first-ever developmental project that seeks to create career intentionality and employability among underprivileged young girls. A non-profit initiative of Avtar, Project Puthri aims to help girls from economically disadvantaged backgrounds break free from domestic labour and pursue careers in the professional sector. If there is one impactful strategy that can help us achieve this goal, it is instilling career intentionality in girls.

If done right, ICP can help women navigate their careers with purposeful progression. I've had a first-hand view of how effective this concept can be. Over the past few years since we uncovered the concept of ICP, several leaders and organizations have approached us, seeking help in harnessing their employees' full potential and ICP has proven to be valuable every single time.

For example, in mid-2022, a mid-sized IT firm approached us to evaluate employee talent and their career preparedness. Nusrat was among their near-100-person workforce. A senior data analyst, Nusrat had been with the company for close to five years. The people managers in the company had identified Nusrat as a 'high potential' employee but believed there could be room for improvement with respect to her productivity and people skills.

One afternoon in November 2022, I sat down with Nusrat for an informal chat in their office. A cheerful but slightly reserved thirty-four-year-old Nusrat came across as someone totally at ease with her work responsibilities. As a mother of two, she had a hectic schedule at home and worked from home most days of the week, going into the office primarily to attend meetings.

About an hour into the discussion, I was able to conclude that she ranked low on most of the tenets of career intentionality but had the potential to be a star performer if provided with the right guidance to overcome this shortcoming.

I noted down the following points after our discussion:

- Nusrat was good at her work, but being a little too comfortable with it, she no longer found it stimulating. As a result, this seemed to affect her productivity.
- She had a very busy schedule at home, because of which she had pushed learning and upskilling to the backburner.
- Given her gruelling chore list, she chose to work from home most days, leaving her with no time to connect with mentors, network with her peers or build a strong relationship with her manager—each of which, as we know, are important tenets of career intentionality.

Here is the step-by-step action plan I came up with for Nusrat to build her career intentionality quotient and help her perform better at work while simultaneously attaining her highest potential.

Action task	How It Can Help/Suggestions for Execution
Identify your strengths and interests.	Self-awareness is the foremost step in ICP. Reflect on the following: • What are you good at? Analysing and managing data are clearly your strengths. Are there other strong points that you have largely left unexplored? • Have you explored new avenues to employ your existing strengths? • Are there any new skills that you would like to develop? • What truly sparks your interest? It could be art and design, content creation or even social impact.
Find ways to network with your peers.	• Though in-person networking is more effective, explore internal and external virtual networking events since time is a constraint. Aim to attend at least two networking events in a month. • Try to go into the office at least twice a week for a few hours a day. Remember, lunch breaks are a great opportunity to connect. • Leave your child at a nearby childcare centre for a couple of hours. Talk to your HR about possible tie-ups that your company may have with childcare centres within reach. • If you need to travel a long distance for work, consider moving close by or looking for opportunities closer to home, simply because integrating work and life is easier with a short commute. (This may not always be possible, but if you can manage this, it can truly be a game changer!)

Action task	How It Can Help/Suggestions for Execution
Request for a one-on-one meeting with your manager at least once a week.	• The meetings need not be long—about twenty to thirty minutes will do. • Write down key talking points before every meeting—you could cover project updates, your manager's feedback about your work, your feedback about the project, your concerns, your strengths and interests and how they can be utilized better, projects in the pipeline and the overall objective of the team. • Though in-person meetings are better, pick a format that suits both of you. Sometimes even a phone call will do. But be sure to meet your manager in person at least once a month. • Be open and honest and do not shy away from discussing difficult subjects such as project challenges, workload and career stagnation. Also, express appreciation for your manager's insights.

Now, back to my meeting with Jo at the Google office in Hyderabad. As we go through the plans for piloting DigiPivot, we talk about Jo's life experiences and the origin of her unmistakable drive to be career-intentional. Career intentionality can be developed by practising the six tenets we spoke about earlier, but for some people, it is naturally created through their life experiences. Jo belongs to the latter set. She is from a rural area in west Japan and the third daughter in a community that cherished boys as being more important for the longevity and sustenance of families. She was born left-handed, and with grey hair at the age of four, she looked different from the other children. While her parents were her biggest advocates, she was a painfully shy child due to low self-esteem and a lack of confidence. She loved reading so much that she would hyper-focus on books and lose herself in them. She began teaching herself English so she could read books in the language and over time, she actually became a proficient English language teacher.

Her initial career choices, from being a teacher to a translator to an academic assistant, gave her both good and bad experiences. The last career stop in academia was a bitter one for Jo, where she faced harassment of different kinds—emotional, sexual and work-related. She decided to shift gears to HR consulting, a move that turned out to be a fabulous one and through which she landed a job at Google within a few years. She did not forget her journey and chose to work on projects where the large corporation's resources could be utilized to build a bridge for historically underrepresented people (women and non-binary) and to help them be ready for high-paying corporate jobs. In partnership with Avtar, Jo was instrumental in the realization of DigiPivot, which, as she puts it, 'is a vision-come-true programme for me!'

Jo describes career intentionality as 'having a vision of what a great career looks like that works for YOU'. She advocates coaching and self-awareness on women's own non-conscious gender conditioning based on societal norms, which is highly prevalent, especially in APAC countries such as Japan and India.

Whenever you are facing a career slump, here are three things that Jo advises:

1. **Take a step back and think of your career as a long-term journey.** Great change may not be happening daily or even monthly, but if you take one day at a time and make each day count, you will see that you have made awesome progress when you look back one year from now.

2. **Don't compare your career or compete with others.** You are on this unique journey of your own; the path is ready only for you and your learning.

3. **Maintain higher perspectives and don't take things personally.** There are always opportunities to learn from the lows and also pave the way for others who come after you.

Coming back to Nusrat, I met her for the second time in December 2022 after the two-week break, which she had effectively used to reflect deeply on her goals, passions and the daily logistics of managing her career and family. She had realized that she needed to dedicate more energy towards building relationships with her manager, peers and team and was ready to explore childcare options for her younger one, which would allow her to go into the office more frequently. She had also understood that if she treated her career as a series of learning points, many more fulfilling work opportunities would open up for her. I could see a distinct improvement in her demeanour—she expressed keenness to catapult her career forward and wanted to get back to her hobbies, especially writing and art. We parted ways and she promised to keep in touch.

A couple of months ago, as I was going through the profiles of the final list of selected candidates for DigiPivot's 2023 cohort, Nusrat's name caught my attention. She had cleared the arduous selection process for the scholarship. When I spoke to her, her excitement was palpable. With DigiPivot, she was looking forward to exploring ways to mesh her interest in writing and content creation with her proficiency in data to delve into the field of digital marketing.

Nusrat's transformation reaffirmed my belief, yet again, in the power of ICP in facilitating meaningful and efficient career progress. On that note, I want to tell you, dear reader, that you are the architect of your own career. Your focus should be on mindful progress, not perfection or comparison. Career intentionality can take you places—believe me, it has done so for me and countless others.

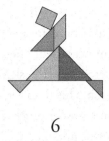

6

Finding Your Ideal Job

Ayesha is keying in bills on the computer at her father's shop near Cloth Market in Chandni Chowk, Old Delhi. It's a warm day in March 2022 and the fan seems to be working overtime. A beautiful metal paperweight in the shape of an eagle holds the stack of bills down as she pulls one, peers at it and begins typing into the keyboard, searching for information as her head bobs between the screen and the invoice. Her tea—'green tea for *chhota* (younger) memsahib!'—is turning cold and her father, sitting a little further on a comfortable sofa meant for customers, sipping his own masala chai, looks at her with exasperation. 'Why don't you finish that tea?' he asks. 'Let me complete this set and then I will,' replies Ayesha patiently. 'Is there anything I say that you are willing to listen to?' he demands. Ayesha's reply is just a smile. He sighs and continues speaking to me, complaining about Ayesha. 'She is a software engineer. From a very good college too! I didn't even have to pay any capitation—she got through merit. But look what she is doing. Sitting in this shop and typing bills. She refuses to go out and find a job.' I had come to buy curtains for a friend in Delhi and after a successful transaction, I am drinking refreshing hot elaichi tea with Mr Azad, who owns Imperial Curtain Mart. We are discussing work prospects for his daughter, Ayesha. 'Why don't you want her to work here? You need someone to take care of your business too, right?' I ask Mr Azad. He removes the topi (skull cap) and scratches his head thoughtfully. 'No, madam. I prefer that she work in a proper office. Businesses like these are tough for women.' I look around the shop. It is filled with bundles of fabric—sofa covers, curtains, bedspreads and carpets hog every inch of the space. Mr Azad mentions that he inherited the shop from his father, who had set it up in pre-Independence India. It's a 500-square-foot shop in a by-lane and with the steady flow of passers-by, there is just enough space on the road for a couple of two-wheelers and the occasional freight auto. The street houses several curtain shops, outlets selling fabrics of different kinds and tailoring units offering bespoke wedding suits and lehengas. It's a happy bustle in a neighbourhood that is familiar and friendly. I consider embarking on a discussion with Mr Azad to convince him that his daughter could very well manage a shop where she has literally grown up. But it is a discussion fraught with too many complexities and one that I can't finish in just the fifteen minutes I have on hand. So I leave it for another day.

'You are keen on pursuing a career, right?' I ask Ayesha. It is important to understand if she really wants a job. Landing your ideal job comes second to understanding why you really wish to work. Many women quit the workplace because their reasons for starting work begin losing steam as time goes by. Looking for jobs is an arduous task in itself and if you don't know where you wish to go, then all routes will end up complicating the journey. 'Yes, of course, ma'am,' replies Ayesha. She is twenty-three and a BTech graduate in computer science. She has a strong educational background, having completed her schooling at one of Delhi's better institutions, and her clear diction and confident choice of words reveal that she has learned well. 'My college offered campus placement, but all the companies that I was interested in were from outside Delhi. And I did not want to travel outside,' she explains.

'Was it you who did not wish to live outside Delhi or was it your dad's decision?' I ask, looking at Mr Azad. 'Well, there are enough jobs right here, no?' counters Mr Azad. And then adds, after thinking, 'It depends on the kind of job, Madam.' 'I would say it was both of us who decided that I shouldn't move out for work,' confesses Ayesha. She has tried speaking to a few of her father's friends and the contacts referred by her faculty at the engineering college where she studied and she has also applied to some jobs via LinkedIn. She has received zero responses to date, which has resulted in Ayesha assisting her dad in the accounting process at the shop. Even though Mr Azad has grudgingly agreed, he is not happy with this. He asks me to help her find a job. And we get down to putting together a plan.

Finding your ideal job has many interlinked parts and it is important to remember that during the early career stage (like Ayesha is in), the priority is to get a job that aligns with your education. Only later—in the next three to four years—does the actual definition of what an 'ideal' job emerges. Ayesha emails me to set up a time for a Zoom session in which we chalk out her job search strategy.

The foundational prep work that Ayesha must first action is as follows:

- Determine the skills and education that you can offer and that will make you stand out to potential employers. True, in your early career stage (and definitely in your first job), it is difficult to list out an elaborate bouquet of skills, but it is important to introspect on what you bring to the table. Think of what you really enjoy doing, what your education truly taught you and the combination of these two, which is fungible. In Ayesha's case, this reflection made her realize that while she had learned programming, she also liked numbers. This additional awareness helped her shortlist jobs at the intersection of her interests and her qualifications.

- Then comes the preparation of your resume. A resume is a great marketing document. A simple search on the Internet will reveal hundreds of different templates. My vote is for a single-page profile that is concise, factual and interesting. In today's age of AI shortlists, the keywords that you use to define your skills are key to making your CV both functional and optimized. Avoid outlandish language and stick to your own authentic expression. Ayesha chose to customize her CV for each job she applied for, so it was a little more aligned with what the employer was looking for.

- With the area of work chosen and your resume drafted, it is time to boost your search. Do remember that a job search, especially for your first job, is a coming together of opportunity and luck. For this to happen, you need to be discoverable in many places. Ayesha looked at the following routes:

  o One, she applied for relevant roles directly on company websites.
  o Two, she posted her profile on job boards found on LinkedIn and Foundit.
  o Three, she logged onto myAvtar (a diversity job portal that specifically identifies underrepresented talent for

companies steeped in DEI) and signed up to speak to a counsellor who could guide her on her job search.

- Next, Ayesha focused on how she was engaging on social media. She did a quick audit of the platforms she was present on (LinkedIn, Instagram and Facebook) and whether she was attracting the kind of followers that would help her search. She drafted posts for each platform that highlighted her interests and the kinds of news she consumed. Additionally, she also connected with people who would help her job search—people in recruitment and workers in other fields that are in need of programming personnel—by sending brief, professional messages that showed her keenness to work.

- After identifying her preferred job roles, drafting her resume and applying to positions, Ayesha focused on staying organized. She created folders in which she had the different versions of CVs that she had sent to varied companies. She maintained a record of all her emails and created calendar bring-ups to remind her when she had to follow up.

Within the next few weeks, Ayesha began receiving replies to her applications. She was surprised and thrilled at the number of responses she received, as she had frankly not expected to hear back from so many companies. Her excitement was palpable when I told her that corporate India is progressing in a positive direction when it comes to women's employment. Avtar's work in the field of DEI shows that companies are increasingly prioritizing DEI and putting in place a structured approach to foster gender diversity and equity. The 'Best Companies for Women in India' study by Avtar and Seramount has consistently shown that the top companies are investing in diverse hiring initiatives, family-friendly policies, regular diversity assessment and second-career programmes to attract women and provide an equitable work setting.[1] With the favourable change in the landscape of women's employment and the systematic manner in which Ayesha approached her job search, it was but natural that she received callbacks. It was now time for Ayesha to assess each opportunity.

Jobs are attractive to different people for different reasons. At Avtar, we ask over 166 questions to determine how interested you are in a job and how that particular role matches your skills. Arriving at a clear match between what you want and what the job offers is a fabulous thing! To help Ayesha select those jobs that she could further engage in and possibly move to the interview stage, I asked her to assess them on the below parameters. These factors are equally important for men too, but in the case of women, they assume greater significance simply due to the fact that each of these could be a potential derailer if not assessed properly:

- Job description
- Brand identity
- Opportunities for growth
- Geography
- Work–non-work integration
- Compensation

Let us go over each factor in detail.

Job description: It is important to completely wrap your mind around what exactly the job expects from you. A solid understanding of the job makes sure that you are clear and prepared for the highs and lows of the role. So go through the job description thoroughly and understand how the company benefits from this role. Do online research to see what others say about that particular function and evaluate if you are suited for the role. If you are working with a consultant, then obtain their expert opinion on this and also learn to detect if the job is being hard-sold to you.

Brand identity: This refers to the general reputation that the company you are applying to enjoys. Simple searches on Google and X will tell you if the company has a good brand identity. A company's employee value proposition is a composite of several things, such as brand value, the 'coolness' of the space, the kind of funding it attracts and the type of people that work there. Ayesha also took into consideration the company's placement on lists such as the 'Best Companies for Women in India (BCWI)' by Avtar and Seramount, the 'World's Best Workplaces' by Great Place To Work and 'Best Companies to Work for in India' by *Business Today*. A BCWI organization has very progressive policies, strong values, a great book of business to ensure sustainability and highly valuable goodwill.

Opportunities for growth: Another important factor you must consider before applying for a job is the potential for advancement in that role. By growth, I am not referring to a mere change in designation every couple of years, but also the learnings and skill sets you would be able to accumulate.

Geography: Deliberate on whether you would prefer an onsite role, a remote one or a hybrid arrangement before accepting an offer. Some points that you must consider in this regard are your work style, personality, responsibilities at home, the job's requirement for onsite presence, your commute and the company's culture concerning remote work.

Work–non-work integration: Consider the demands of the job and evaluate how the working hours, the commute to work and the degree of flexibility that the role offers will affect your personal life.

Compensation: Analyse the compensation offered for the role you are applying for, not just in terms of money but also other benefits, such as healthcare plans and other subsidiary perks.

Ayesha keenly listens as I discuss each of the above parameters in detail with her, taking notes diligently. A couple of months later, I receive a call from her. I can sense her excitement when she exclaims, 'Doctor, I am living my dream!' She has secured a job as a junior data scientist at a market research firm in Delhi and she is eager to put her programming, analytical and research skills to good use. I congratulate her and wish her the very best. She thanks me, confirms Avtar's mailing address and hangs up, promising to keep in touch. Three weeks later, I receive a package from Ayesha Azad in Delhi. I open it to find a beautiful Phulkari sari with exquisite embroidery, along with a handwritten note that reads: 'Doctor, a small token of gratitude for helping me land my dream job. Your insightful guidance will always stay with me.' Needless to say, the thoughtful gift, the note and, above all, the news of Ayesha landing her ideal job made my day.

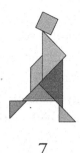

7

Home or Career—Which Should You Choose?

'Dr Rajesh, can we have just fifteen minutes of your time, please? Our CEO wants to personally discuss something very important with you.' I receive a call late in the evening from Priyam, executive assistant to the CEO of one of India's upcoming software development companies, a very prominent client of ours and I cannot refuse. It is 2018 and I am straddling a bunch of various commitments, paramount of which is the authoring of my first book, *The 99 Day Diversity Challenge*,[1] and I am racing to complete the first draft of the manuscript. I know that no conversation, especially with a CEO and more so when it is personal, can be limited to just fifteen minutes and a request like this means that my daily target of writing 1000 words would have to take a backseat that day. 'Sure, Priyam,' I say. There is great relief in Priyam's voice as he replies, 'Thanks a bunch, doctor, really obliged to you. I truly appreciate your taking the time.' I sigh and get ready to take the call. After all, a company that hires over 500 women each year and provides us with the opportunity to train all of them on career intentionality is not to be taken lightly.

'Hello doctor!' Gurbaksh's voice booms over the phone and I recall the tall, charismatic leader who rose the ranks from a frontline salesman to become the CEO of the company. He commands the utter loyalty of his team and the success of the DEI agenda at his company is entirely the result of his lighthouse leadership. His story is powerful and exemplary and I recall him being very grounded and completely committed to the cause of gender diversity during the session that I led for his direct reports. One of the goals that he had set for the company was to reach 50 per cent women's workforce participation and I wonder whether he is personally calling to share the good news about his company having made it. 'I will not take more than fifteen minutes, I promise!' he says. 'It's great to hear from you, Gurbaksh!' I respond, not untruthfully. 'Tell me, what's the news?' There is a brief silence before Gurbaksh speaks. 'Doctor, I need your help,' he says. The sudden dip in the energy of his voice informs me that this is not going to be a happy call. 'Sure, go ahead, Gurbaksh,' I reply.

Gurbaksh continues in a tone that reveals his concern and anxiety, 'My daughter, Roop, who has completed her BCom from Lady Sri Ram College (LSR), was going to apply for post-grad courses abroad. She is a very good student and I was confident she would get into one of the Ivy League colleges. But she just dropped a bombshell this morning. She tells me that she does not want to study further and wants to get married and be a housewife.' I am able to understand Gurbaksh's apprehension. At the same time, I also understand that all choices are acceptable and that if his daughter wishes to stay at home, she should be able to do exactly that. I share my thoughts with him. 'I know fully well that it is her choice, doctor. But I am concerned. Why would she not want an identity of her own and financial independence?

I know that there are several cousins of hers who are homemakers, but they live in the heartland of Punjab. Roop lives in Delhi and is a very smart and knowledgeable girl,' retorts Gurbaksh. 'Gurbaksh, being smart and knowledgeable does not preclude a choice to want to do something different. Perhaps Roop wants to be unique; maybe she does not want to follow the herd and pursue a career,' I try reasoning. 'Getting married, staying at home and being a housewife is exactly what the herd does, doctor! That is what the majority of the women in our country do!' thunders Gurbaksh. 'If this was her choice all along, why did she put herself through so much strain to get into LSR, which is one of India's top colleges for women?' he demands. I understand Gurbaksh's worry. For a leader who believes so passionately as he does in gender inclusion and the empowerment of women, this must have come as a definite blow. 'Her rationale is worrying me, doctor,' he continues. 'Roop believes that she can be a good mother only if she is a full-time homemaker. I need you to speak to her, doctor,' he says. I promise that I will.

The NFHS-5 reveals that nearly 70 per cent of women in India are homemakers.[2] While various factors contribute to this, I sometimes wonder if one of the main reasons for this sizeable demographic of women to choose to remain at home is because they still believe that being a mother and pursuing a career is an either–or situation. Is life a multiple-choice question with just one possible answer or choice? Are 'baby' and 'career' mutually exclusive choices with no option to choose 'both'?

It is not just the women who feel this way; it is also the family and society that still largely believe that a woman must give up her desire to become a mother if she wants a fulfilling career and vice versa. While Gurbaksh, being an exception to that rule, deems it important for his daughter to pursue a career while also being happily married and a mother to his grandchildren, the stories of a lot of young women that I have met in the last few years substantiate this point.

Maria, a mother of two who had registered in one of Avtar's programmes as a second-career woman in 2018, shared with me that getting back to corporate work was a very big deal for her. Her father had always told her that if she was bent on earning some money, she must become a preschool teacher because he felt that, as a Pre-K educator, Maria would be able to get back home by 2 p.m. before her own kids got back from school. 'He meant well for me; I know that,' says Maria. 'So I have grown up thinking that no other option is possible for mothers and that women pursuing other careers are falling short as mothers.' So Maria ended up doing a bachelor's degree in humanities at a private college, not because she loved the subject but simply because she needed to have that basic degree. 'I have always loved engineering. But my father felt that it was too much effort and investment if the person was eventually going to become a nursery schoolteacher.'

Many still view women's careers as superfluous. Diva Dhar, a researcher from Oxford University who published a paper titled 'Indian Matchmaking: Are Working Women Penalized in the Marriage Market in India?' in 2021 has some disappointing findings to share. The most popular women on the matrimonial sites that Diva explored were those who do not work and have no interest in working and nearly 70 per cent of men respond to these profiles, the study reveals, and there is a drastic drop in the number of men who respond to women who want to work after marriage.[3]

Nisha, a data scientist whom I met at a 'Women in Tech' conference in Bhubaneshwar, candidly shared her matchmaking experience with me. 'My parents had registered my profile on a couple of top matrimonial sites. There was this one particular interaction with a Boston-based guy that I can never forget,' she said. The man who was a top scientist in the field of cancer research seemed progressive initially, but as they got talking, her opinion changed. He tried telling her subtly more than once that only one person in the relationship could commit fully to a career. 'He had very high regard for his profession and big dreams but wanted his wife to be a homemaker because he believed that it would help him forge ahead in his professional path.' That was enough for Nisha to realize that this person was not right for her, but she added that there was pressure from her parents to not give up on him so soon. 'I am so glad that I stood my ground,' says Nisha, now an expert in data science.

The person that Nisha said no to is certainly not alone in thinking that men's careers must always take precedence over those of women. Rashi, an exceptionally talented acrylic pour painting artist, shares her story, which has a similar narrative. Growing up in a middle-class family, she witnessed her parents always prioritizing her brother's learning needs over hers. She says, 'My brother would attend Indian Institute of Technology (IIT) coaching classes, math tuition and chess classes, while I have never attended any class in my life. My art is self-taught. I stopped with a BA while my parents used all their savings to send my brother abroad for higher education.'

But why do people (both women and men) view women's employment as pointless when there is a very strong business case to support it? Three main reasons contribute to this:

1. **Childhood conditioning:** Many of our mothers were homemakers and we have internalized these traditional gender roles. So, right from toys and colours of clothing to

the activities we plan for our boys and girls, we make very different choices and we fail to equip our daughters with many key life skills.

Sania, a mother of three, helps her husband run a department store on a street next to where the Avtar office is located. I visit the store very often on account of the amazing range of healthy snacks that Sania stocks. Being a great conversationalist, she's shared snippets of her life with me on various occasions. 'My parents always wanted me to learn to cook well and maintain a house, ma'am', she once said, adding, 'and I am a great cook thanks to them. But I wish they had taught me other things too. I don't know cycling; I am not very good with numbers or technology and I can't do home repairs.' While I told her that it's never too late to acquire new skills and pushed her to learn them one by one, I couldn't help but lament the fact that men and women kick off from very uneven positions, primarily due to our ingrained beliefs.

2. **Tendency to lean towards the less demanding option:** Letting go of age-old gender roles is a big change and humans in general tend to resist change. Besides, sticking to traditional gender roles may seem like a less taxing option.

   To illustrate, a majority of women take on three kinds of responsibilities at home:

   • Cognitive labour: planning playdates, meals, etc.
   • Emotional labour: regulating the family's emotions (basically being the fixers of unpleasant situations)
   • Physical labour: doing the actual work (meal prep, grocery shopping, etc.)

If a woman pursues professional work, this burden of cognitive, emotional and physical labour on men tends to go up, which is viewed as unnecessary and avoidable stress on men. A working woman has professional commitments too, in addition to all the above responsibilities (which are significant themselves). 'Responsibility fatigue' is real; excessive responsibility can indeed run you down. So, sometimes it feels like clinging to the status quo is the smoother and easier option for both men and women.

For instance, Lizzie, a homemaker and mother of two, prefers to adhere to the established gender norms for precisely this reason. Lizzie returned to work after a career break of six years when her kids were six and two, but she soon quit. She admits to finding conversations about gender equality and women's financial independence inspiring. 'But when I started working, it elevated everyone's stress levels, including mine. My kids weren't happy with the reduced attention from me, my husband couldn't give his job the focus it needed and neither could I,' she says. She handed in her resignation within just two months. 'The stress just wasn't worth it. I honestly wonder if it is practical for both parents to wholeheartedly dedicate themselves to their careers without making major compromises,' she adds.

Lizzie's concern is a widespread one. A considerable number of people believe that things were much less complicated when men and women unquestioningly stuck to their gender roles. But there is emerging research on the immense benefits of gender equality and women entering the workforce: kids of working moms grow into happy adults and have higher self-esteem;[4] diverse companies are more innovative and hence more profitable;[5] having women in a team leads to enhanced collaboration, problem-solving, and decision-making;[6] and gender equality leads to reduced poverty, economic growth and sustainable development.[7] Clearly, the case for gender equality is convincing, but we must also explore ways to make this progressive landscape work for everyone so that women do not feel forced to choose between career and home. Managing a home and career is not easy, but it is definitely possible and gets easier with time.

Circling back to Gurbaksh's daughter, Roop, I decided to have a long conversation with her on a weekend. As I speak to her, I realize that contrary to what Gurbaksh believes, Roop is not against higher education. She is open to studying further. However, she does believe that a successful career cannot be without strings attached. The role models around her—her mother and her aunts—are homemakers whose lives have been dedicated to being the bulwark of the family and Roop is convinced of her decision on account of a strong identification with her mother. When children witness positive role modelling from their parents, it prompts them to follow their example and 'identify' with them. Those who believe that their parents made mistakes and don't want to follow the same pattern 'react' against them. 'I know that Dad is very upset with me, doctor,' she shares. I realize that Roop is not jumping into a verdict irrationally. 'But I am very clear. I believe that attempting to do everything is a zero-sum game,' she says. Roop goes on to reveal that she loves children. 'I want to have at least two or three kids. That's how it is in my own family and that of my uncles and aunts. I know that Mummy, also well-educated, decided not to pursue a career because she wanted to bring up my two brothers and me well, giving us all her attention. I can see the difference that having a full-time, stay-at-home mom makes to the lives of children,' states Roop with conviction. Her confidence in her decision is so strong that it's tough to even get her to think differently and step back from an idea that she views as a foregone conclusion. I use all the data in my possession to make a compelling case. After two conversations, during which I provoke her to think deeply about what I said, Roop decides to reconsider.

What Did I Tell Roop?

I shared with her the story of Hema, whom we met in Chapter 3. In fact, whenever I address a group of women who are at the crossroads of determining their path amidst various challenges, I recall Hema's words. When a woman works, it has a profound positive impact on her family as well as the nation. First, let's consider how it shapes the family:

- A widely cited study conducted by a professor of business administration at Harvard states that girls raised by working mothers are more likely to pursue careers themselves.[8] Not just that, these girls are more likely to earn higher wages and hold supervisory roles too, compared to girls raised by full-time, stay-at-home moms. The same study also states that boys raised by working mothers have a better understanding of gender equality and are more likely to contribute to housework.

- A working mother also serves as a role model for her children and demonstrates to them the value of independence and self-reliance and the skills of time management and prioritization.

- Furthermore, research by the World Bank reveals that when women earn, they are more likely than men to invest in

household needs and in their children's health, education and
overall growth.[9]

* On the other hand, when women are financially dependent
on their spouse or family, we know that they are likely to
possess restricted decision-making power, which could lead to
reduced self-esteem, making them more vulnerable to abuse.

On the topic of caregiving, here are some of the tips that I shared
with Roop, which can help women navigate home and work
without too much stress.

1. **Think long-term:** Any change is tough in the beginning.
   When a new mom starts work after a break, it can be
   overwhelming. But once you settle into your new work role
   and your child grows a little older, trust me, things will get
   a little easier. Stay attuned to your long-haul aspirations by
   writing them down and revisiting them every now and then.

2. **Know that it cannot be a fifty–fifty split:** It is tough for
   any couple to always split home and childcare responsibilities
   in half, as it is equally challenging for both parents to
   wholeheartedly dedicate themselves to their profession at
   the same time, because this will result in intense stress and
   burnout. Michelle Obama explains this point very well in a
   November 2022 talk with the National Public Radio (NPR).
   She says, 'Marriage is never fifty–fifty. But over the course
   of the entire relationship, you may have fifty–fifty over
   time.' She shares that in her marriage, at any given point,
   one of them was always giving way more than the other.
   It is important for couples to take turns prioritizing their
   careers and mutually supporting each other in whatever way
   possible.[10]

3. **Learn to integrate work and life:** There are ways to seamlessly blend work and family responsibilities by opting for a role that offers flexibility, putting technology to good use and so on, and, if done effectively, managing work and home needn't be too stressful. Chapter 15, 'The Fallacy of Balance', examines work–life integration in depth with practical tips to achieve seamless integration.

4. **Explore flexible work options:** Sometimes a break may be inevitable, but it is critical to make it count—we dive deep into this in Chapter 17, 'When Is It Time for a Career Break?'. Also, try to keep your break short. If returning to full-time work does not seem feasible, know that part-time and freelancing options are available aplenty today. Michelle Obama, in her chat with NPR, says, 'I had to take my foot off my career gas pedal, never putting on the brake, but slowing up a little bit.'[11] Slow down, but never lose touch with your work.

5. **Let go of social conditioning:** How do we break free from biases, stereotypes and societal expectations? I get asked this question every time I am invited to speak at forums for women. My answer is role models (to be more specific, female role models) because seeing is believing. Role models have three core benefits for women:

- They represent what is possible.
- They encourage us to make choices.
- They show us that we are not alone.

6. **Build a support system:** A solid support structure is critical if a woman wants to pursue a career and the most important person in your network of support is your partner.

Philanthropist, writer and former COO of Meta Platforms, Sheryl Sandberg, says in her TED Talk, 'Make your partner a real partner.'[12] Your spouse must take on unpaid housework along with you. I understand that this is easier said than done given the patriarchal setup, but there are ways to make this happen gradually, with continuous effort. We explore ways to secure the support of your spouse and family while maintaining a harmonious relationship in Chapter 10, 'Housewives and Feminists'. Remember, you need reliable support at work too—in Chapter 11, 'The Work Family', we look at ways you can create allies, stakeholders and your personal board of directors who can back you every step of your professional journey.

Look around you and you will find at least a couple of women and families who are making it work beautifully. At Avtar, almost 70 per cent of our women employees are mothers and we have seen time and again that they flourish in supportive environments.

If you do not have the inclination to pursue a career, that is perfectly okay. But do not make that choice because you think it is not possible for you to do both. If you have tried it and given up, it is probably because the situation at work or home or in both places was not ideal or you likely gave up too soon.

As the Career Doctor, let me assure you that with some strategic steps, it need not be home OR career, it can certainly be home AND career.

8

Guilt-Edged Lives

I was asked about 'Guilt' for the very first time when I addressed a women's day event at Accenture in 2007. Those were days when the Indian woman's career was just emerging out of oblivion and we were talking about everything that would make or break them. Once we opened the box of guilt, the questions flew fast and furious: Is guilt a negative emotion? How do I erase guilt from my mind? Which is worse, guilt or regret? Should I become a people pleaser?

It was a discussion I will never forget. We spoke about the anatomy of guilt, how it manifests, the difference between guilt and shame and the route to walking the razor's edge of winning society's approval while simultaneously being who you want to be. Ever since that energetic discussion in March 2007, there has been no discussion about women or women's careers that I lead, where guilt has not come up as a topic of contention.

Guilt plays a very big role in the lives of women, especially Indian women. It starts when you are a young girl, travels with you during teenage and adolescence, gets entrenched when you are a mother and unless you make a lot of effort to become self-aware and shake off its hold, guilt is your forever and ever companion. It takes many forms—motherly guilt, daughterly guilt, guilt of being a less-than-perfect wife, guilt of being a not-too-great professional and even guilt of being an absent grandmom—yeah, all kinds. We lead guilt-edged lives, indeed.

I had taken a career break simply because of the guilt I felt at leaving my nine-month-old son with my then-recently widowed mother-in-law, who was grieving her husband's loss. And I am not alone. Over the years of my experience in the realm of women's workforce participation, I have seen that nearly half the number of women who take a break do so out of guilt. Women professionals often lead subpar lives because they feel guilty about some aspect of their lives, where they feel they are failing in their duty.

Whenever I discuss guilt, I go back to the story of Sudha, whom I met on a flight from Delhi to Chennai. It was 2008 and I had just then become a frequent flyer by virtue of all the training sessions that I was conducting for India Inc. from Kashmir to Kanyakumari—well, not those two places particularly, but you get the drift. While my clients paid the regular economy fare for me, there would be times when, by sheer luck of the draw, at the boarding gate, I would get a free upgrade to business class. Flying business class on the longer flights is a delight, especially after a gruelling day of diversity interventions.

On one such occasion, as I settled into my upgraded aisle seat and stretched my legs with immense gratitude, I noticed a well-groomed woman with a quiet aura of intensity, at the window. She was probably in her late thirties or early forties, with streaks of grey in her long, plaited hair. She typed furiously, pounding away on her laptop keypad for the next thirty minutes or so.

It was 9 p.m. and I marvelled at her focus as she translated her thoughts into words, filling page after page of text. I thought she was perhaps an author, racing to meet a deadline.

The aircraft hit a bit of turbulence and I woke up with a start to realize that I had dozed off. The lights were dim, but not so dim that I couldn't see Sudha weeping. Shoulders hunched and whimpering, she sobbed into her napkin until the hiccups took over. In the quiet of the night, inside the hushed silence of the cabin, her hiccups startled her and me, too. She caught my eye by way of apology and I instinctively reached out to pat her hand. With that gesture of consolation, Sudha allowed herself to give free rein to her sorrow and the tears poured as she shared her story. She had just typed out her resignation from a high-paying, marquee job at one of India's top companies on account of a 'hypertensive crisis', where her blood pressure (BP) would not drop below 180/110.

A brilliant student from a middle-class family, Sudha studied engineering from IIT and business management from the Indian Institute of Management (IIM) to land a job in sales at one of India's iconic FMCG companies. She was fiercely career-oriented, making it conditional even when her parents brought up the topic of her wedding. She wanted to own her individuality and make sure her education at two of India's premier institutions did not go to waste.

Marriage followed and while her husband was a supportive chap, she lived in a conservative joint family where she was expected to perform the roles of wife and daughter-in-law to perfection. This included cooking every single meal for the family, even if she was not around to serve them throughout the day. Her mother had done this, as had her mother before her. Of course, they did not pursue a career outside the home, but should that matter? She held a degree in business management, which neither of them had—she was an improved version; she would crack this.

Sudha took the demands in stride and established a punishing routine, which involved her waking up at 4 a.m. to cook and manage the household, working through the day and ending her chores at 11 p.m. at night. When she had to travel for work, she would cook every single meal for days in advance, label them and put them in the refrigerator with instructions. She wanted to prove to herself and her family that she could do it all. If, on the off chance, she couldn't do it, she felt guilty and miserable. During times of international travel, she would cook for weeks. Couldn't her husband and parents-in-law have managed for a few days in her absence? Well, they certainly could have, but Sudha never knew because she never asked. She did not want to feel guilty for being remiss in her duties.

While this may seem like something that many of us do, what was special in Sudha's case was that she did this not just for one or two, but for seventeen years! Yes, for seventeen long years, she cooked while balancing a hectic corporate job. Throughout her career, raising her two children, living in three cities and getting promoted to vice president, Sudha cooked three meals plus organized snacks, juice, etc., called and gave instructions to her children, parents-in-law and husband regarding heating up food, all this while defying unimaginable exhaustion and sleep deprivation.

About two months before I met her on the flight, Sudha felt a sense of confusion and severe anxiety while addressing a meeting and her vision became blurred. She woke up in a hospital room, where her husband informed her that her BP had shot up and she had fallen into a dead faint. He blamed her work pressure for having caused her high BP and gave her an ultimatum to quit her job. As Sudha reflected deeply, she realized that it was not just her work that had led to this but also her guilt.

As I heard her story flabbergasted, I wondered why it had come to this. Sudha was a business head and a mature woman leader who was looked upon as a role model. Why did she cook every single meal? Why did she not appoint a cook?—She could certainly afford one. Why did she not speak about her troubles to her husband or children? Why did she build so much stress into her day?

When the former prime minister of New Zealand, Jacinda Arden, referred to her constant feeling of guilt over not being there for her daughter, she conveyed the challenge that most women go through. Guilt is a strange phenomenon. And it manifests itself among women, especially Indian women, in a thorough manner; no holds barred. I say this, not just as an expert on women's careers but as a mother and daughter myself, with guilt having determined many of my actions. The deep conditioning of daughters as caregivers for the family compels us to feel that if something or someone else isn't all right, we are the ones that are responsible and hence it is our duty to fix it. If we want something for ourselves, that makes us guilty too, as if, by so wanting, we are failing in our care for everyone around us. We feel guilty for falling ill, for being silent, for being less than perfect, for pursuing careers, for not pursuing careers—quite simply, for almost everything. It seems that our most frequent expressive state is guilt.

- **What guilt feels like:** In Sudha's case, guilt manifested as critically elevated blood pressure. I have observed that guilt also presents itself as anxiety, a knot in the stomach, a constant preoccupation with the past, sleeplessness and even depression. Guilt takes its origins from various influences—religion, early childhood experiences, culture and societal moorings. As we spoke, I realized that Sudha's mother had a profound influence on why Sudha made the decision to behave the way she did.

And guilt is a tiring emotion. It saps our energy, eats up our bandwidth, affects our mental and physical health and often causes irreparable damage to our lives. While the best companies for women in India offer a plethora of policies and enablers for women in the workplace, there is no manual on guilt. So how do we manoeuvre our way through the maze?

- **Get to the source:** I once asked the late Nirmala Prasad, mother, educator and principal of MOP Vaishnav College for women—a veritable force of nature—how to deal with guilt. Her reply, as succinct as always, was: 'Cut out that voice in your head.'

  Whenever you feel guilty, ask yourself this: should you listen to the voices in your head that tell you what to do or should you listen to your own voice? Also, reflect on why you feel guilty about not attending the fifteenth family event, even though you attended the last fourteen. Ask yourself why, even after spending great memory-building time with your kids, you feel like a failed mom for not picking them up from school at the instant of the bell. Ask yourself why even though your body is literally begging for rest, you must cook twenty-eight dishes for four days and stack them in the fridge. Whom are you trying to please? Ask yourself this. Get to the root of these thoughts. Do you feel judged? Is it your early childhood conditioning? Start the process of becoming self-aware by recording your feelings in a journal. Over time, you will realize that your guilt is a reaction to a belief system that is largely irrelevant.

• **Take charge of rating yourself:** Our guilt stems from the way people around us—those very close to us—determine what is good and bad. Our early childhood conditioning leaves deep imprints, which make us give away our right to create an identity that is our own. While the advice of our mothers, teachers or mentors has often been for our absolute good and clearly helped us stay alive, survive and thrive, not everything needs to be embedded within your belief system. Start taking charge of your scorecard. This may be challenging at first, but over time, as your intentions are clear to those who matter to you, the scorecard will swing in your favour. Communicate simply but powerfully that your identity is your choice and that your parenting, daughterly duties or wifely pursuits are entirely dependent on your determination.

• **Self-compassion is essential to being your best:** My mother would often say, 'You can only paint a picture if you have a wall to do so.' Self-compassion, or self-love, is a highly neglected concept in many Indian cultures. The stereotype of the sacrificing mom is so glorified that if we set aside an hour each morning just to refresh our bodies or minds, we view that as an extravagant luxury. The negative emotion of guilt can be countered only by creating a positive narrative for yourself. What are the good things that you have accomplished? Have you secured the future of your child with your income? Have you helped your colleagues through tough times? Another crucial step is to build empathy and compassion for yourself. How do you do that? One of the former heads of a leading bank has stated that she would look at herself in the mirror every day and state three positive traits of her reflection. Is it that simplistic? Perhaps, yes. But it is also amazingly reassuring.

- **Guilt as a corrective mechanism:** At Accenture, when I was asked if guilt is a negative emotion, my answer was 'No'. I firmly believe that guilt is not a negative emotion. Guilt may be provocative, but it is also a healthy emotion—a feeling that pushes you to think. Experiencing guilt reveals that you have been raised with values, ethics and rules. It means that you developed a sense of right and wrong in your childhood, that you are very observant and that you paid attention to what your parents or other influential figures in your life had to say. Guilt reminds you that you may need to make amends, apologize or balance out certain things.

- **Using the guilt matrix:** Often, we use a simple guilt matrix while counselling women professionals. Before we get to that, here's a simple illustration of the different types of guilt:

Types of Guilt	Healthy Guilt		Unhealthy Guilt		
	True Guilt (When you have genuinely violated your ethical standards)	**Empathy-Based Guilt** (When you feel guilty for not helping or caring for someone in need)	**Misplaced Guilt** (When you feel guilty for things that are beyond your control)	**Societal Guilt** (When you feel guilty about not conforming to social norms)	**Shame-Based Guilt** (When you feel guilty for not living up to unreasonable internalized expectations from yourself)
Is the guilt rational?	Yes	Yes	Sometimes, Yes	No	No

	True Guilt	Empathy-Based Guilt	Misplaced Guilt	Societal/Shame-Based Guilt
Example	You promise your child pasta for dinner, but you don't keep your word because you are just not in the mood to cook pasta.	Your elderly mother is unwell, but you are stuck at work and unable to get back home and attend to her.	You miss your child's performance at a school event because of a critical work meeting that you absolutely cannot miss.	You are unable to cook and serve three fresh meals on a daily basis for your kids, husband and parents-in-law because of your demanding work commitments.
Action	Accept, Forgive yourself, Apologize, Take corrective action and try not to repeat it.	Accept, Forgive yourself, Apologize and support the person in whatever way possible.	Apologize, but prioritize your well-being and consciously direct your attention towards the positive aspects of your relationship with the person.	Unlearn societal rules, understand the root cause of your guilt, recognize that it is not possible to meet all expectations and practise self-care and self-compassion.

Coming to the guilt matrix, ask yourself these five questions:

- Have you violated your moral standards?
- Was the situation within your control?
- Are you feeling guilty because you have failed to meet societal expectations?

- Are your expectations from yourself reasonable?
- Do the people you feel you have let down really need your support?

Sudha's guilt matrix looks somewhat like this:

Self-Reflective questions	Have you violated your moral standards?	Was the situation within your control?	Are you feeling guilty because you have failed to meet societal expectations?	Are your expectations from yourself reasonable?	Do the people you feel you have let down really need your support?
Sudha's answers (in most situations)	No	No	Yes	No	No
Action Sudha could have taken	Unlearned societal rules, understood the root cause of her guilt, recognized that it is not possible to meet all expectations, focused on the positive aspects of her relationship with her family and practised self-care and self-compassion.				

Understanding your feelings of guilt by writing down what you feel is of tremendous help. Explore your emotions with curiosity instead of judgement. You may not get to the root right away, but unravelling the knot will help you solve the problem with greater gentleness and self-compassion.

Remember this: when approached constructively, guilt is a reminder that you can do better. Rather than getting caught in its trap, not knowing what to do or rushing into hasty actions, if you detach yourself from its thrall and observe what your guilt is trying to tell you, there can be a lot to learn.

The Career Doctor's list of actions for dealing with guilt:

1. Understand where your guilt is stemming from and question its validity.
2. Develop your own sense of assessing yourself—you are the arbiter of your scoreboard.
3. Practice self-compassion—go easy on yourself.
4. Utilize the learning moments that guilt provides—it reveals that you have standards and will abide by them.

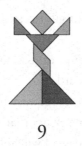

9

Superwoman Syndrome

It is a chilly September day in Delhi in 2010, especially for a Chennaiite like me. I am at the Vital Voices conference on women's empowerment curated by a passionate group of folks led by Sushma Narain from the American consulate. Founded by the former first lady of the USA, Hillary Clinton, Vital Voices is a global non-profit organization that works on amplifying the voices of women worldwide and this is their inaugural conference in India. My talk is part of the closing plenary, after two days of a brilliant exchange of ideas by some of the world's most prolific guiding lights on women's empowerment. I am thrilled to share the stage with Dr Tara Thiagarajan, the chief managing director (CMD) of Madura Microfinance, Naila Choudhry, chairman of the Dhaka-based Teleconsult group, and Luna Shamsuddoha, founder of Dohatec New Media in Bangladesh. Canadian journalist and CNN correspondent at the time, Zain Verjee, looks resplendent in a peacock-blue gown as she moderates the proceedings.

Dr Tara's Madura Microfinance (now acquired by Credit Grameen Bank) has provided the power of microfinance and funding to millions of women in Tamil Nadu. I've personally witnessed her passion, with Avtar having designed and managed a recruitment drive (more about this in Chapter 25) for Madura in 2009 to hire over 500 first-generation women credit advisers from the hamlets of Tamil Nadu. Luna (who sadly passed away in 2021) was the first female chairman of the Bangladeshi state-owned Janata Bank. A first-generation entrepreneur, Luna was also a director of the Bangladesh Association of Software and Information Services (BASIS). Naila has a prolific career as an international adviser, board member and propeller of the socio-economic development of women through technology and consulting. The conference reminds me of the amazing power of the feminine and the manner in which self-empowered women can create tectonic shifts in the world around them. Luna, Dr Tara and Naila are brilliant leaders who have changed the way communities around them function and each of them is also a committed mother, wife and daughter. They are national icons of repute, having built sustained programmes that have changed lives and destinies for many. One could refer to them as superwomen.

Post-conference, I'm catching up with Manya, a top human resources (HR) professional at one of our client firms, whom we had worked with a few years ago. She is an interesting example of a technical professional (a BTech graduate from NIT Rourkela) who transitioned into HR. Manya has stayed in touch and made the long trek, braving the heavy Delhi traffic, to meet me to share a few updates and take my advice. She is waiting in the lobby and upon seeing me, she rushes over to give me a tight hug, her eyes glistening with unshed tears. I am not surprised at the emotion, as she informed me in her message requesting to meet that she is going through a rough patch in her marriage as well as her career. I order some hot masala chai and biscuits and we speak about the weather, the traffic, generic work updates and a few other pointless topics while slowly circling the real reason why Manya wanted to meet me. After a great deal of thought and a lot of silence, she finally opens up, 'I am going through a very tough phase, doctor. I am being called a Superwoman and I hate it.'

Manya grew up on the National Institute of Technology (NIT) university campus in Rourkela, Odisha. Her father was a lecturer and her mother was a schoolteacher on the same campus. 'Probably because of the support and encouragement I received, I was a great student and always a class topper. Friends of my parents would always say that I would end up at NIT Rourkela itself, on account of my academic excellence. And indeed, I did!' Manya's face lights up with joy as she recalls how she concluded a stellar student life by being one of the few women to take up mechanical engineering and join an earth-moving company as a production engineer in charge of a line of bulldozers. The icing on the cake was that she landed a job in Rourkela at a prestigious company that everyone admired. 'Perhaps too many good things happened too soon, doctor,' ruminates Manya as she continues sharing her tale. Her focus and determination at school and college followed her into the workplace and she quickly rose up the ranks.

Given that she had the support of her proud parents, who wanted her success as much, if not more, than she did, Manya gave herself fully to work. Her mother did not allow Manya to shirk her responsibilities around the home and ensured that she learned cooking, managing home upkeep and all the rituals and activities around the festivals that her family celebrated. Within the next couple of years at work, Manya was promoted to a more senior role with greater responsibility. Her penchant for perfection and need for success ensured that she aced the role and by then, her parents began the process of identifying a suitable life partner for her. Since her husband, Ajay, also an engineer, worked in Delhi, Manya requested a transfer, which was readily granted by her organization. A few years later, Manya and Ajay became parents to a baby boy and life continued in its undulating way.

Slowly, the pressure began building in Manya's life. Despite holding a demanding job and bringing in over 50 per cent of the family income, Manya noticed that her husband and in-laws looked at her primary role as fulfilling her family responsibilities. When Manya raised this with her mother, the advice she received was that married women and more specifically, mothers, are the primary stakeholders in the home and the first to be blamed for any mishaps in their households. Manya decided to bind herself into a more exacting routine in order to keep up the quality of her family life and also manage her career.

Over the next decade, she apportioned time to cook for her family, care for her husband's parents and her own parents, manage her son Varun's schoolwork and ensure that her home was spotlessly maintained. She was the go-to person in her family circle for any help or support and she was also an agony aunt to her friends. Meanwhile, on the work front, she moved from her original technical arena to HR and decided to learn the subject afresh. She completed an online diploma in human resources and loved the subject so much that she signed up for a global resource group, which meant a few hours of work a week at midnight. With occasional health hiccups and a generally accepted notion that the sharing of workload would be skewed at home, Manya admitted to feeling a sense of futility in playing all the roles in her life to perfection.

One day, Manya received a call from Inez, her boss's daughter, to help plan her wedding. 'Dad said that you are the best person to ask. He often praises you, saying you are the best colleague, the best mother, the best professional and the best support! You are indeed a superwoman!' said Inez. The coin dropped as Manya realized it was not a compliment but a moment of truth. She realized that she was a victim of the 'Superwoman Syndrome'.

The superwoman syndrome is a socially perpetuated phenomenon where women are pressured to assume different roles, shoulder the responsibilities that come with those roles and perform them to perfection. They are glorified for overworking and lauded for not compromising on any of their expected duties. Sadly, for most women, not being a superwoman is not a choice. A sizeable number of these women are proud of the fact that they are super achievers. Considering that we are inundated with misleading ads and movies that put women on a pedestal, this is hardly surprising. A mother soothing her crying child, preparing breakfast for the family, helping her husband find his socks and handing her mother-in-law her medicines—all at the same time—before rushing to work and excelling in all her professional endeavours is an all-too-familiar narrative, is it not?

We do not realize the harmful implications of wanting to take on responsibility for everything and wanting to excel in everything we do. Studies show that women with this syndrome are more likely to experience anxiety, distress and feelings of inadequacy, neglecting sleep, nutrition and health, which in turn could put a massive strain on marital relationships. This sense of hyper-competence seen in some women perpetuates gender stereotypes and affects other women who desperately want to free themselves from unfair societal expectations. It impacts our future generations too—girls and boys who grow up around 'superwomen' are likely to stick to inequitable gender norms.

These tendencies of excessive self-reliance and perfectionism are clearly detrimental to everyone, but we have been unable to cut loose from them for years. Though women entered the workforce in large numbers during the Industrial Revolution in the late eighteenth century, it was only in the 1960s and the 1970s during the feminist movement that it was even recognized that women were overworked and underpaid and were in fact doing two shifts—one at work and another at home. The concept of double shift is widely attributed to Arlie Russell Hochschild, an American professor of sociology, who, in her book *The Second Shift*,[1] explored in depth the 'leisure gap' between men and women. Data from the Office of National Statistics, UK, reveals that men enjoy two years more leisure time than women over their professional journey, which stretches over a span of roughly forty years.[2] That is a lot, don't you think?

How do we get women like Manya to take it easy? Here's the Career Doctor's advice:

The first step is recognizing the signs of superwoman syndrome. Here's a simple self-audit to check if you are showing any evidence of it.

- **Are you a perfectionist?** Do you crave doing things perfectly because anything less would mean that you are not good enough? Do you feel inadequate when you are unable to give it your all?
- **Do you have a poor work–life balance?** Are the lines between your work life and your personal life blurred? Do you often

carry your work home to stay well ahead of your deadlines and thus extend your working hours?

- **Do you have trouble setting boundaries?** Do you find it difficult to say 'No'?
- **Are you experiencing burnout?** Do you have a constant feeling of exhaustion from a lack of sleep and self-care?
- **Are you extremely self-reliant?** Do you feel ashamed to ask for help and believe that you can manage anything independently?
- **Do you neglect your health?** Do you feel guilty when you sleep extra hours? Do you think setting aside time for relaxation or physical fitness is a luxury? Do you tend to prioritize everyone else's nutritional needs while not caring about what you eat?

If you've answered 'Yes' to all or most of the above questions, here's a four-pronged approach to help you tackle the four main markers of the superwoman syndrome:

The Four Markers of Superwoman Syndrome	Action
1. The need to always be perfect	<ul><li>Focus on your effort and progress instead of outcomes.</li><li>Set aside a fixed time for a task and do not exceed the time frame, even if you think the result is not perfect.</li><li>Make sure your goals are realistic.</li></ul>
2. Excessive self-reliance	<ul><li>Identify a support network at home and at work. It could even be just two to three people.</li><li>Take conscious steps to seek help.</li><li>Start by reaching out with small requests for help.</li></ul>

The Four Markers of Superwoman Syndrome	Action
3. Difficulty setting boundaries	• Do not respond to requests right away. Say that you will get back after checking on your schedule. This will give you time to check your availability and discourage you from taking on more work than you can handle. It will also help you reflect on whether you want to do the task and think of ways to politely decline the request. It will also encourage the other person to explore alternative options to get the work done. • Practice firm communication in front of the mirror and practice saying 'No' with your close circle in relaxed circumstances. • Use 'I' statements while refusing requests. For example: 'Unfortunately, I have a packed schedule tomorrow' instead of 'You are asking me to do a lot more than I can manage'. • Be polite, but do not apologize for declining unreasonable requests. You could say something like, 'Thanks for thinking of me, but my current schedule does not allow time for this.'
4. Experiencing guilt over putting yourself first	• Make a list of activities that bring you joy. • Schedule some 'me time' in your calendar and let everyone know about this time window that you have allocated for yourself. Begin with just twenty minutes and spend them doing something you enjoy. • Be consistent in setting aside this 'me time'.

Undoing the effects of the superwoman syndrome is not impossible. It takes time, patience and a lot of self-love.

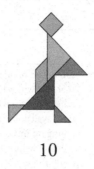

10

Housewives and Feminists

Sarala is visibly disturbed.

I offer her a glass of water. She takes a sip and looks at me with unhappiness in her eyes. I remember her dancing to *Enjoy Enjaami* with enthusiasm at Avtar's anniversary celebrations in December 2022. I would rib her for her rumbunctious laughter, which could be heard a mile away. A recruiter by profession, thirty-six-year-old Sarala joined Avtar in early 2022. Being the mother of a four-year-old, she opted to work remotely, three days a week. Her logic was that remote working would help her balance her career and childcare responsibilities. But in just about five months, she switched to full-time onsite work because she realized that her work-from-home days were significantly more frenzied than her work-from-office days.

Fast forward to August 2023 and Sarala has just resigned. 'I don't want to quit', she says, adding, 'but it has become very tough.' Sarala's resignation is not unexpected; she has been facing challenges managing her personal and work responsibilities. Her manager and divisional leader have spoken to her, but since she remains steadfast in her decision, they have requested my intervention. It is important that I speak to Sarala because she is a brilliant recruiter, one who is very good at identifying the right opportunities for underrepresented talent. In her eighteen months with Avtar, Sarala has placed over 300 women across different companies. Her income is important to her family and even more crucial for Sarala herself. She pays her son's school fees and sends money for her widowed mother's living expenses. But she is also one of the many millions of women desperately trying to handle the multiple responsibilities of running a home and managing a career. Her eyes well up as she tries to make sense of her situation.

'The COVID times were better, ma'am,' she says. 'Everyone at home realized the extent of work I had to do and they all pulled their load. At that time, it was possible for me to be both a housewife and a career woman.' The 'everyone' she is referring to are her husband and mother-in-law. But things were back to square one now—it had become her sole responsibility to keep the house and family running. 'I want equality, ma'am; equality in chore distribution. I want my husband to help me, not as a favour to me but because the home is his too,' she says. But Sarala's husband is not up for housework and wants Sarala to remain a housewife. He is not alone—he echoes the sentiments of the majority of men. Studies show that most men in India prefer that their wives stay home. 'Isn't my financial independence equally important to the family, ma'am? And if I protest even a little bit, I am scolded for being a feminist,' says Sarala exasperatedly.

As Sarala mentions the f-word, my mind goes over the times when I have been called a feminist and not as a compliment. Feminism is a much-maligned concept. A 2022 study conducted by the Global Institute for Women's Leadership and the research firm Ipsos found that 32 per cent of men surveyed believe that feminism does more harm than good; 33 per cent of them believe that masculinity is under threat; and 23 per cent feel feminism has made men fall behind socially, economically and politically.[1]

During my interactions with various people post-trainings and workshops, I have been exposed to the many unbelievable misconceptions that both men and women have about feminism, such as 'Feminism means disrespect for men', 'Feminists hate men' and 'Feminists disrespect culture'. I attribute this pervasive misunderstanding of feminism to two reasons primarily: first, people's general resistance to change—to fully embrace feminism, one must substantially alter one's beliefs and conduct; and second, the media's distorted portrayal of feminism—showing feminists as man-haters, making jokes out of feminist ideas in an attempt at creating humour and sometimes over-simplifying it and missing its nuances.

I am not going to elaborate on the intricacies of feminism here, but in the simplest terms, feminism is equality for men and women, where women have access to the same rights, opportunities and respect as men. Anti-feminists often argue that men and women are not the 'same' physically, hence equality between the two genders is not possible. Kathy Caprino, a career coach, explains why this argument is erroneous, with a good example in a *Forbes* article ('What is Feminism, and Why Do So Many Women and Men Hate It?').[2] Imagine there are two young boys, one physically weaker and smaller than the other. Asks Caprino if we would be denying the weaker boy respect and access to resources because he is weak. So, one fundamental point to grasp is that feminism is not about achieving sameness but equality.

On the work front, feminism translates to equal pay, equal representation in leadership positions, fair hiring and appraisal practices free of bias and stereotyping and the provision of enablers such as flexibility to ensure that men and women can achieve equal outcomes. At home, feminism means the sharing of childcare and housework responsibilities between partners; creating a pleasant environment where there is mutual respect; ensuring that both the man and the woman have an equal say in financial and family matters; and joint decision-making after respectful discussions. If we look at the historical narrative of gender equality in domestic settings, we know that the household landscape has been skewed in favour of men. Husbands made decisions that wives adhered to unquestioningly and wives stayed home, shouldering all household responsibilities and attending to the kids, which made it possible for the husbands to shine in their professions. If there were exceptions to this household dynamic, it was a minuscule percentage. Most men wanted their wives to remain housewives.

Whenever I hear the word 'housewife', I am reminded of C.K. Kumaravel (CKK), founder of the Naturals chain of salons and spas. CKK is an archetypal male ally. He believes in the limitless, untapped power of women. 'Women can never be equal to men— they are infinitely better,' laughs CKK, as we brainstorm about his initiative 'Homepreneur Awards' in the beautiful conference room of Naturals' corporate office in mid-2018. His personal vision is to create an India where today's freedom fighters—entrepreneurs— are able to guide our nation to become a developed one and if those entrepreneurs are women, CKK is doubly thrilled. 'Women possess strengths and qualities that often surpass those of their male counterparts,' says CKK. 'Their resilience in the face of adversity is unparalleled. I find their entrepreneurial spirit to have lasting effects on our society,' he adds. The Naturals salon was his spouse Veena's idea and when she broached it in 2000, he enthusiastically joined her in the adventure. Today, two decades later, Naturals has over 700 stores across over twenty states in India and is among the most successful franchises in the beauty business.

CKK abhors the term 'housewife' and wishes to eradicate it from the English vocabulary. He does not mince words while stating that women who do unpaid work at home, thereby enabling everyone else to earn money, deserve their economic independence too. Not for him are the accounting jugglers who attribute a notional value to a woman's work, without actually giving her the opportunity to earn and make money. 'History has consistently made the woman financially weak and dependent on the man,' he says with fervour. 'If there is a woman in your house, in the role of a mother, daughter, sister or wife, it is a man's responsibility to make that woman financially independent,' asserts CKK. In every talk that he has delivered, every interview he has given and every initiative that he has created (such as the Homepreneur Awards), CKK speaks about how financial independence is crucial for women. 'Money in the hands of women can build a family; it can build a country,' he states. CKK's mother, R.C. Hemalatha, a powerhouse of energy, raised him after his father passed away when he was barely twelve years old. Says CKK, 'When my father died, my mother called all of us and announced that starting from that day, she would be both mother and father to us. My mother became an entrepreneur and broke the belief of the time that women could only be housewives.'

Women like Hemalatha are a rarity. Most women in post-independent India seemed to accept the assigned gender roles submissively and focused their time and energies on being housewives. It was the influx of education and economic liberalization that brought about a sea change. This has led everyone—from mothers (who did not have the opportunity themselves) to concerned dads and teachers, to leaders and the media—to tell our girls that whatever happens, they must build a career for themselves. And, obediently, the young, educated women did land a job and started out enthusiastically.

Unfortunately, societal norms still saddle women with almost the full responsibility of running the house. This results in one or both of the following outcomes for working women: it causes burnout and forces women to quit working and abandon their career aspirations. The 2022 Women@Work study by Deloitte reveals that nearly half of the women surveyed feel burned out and concludes that this burnout is the top factor driving a lot of women to leave their current jobs.[3] We must understand that this burnout that women feel is not exclusively the outcome of an unsupportive work environment.

An equally prominent reason for women's burnout is the tilted situation at home. Kate Mangino, a gender expert, says in an interview with the *Guardian* in August 2022, that women do 65 per cent of the household chores.[4] She further explains how household tasks are usually split between men and women—while women take on all the routine tasks such as cooking and cleaning, men tend to do 'intermittent tasks' that don't need to be done every day. For example, in the Indian context, intermittent tasks could be booking travel tickets and monthly cleaning of ceiling fans and mosquito nets. So, men have the leeway to postpone these tasks and pick a suitable day to do them, while there is no escape for women from the critical everyday chores. Mangino says that in addition to this daily chore load, women shoulder the burden of 'cognitive labour', which includes tasks such as remembering important dates, organizing family get-togethers, mapping out grocery buying and so on.

'Why did working from home not suit you?' I ask Sarala. I am still attempting to uncover the key reasons for her decision. 'My family doesn't realize that working from home means that those six to eight hours are actually working hours,' she says. Sarala began to notice that the tasks that her extended family was seeing to when she was in office got foisted upon her on the days she worked from home. Though these were simple tasks such as preparing tea for the entire family, folding clothes or clearing up after lunch, they did add up, taking up a sizeable amount of Sarala's time and energy. While this upset her, she also realized that her family didn't have a deliberate or ill-natured intent while handing over these extra responsibilities to her. She says, 'They did it because, to them, I am the "housewife" and they genuinely and almost subconsciously believed that I would want to do these tasks whenever I am home.' And here's the clincher: Sarala admits that sometimes she personally felt obligated to take that chore away from someone else and do it herself, almost as if it were muscle memory. 'I don't want to completely stop doing my household chores, ma'am. I don't want my work to cause problems in my marriage. I just want a little bit of help at home, especially from my husband.'

This, unfortunately, is the reality of most marital relationships. Things did improve marginally during the pandemic lockdown in 2020 when kids were home from dawn to dusk and families were void of any external help. Avtar conducted a study in 2021 to examine how this radical change in circumstances changed the dynamics at home and our findings were reasonably encouraging.[5] Of the 300-plus people we surveyed, 35 per cent of men said that their contribution to home chores (which includes the 3Cs—Cooking, Cleaning and Caring) had increased substantially since the lockdown. And 31 per cent of Gen Y men reported near-equal load sharing at home. But the same study also revealed that 52 per cent of men in joint families spent no time or less than an hour on housework.

But with the pandemic well in the rearview, a considerable proportion of women have likely gone back to almost single-handedly running the home, teetering on the verge of burnout. Many organizations are making a sincere attempt to address women's burnout in a bunch of ways, such as by offering flexible work arrangements and remote work options and fostering a culture that encourages employees to disconnect from work. But sometimes, these special enablers can end up creating problems because women who work from home or who have flexible schedules are often expected to take on an enormous load at home.

So, are enablers such as flexibility doing more harm than good for women? And should they come to an end? Certainly not. But along with these catalysts at work, we need to witness a critical change at home: men must embrace housework and childcare as much as women. Bridging the gender gap at work can happen only if we bridge the chore gap at home. Let's be clear: we need to go beyond the concept of mere 'help' from men when it comes to housework or childcare. We need men to take complete ownership of house tasks and be on par with women at home.

I simply cannot stress enough the importance of fair teamwork at home and I must admit that things are gradually improving. For instance, I see millennial dads being very involved in childcare these days. And the media is displaying an interest in broadcasting the message of gender equality, too. For example, Procter & Gamble's #Sharetheload campaign highlights gender disparity at home in a very engaging and relatable way. But we have a long way to go. A 2022 report by UN Women states that at the current rate of progress, it may take almost 300 years to achieve full gender equality.[6] So, it is imperative that each one of us—both men and women—take up the responsibility to drive change.

Coming back to Sarala's challenge, after a long and probing conversation, we understood that her decision to quit was a complex one compounded by the pressure of housework and because in the next two months, she was expected to attend a few family events, where her contribution as the daughter-in-law of the house was significant. The first thing we did was give her a sabbatical of four months, during which she could complete all of this without guilt. India needs every Sarala to be in the workforce and if a four-month break is going to ensure another fifteen to twenty years of active earning for her, that's a small price for a big win. Next, we connected her with a career counsellor who would support her in sorting out her planning and responses on how to perform her work without derailing things at home.

But that was just half the solution. How could Sarala get her spouse to contribute his fair share at home? The answer is Communication, Communication and Communication, at every stage. Here are the Career Doctor's tips for Sarala to change the chore dynamics at home. Let me split the action into two parts—preliminary work and actioning—because embracing equality at home cannot happen overnight, it requires groundwork.

Preliminary work	Actioning
• Talk to your spouse openly about what gender equality means to you and how it can positively impact the entire family. • Share research-based evidence with your husband on the benefits of gender equality. You could expose him to studies on the economic benefits of gender equality, how equality positively impacts parenting and child development, the mental health impact of gender equality and the like. • Watch podcasts and movies together that nuancedly portray the injustice of gender imbalance at home. • Introduce your spouse to friends and family members who champion gender equality and can shed light on its importance. • If needed, seek counselling from a trained therapist who can help facilitate productive discussions on how gender dynamics have changed over the years, the benefits of equality and so on.	• Jointly brainstorm ways to equally split house chores between the two of you— it is critical that this be a joint activity. • When you split chores, ensure that both of you get adequate free time. Consider both of your strengths and preferences and split chores accordingly to keep boredom or discomfort to a minimum. Rotate tasks every month if both of you prefer or dislike a particular task. • Share the physical load as well as the mental load. The mental load could include tasks such as planning meals, arranging kids' activities, keeping a record of grocery supplies and so on. • Appreciate your partner's efforts and contributions. Come up with incentives to motivate both of you to do your share of housework. For example, consider an activity that both of you can do together once the tasks are completed. • Remember, sharing the load needs continuous effort and engagement from both sides (and hence a lot of patience!), for we are trying to reverse years of conditioning. Experts recommend using 'I' statements while resolving conflicts, where you primarily focus on your needs and steer clear of blame. Also, understand that a fifty–fifty split may not work initially (that should be your end goal, though).

Indian women are often the 'trailing spouse' in an economic equation—they earn significantly less than their husbands. This means that the decision for women to be taken out of the workplace to focus fully on housework does not cause a deep financial dent in the family. As such, for women to have time to grow into their careers and begin contributing equally, if not more than their spouse, it is important for them to stay in the workplace.

I often tell the women I mentor that if their spouse's professional work does not leave them any time to contribute to housework, they should hire external help for all the 3Cs, if needed. This step could also need the spouse's buy-in, especially in the Indian context. So again, openly discuss why it is needed and how it can help the whole household, particularly in the long run. Hiring external help may seem like a huge investment when you are starting out and you may even be spending an amount nearly equal to your earnings. But that's okay. In a few years, when you've established yourself in your profession, you will look back with deep satisfaction at the positive transformation you've brought about for yourself, your organization and your nation. And you will proudly say like I do, 'Behind every successful woman is reliable household help!'

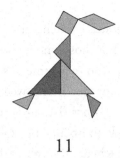

11

The Work Family

I clearly remember the winter of 1999 because that was when a routine test at my son's school revealed that he was dyslexic. For the next decade, as much as I worked for the cause of women's participation in the workforce through Avtar, it was learning about dyslexia and understanding how to support a child with a learning disability that became my passion. Later when, as a teenager, he discovered his talent for communication, abstract thinking and problem-solving and answered all his written exams without the special support that dyslexic children require, it was a victory unmatched in my life. There are many mothers with neurodiverse children who have gone through the demanding experience of getting their child mainstreamed and self-reliant, but I would give credit for easing my journey to an extended network of allies. My colleagues at work and a set of very dependable family members transformed into an empowering fortification around me that proved to me the power of allyship.

Some stories are deeply moving and transformative, and the 2008 movie *Taare Zameen Par* is one that reminded me of the importance of Ram Shankar's role, played by Aamir Khan, in everyone's life. My son and I watched the movie together and it left both of us in tears. For those who missed it, the story is about eight-year-old Ishaan, who encounters scorn from everyone, including his parents, for not doing well at school and being inferior to his 'genius' brother. Ishaan is sent away to boarding school and there he finds an isolated but solid voice of support in Ram Shankar, his art teacher, who realizes that Ishaan may have a learning disability. And the presence of just one earnest guide and cheerleader transforms Ishaan! Who can forget the closing scene when a jubilant Ishaan runs towards his art teacher, who joyfully props him up in the air?

I liken our work at Avtar to the role of Ram Shankar. If one lone person can radically reshape another's destiny, imagine the power of multiple support avenues for children, women, LGBTQ+ individuals and other marginalized groups. As a woman, think of the incredible benefits of having several sources of support, particularly in the workplace. Imagine having a set of people at work who vocally support you, guide you in overcoming challenges, provide you with useful work-related tools and take a keen interest in your professional progress. They are called allies. An ally is someone who uses their power or privilege to help others, particularly those from marginalized sections.

Allyship in the workplace is a fairly new concept, though the concept of allyship itself goes far back in history, right from the abolitionist movement in the nineteenth century, where a considerable number of whites joined hands with African–Americans and fought their fight. Later, during the women's suffrage movement in the late nineteenth and early twentieth centuries, male allies fought for women's right to vote and more recently, in the LGBTQ+ movement, heterosexual individuals have been championing LGBTQ+ rights.

When it comes to allyship in the workplace, let's broadly understand what it entails. While anyone can be an ally, allies are usually people with privilege, so men can make great allies to women and help promote gender equality. When it comes to male allyship, I believe that the first step is acknowledging that most women face discrimination and bias at work and that men's support can help women overcome these challenges more easily. Women can be great allies to each other too. (We discuss this in Chapter 25.)

How can male allies help you? As a woman facing issues such as unfair pay, lack of flexibility, stereotyping and imposter thoughts, imagine having male allies who:

- Amplify your voice in advocating for your needs.
- Call out sexist behaviour and the biased work culture.
- Demand fair pay for all with equitable and transparent appraisal procedures.
- Listen to your problems without judgement, offering emotional support.
- Provide work-related resources to help you work more efficiently and make steady professional progress.

In the course of my work, I have encountered numerous male allies who fully understand the value of gender equality. Raman Ramachandran, dean and director of K.J. Somaiya Institute of Management, Mumbai, is a model example of a male ally. A Keralite by birth, Raman says that he grew up witnessing gender parity in his family. But it was during his PhD days in Australia that he began to fully appreciate gender equality, thanks to Pru Lamotte, his landlady. Raman recalls that Pru conducted an in-depth interview before renting out her place to him and mandated that words like 'mankind' were not allowed in her house. 'I was taken aback. I argued that the use of such words does not necessarily reflect an individual's gender bias,' says Raman. But over the next four years, being a tenant at Pru's, he gradually understood the importance of gender-neutral language in promoting equality. 'I became a strong believer in women's rights thanks to Pru and her friends,' says Raman. There has been no looking back since then. Raman, who was chairman and MD of the BASF group of companies when I first met him in 2015, has been a vocal advocate for gender equality, pushing for enablers such as childcare support, work-from-home policies, skill development for women and more.

Another inspiring example of a male ally is Pavan Mocherla, executive vice president of Becton Dickinson (BD). Pavan, one year my junior at B-School and my quizzing teammate, says that his spouse, who comes from an all-girls family, helped shape his worldview about equality and inclusion. Especially after becoming a father to a girl, gender equality has gained a new level of importance for him. He has devoted a lot of time and energy towards understanding the various challenges that women face at work and has spearheaded numerous programmes at BD to support women. Male allies can undoubtedly have a tangible impact on women's advancement and allyship, in general, can bolster physical and emotional security in the workplace and enable everyone to perform to their fullest.

At Avtar, we have always encouraged employees to check in on each other and extend help to one another in any way feasible. I have witnessed up close the incredibly positive effect of a nurturing environment. In my own case, my colleagues have covered for me in critical meetings when I had to spend time at home on account of caregiving and they've even travelled on my behalf to represent Avtar when it was difficult for me to do so. For almost the first decade of Avtar, I left the office at 3 p.m. and started working from home from 5 p.m. to 9 p.m., after taking care of my household chores and supporting my children with their school work. And in the interim, my colleagues would manage any firefighting that needed to be done. And this is not just specific to me. Indrani joined Avtar as an HR analyst in early 2021. As a single mom returning to the workplace after a six-year career break, she had her share of challenges. But her colleagues—both male and female—have always striven to make her feel at home. They are mindful of her responsibilities at home, always schedule team meetings after checking her availability, share helpful tips and resources to ensure she works effectively and lend a sympathetic ear to her problems at home. Indrani says, 'The workplace is my safe space now. I value my work family so much!'

Ah, the term 'work family'. There has been a lot of debate recently among organizational experts and the masses about whether colleagues and bosses in the workplace can really become one's family. The general opposition to the notion of colleagues becoming family is understandable, particularly in today's context, because people switch jobs frequently, there's fierce competition between workers to pull ahead and companies lay off people arbitrarily and without due process.

But I see the setting a little differently. I agree that the whole workforce in an organization may not be one big, happy family unit and that is okay. It is similar to how we share a close bond with our core family circle and a slightly detached relationship with most members of our extended family while still upholding the family clan's values and esteem. It is much the same here. Find that close group at work who are like family—people who can offer an unbiased ear, support you in times of crisis and propel you towards progress. And build a professional relationship with the others in the organization.

Identifying that close circle is a game changer, I promise. Your allies will help boost your morale, mental health and performance. Many top companies recognize that allyship is a trump card when it comes to employee growth and retention. The annual 'Best Companies for Women in India' study conducted by Avtar and Seramount reveals year after year that the majority of the 'best' companies have specially designed programmes that men can make use of for mentoring female colleagues.

Here is a four-step method to help you find your allies or your core group of support:

Step 1: Build friendly relations with your team members and colleagues. It is important that you initiate conversations, remember names, show interest in their work and lives, socialize over lunch and share personal anecdotes, all while respecting boundaries and displaying a professional demeanour.

Step 2: Broaden your network by attending company events and collaborating on projects and while doing so, make it a point to connect with people from diverse backgrounds.

Step 3: Now, from these connections you make, pick out people whose goals and values align with yours.

Step 4: Reflect on your strengths and how your plusses might help your allies. Offer help whenever you seek support from anyone at work.

So now, can you be an ally? Yes. You can have allies and, at the same time, be an ally to others. Follow this three-pronged framework to be an effective ally:

The 3L Framework:

Learn: Make an effort to understand what your marginalized colleagues need help with. Learning and unlearning are important parts of being an ally.

Lean: Speak up when you see anything problematic. Get involved in conversations that drive systemic changes. Build an ally network—this joined force can help navigate the allyship path at an increased pace.

Leverage: Leverage your existing privileges to bring about effective changes. Even if you fall into the unprivileged category, take small steps such as listening to the experiences of other marginalized colleagues, being a sounding board to them, embracing differences and so on.

But it is important for us to keep in mind the boundaries of allyship. I say this because allyship is a commonly misunderstood concept. Your allies shouldn't be silencing your voice, assuming what you may want, deciding for you or doing the work for you. I have seen male allies speak on behalf of their female colleagues, thereby shutting them down and I've witnessed employees becoming totally dependent on their allies. These are all examples of allyship gone wrong, but, in all probability, done with a well-meaning spirit. Remember, your allies' actions must help you develop, allow you to unlock your full abilities and become a better version of yourself.

While allies are indeed great pillars of support, we must understand that it is not easy for anyone to be an ally because allyship requires considerable effort. An ally needs to be open to learning, receptive to feedback, take active steps to help marginalized colleagues and speak out bravely and this may rub some people the wrong way. Doing all of this while meeting your own work targets and striving for personal progress can get daunting. So, let me be frank. Finding solid allies can take time.

This leads us to the next question: Are there other avenues of support at the workplace? Yes—stakeholders. Identifying your stakeholders and seeking support from them is comparatively easier than finding allies. A stakeholder is someone who benefits when you perform well or progress in your career. One key difference between an ally and a stakeholder is that the former mostly gains unquantifiable advantages from your growth, such as the satisfaction of playing a part in promoting inclusion and a positive reputation, while the latter derives tangible benefits from your development.

For example, any employee's good performance helps the boss in many different ways—achievement of team goals, improved productivity, lower team attrition rate and so on. Thus, your reporting manager is a key stakeholder for you. HR is also an important stakeholder for any worker because employee satisfaction is one of their KRAs. Similarly, identify other people who are likely to benefit from your superior performance. For instance, the various stakeholders for a good designer may include the marketing team, the leadership, product managers, web developers, etc.

Once you have identified your stakeholders, make it a point to spend at least a few minutes every day building pleasant relationships with them by following the same steps that we just discussed in relation to allyship—start conversations, listen actively, display interest in their work and offer support where possible. I guarantee that you will make headway.

Apart from allies and stakeholders, who else needs to be part of your work family? Mentors. It is critical that you create your own personal board of directors keen on advising and guiding you. Many organizations have formal mentorship programmes— the 2023 'Best Companies for Women in India' study reveals that 76 per cent of the 'Best' companies have career sponsorship programmes.[1] So, take advantage of these programmes. If finding a suitable mentor within your organization is a challenge, approach leaders during external networking events or on business platforms like LinkedIn and make sure to customize your connection requests with a crisp and effective message.

If you feel hesitant about seeking help from leaders, remember that mentors stand to benefit too—they gain fresh perspectives from younger employees, get a chance to further hone their leadership skills, shape the future of their industry through these mentorship sessions and more.

Let me reiterate that having a core support group comprising allies, stakeholders and mentors is a necessity for anyone and not an extra. Think about it—studies show that we spend one-third of our lives at work. And a considerable chunk of the time that we spend at home is dedicated to chores and sleep. So, a significant part of your conscious and sharp self is spent among your colleagues. If you have solid relationships with at least a handful of them, wouldn't it make work truly enjoyable for you? On the other hand, if your relationship with all your co-workers is aloof, the risk of feelings of loneliness, stress and burnout is fairly high.

One common reason for many of us feeling alone at work is our hesitation in asking for help. We need to understand that seeking help is a good trait—it is a mark of honesty and an acceptance of vulnerability. Besides, when you reach out to your colleagues and seniors, both to seek and offer help, know that you are playing an active role in your firm's inclusion agenda.

12

Upskilling: Your Passport to a Recession-Resistant Career

If you look at the tiles in your bathroom or kitchen, there is an (almost) invisible paste that holds them in place. It appears invisible because it is usually the same shade as your tiles and neatly fills the gaps between them. The paste that gives a nice, crisp outlook to your wall is not to be confused with mortar, which is the foundation that the tiles sit on. This filler is actually a combination of cement, coloured powder, water and sand. The process of applying this paste to add rigidity and strength to the tile is called grouting. If you want to be a grouting technician, you must know the fine art of mixing these components in the right proportion and also possess the adroit skill of application.

Before you flip the book to check its title and wonder if you have landed by mistake on a guide for construction enthusiasts, hold on. I spoke in detail about grouting only to introduce Josephine to you. Josephine is about forty years old, an energetic mother of two and one of Chennai's finest grouting specialists. She was born in a single-room hut in a slum tenement famous for its seafood, but she no longer lives there. She lives with her husband (a senior mason) and their children in a neat, two-bedroom apartment where (no prizes for guessing) her own grouting skills have been used on the tiled walls.

I met Josephine in August 2020 when she worked on the grouting in my home. Wearing an apron, her hair neatly tied in a bun under a cap and the mandatory mask on, she took a detailed briefing in Tamil from the site supervisor, asking pointed questions (she reminded me of a management consultant!) about the precise tasks at hand before she began her work. I found that she knew more than one language, as she instructed a couple of other workers in Hindi. Quietly, with tremendous attention to detail, Josephine worked for the next two hours. Given that she was not stepping out for a smoke break (unlike her colleagues), I offered her tea and we both sat on the Kadapa slab near the garden and exchanged notes.

Josephine was very excited to know about my work in the space of women's careers and I was super curious to hear her story. She comes from a family of seven children, born to a mother who worked as a domestic helper. Josephine shared that her mother was very hardworking, working in five homes—three in the morning and two in the evening—and returning home late in the night, often buying food from government-run canteens. 'My siblings and I would clamour around her to get our packets and she would watch us eat with a sense of fulfilment. I am happy that she is now retired and lives with me!' Josephine happily mentioned.

'What did you want to be when you grew up, Josephine?' I asked. 'Honestly, at that age, we never had any dreams, ma'am,' shared Josephine. 'But when I work at construction sites these days, I feel I would have made a good engineer!' Her dad was well-meaning (she mentions with fervour how he never abused her mother, unlike other men in the neighbourhood) but an alcoholic. He drove an auto rickshaw and managed to put four of the children through school. But before any of them could go any further and the remaining three children could get any sort of primary education, he passed away in the same auto rickshaw from an overdose of alcohol.

The boys of the family got started on various jobs of menial labour, while the girls went for daily-wage jobs at a local printing press, the flower market and so on. But these jobs were not permanent. When work dried out, the family would struggle to have three square meals. That was when one of Josephine's brothers began training under a mason and the work gave them a steady income almost every day. Josephine decided that she too wanted such a job where she would have sufficient money earned and put away so that even if there was no work for a couple of days, they could manage to get by.

She began accompanying her brother on his masonry assignments as an apprentice (known as *sittraal*, or junior worker in Tamil). She was eleven when she first started, she remembers. She practically did every job on the site. She was strong and agile—a combination that worked very well to make sure she was in demand. She would load and unload bricks and other materials, dig trenches, assist in the mixing of cement, help with the scaffolding and clean up the rubble. When she was nineteen, her brother's friend expressed his desire to marry her and since he had a reasonably secure income, she agreed. 'He doesn't drink, ma'am. That's what I like most about him,' smiled Josephine.

This is tough physical work, demanding a lot of effort. How did she manage during her pregnancy? That's when Josephine spoke about upskilling. She shared that when she got pregnant the first time, it was difficult for her to do the (literal) heavy lifting. She noticed that the grouting work paid well, was comparatively lighter and that the grouting specialists were respected too. She began spending more time assisting the chief grouting technician. One day, in early 2008, when he took ill and was on leave, Josephine completed the work all by herself, which greatly impressed the site engineer and from the next day onwards, Josephine was assigned to grouting work.

Over the next few years, she began building skills within the space of grouting expertise. She learned about colour palettes and how to mix powders to arrive at the exact shade of paste; created a toolkit with specific equipment that she had seen at other sites; and even learned how to use epoxy chemicals. In addition, she began using her knowledge to prepare groundwork appropriately to save time and money. In the next couple of years, she started insisting that she should be involved in the planning stage itself so that she could suggest colour options. 'I want to start a grouting academy for girls from my slum, ma'am,' shared Josephine. 'I believe that this kind of skilled work will really help them.' Josephine is genuinely convinced of this because she is respected at work, makes decent money to put her two children in playschool and has also supported the education of her two sisters.

Skills: The Basis of Relevance

The story of the two woodcutters and the paths they used to succeed is a thought-provoking one. The first one, despite working longer hours, was less productive because he used the same blunt instrument to pound away at his job. The more successful one, who was able to deliver double the output of her counterpart, actually spent only half the time at work, as she spent the rest sharpening her axe.

Josephine's story is a powerful illustration of the importance of upskilling. I am talking about technical skills, not soft skills. But don't get me wrong, I am a huge proponent of soft skills. In fact, I believe the term 'soft skills' is a misnomer. There is literally nothing soft about what such skills can do. I believe that soft skills should be renamed strategic skills, given the crucial role they play in women's careers. They procure opportunities, prevent regretted attrition, enable problem-solving and create leadership. However, the focus of Josephine's story is not about the strategic skills; it is about the technical skills that she developed over time. More importantly, the way in which she upskilled herself.

Technical Skills—What Are They?

By way of definition, technical skills are those skills that I refer to as ones that solve a certain kind of problem. Let me be clear: in this context, technical skills aren't just those skills that involve the use of software, data or machinery of some kind. Any skill that helps one become more competent and efficient at his or her work counts as a technical skill. For example, a hairdresser may benefit from learning about the various treatments to improve hair health or the different ways to do hair colour correction. An event planner may find value in learning about efficient and evidence-based methods of logistics management and budgeting.

Every profession requires distinct technical expertise and people in all stages of their careers can derive advantages from this specialized know-how. Let me break it down for you:

1. **Early career stage:** Technical skills increase your employability quotient, productivity and confidence. In the initial career phase, when you are laying the foundation of your career and

creating a name for yourself, these technical skills can be a great value addition. Skills that can improve your knowledge and efficiency will open doors to various career advancement opportunities.

2. **Middle career stage:** This category includes people who are roughly in the thirty-five to fifty-year-old age bracket, where most of them are in management positions or have just been promoted to one and are starting to handle a team of their own. Their assignments also become more intricate. So, if mid-career professionals can focus on technical skills that can widen their domain knowledge, it will greatly enhance their professional competence, thereby making them more confident and well-informed mentors to their subordinates.

     Remember, most people in this phase also have added personal responsibilities, which include attending to the needs of their children and elderly parents. So, technical skills that improve workplace efficiency can lead to a better integration of work and personal life. For example, a marketing manager can use AI to swiftly analyse data and assess risks, thereby saving time as well as train his team of writers, analysts and designers to leverage AI to make work more productive.

3. **Leadership stage:** Sustained upskilling helps leaders thoroughly understand the business situation, thus enabling them to lead with confidence and authority. Not just that, when leaders are up-to-date with the relevant technical skills needed to tackle the volatile business realm, their organizations are in a far better position to adapt to the latest business trends. Leaders who prioritize technical upskilling make better mentors and they are well-placed to choose

potential leaders among their employees too. Besides, when leaders consistently upgrade their skills, they are setting an example for their staff to prioritize upskilling.

There are many real-life examples of leaders who have succeeded mainly because they understood the value of upskilling and prioritized it. For example, Ginni Rommety, former chairman and CEO of IBM, shared in a conversation with the *Harvard Business Review* in March 2023 that 'for many jobs, success depends more on skills and the ability to adapt and learn than on piece-of-paper credentials.'[1] Under her leadership, IBM focused heavily on developing the technical skills of its employees. Her own personal growth within IBM can be attributed in significant part to her enthusiasm and dedication to skill development. Another leader who has always stressed the worth of skill development is Ursula Burns, former CEO of Xerox Corporation, whom we spoke about in Chapter 4 while discussing the skill route to a successful career. Burns, who started as an intern at Xerox Corporation in 1980, rose to become the CEO of the company in 2009 and the first black, woman CEO of a Fortune 500 company—all thanks to her openness to learn.

No industry can afford to neglect upskilling, especially because in most industries, people start with rudimentary technical skills and then progress in their career trajectory by actively upskilling themselves. For instance, take the banking or IT sector: most entry-level positions require only a bachelor's degree in finance, accounting or engineering—nothing more. But as you move up the ranks, you enhance your expertise by attending specific training programmes in new banking or IT technologies, database management, programming languages, regulatory changes, risk management and more. Many banks and IT companies also collaborate with educational institutions and encourage their employees to pursue specialized courses and globally recognized certifications such as financial risk manager (FRM), chartered financial analyst (CFA) and project management professional (PMP), which can boost their domain knowledge.

In some other industries, such as retail, many entry-level positions do not typically demand a bachelor's degree either. Employees in the retail industry ascend their career ladders mainly by learning on the job, staying abreast of industry trends and acquiring new competencies, such as learning efficient ways to manage customer data, exploring the intricacies of digital marketing, becoming proficient in inventory management and so on. So, allow me to restate my point: upskilling is a must-have for all industries.

Now that we recognize the value of upskilling, here's a ten-point hands-on upskilling blueprint:

1. Assess your skills, strengths and weaknesses.
2. Do your research to identify the skills that are most valuable in your field.
3. Identify and write down your skill gaps.
4. Actively explore training programmes and certifications via online courses, webinars, conferences, etc., to address the skills you need to acquire.
5. Connect with your mentors and colleagues to gather input about various learning avenues and game-changing skills in your industry.
6. Make the most of the upskilling opportunities provided by your organization, including mentoring sessions, workshops and access to learning resources.
7. Set clear and short-term goals for yourself.

8. Create a learning plan and set aside time for learning every week or month, depending on your needs and schedule. Remember, upskilling is just as important as your regular work.
9. Make a conscious effort to apply the new skills that you develop.
10. Reflect on your progress and seek feedback from your colleagues.

Often, I use a **skill-development matrix** to help people decide when and how to upskill themselves.

Using the Skill-Development Matrix

Self-Examination	Action to Take If Your Answer Is Yes
Are you experiencing slow career progress or career stagnation?	Acquire new skills related to your current role to deepen your expertise and widen the scope of your work.
Do you feel overwhelmed by your workload or are you taking too long to complete your tasks?	Seek out efficiency-building skills. For example, a researcher can opt for relevant AI-related online courses to become proficient in using AI to cut down on research time.
Do you lack confidence in certain areas of your work?	Upskill yourself in the specific areas where you lack self-belief.
Is your field an evolving one with rapid technological advancements and frequent regulatory changes?	Set quick-term goals and make learning and development a part of your weekly routine.
Do you dislike your work?	Analyse what you find unappealing in your work and explore related areas within your field that lack those aspects. For example, a social media content creator who does not like the constant emphasis on garnering likes and audience engagement can investigate other forms of content creation, such as scriptwriting or technical writing.

Self-Examination	Action to Take If Your Answer Is Yes
Do you have a strong desire to grow and reach higher levels of success?	Meet with organization leaders and mentors on a regular basis to find out what it takes to succeed in your field and focus on developing those specific skills.

Use this matrix to take stock of your skill-enhancement journey. To sum up, here's the Career Doctor's advice on how you can unlock your full potential:

1. Do not hesitate to step out of your comfort zone and embrace new opportunities. It promotes personal growth and helps you discover hidden talents.

2. Adopt a flexible outlook and develop a growth mindset where you welcome feedback and are open to continuously learning and improving. In other words, be comfortable being a beginner at every stage of your life.

3. Learn new skills regularly to evaluate your learning agility and aptitude as you age.

4. Be open to reverse mentoring (where a less experienced employee mentors a senior employee). Remember that younger people are digital natives who can teach you a host of technical skills in an easy and fluid manner.

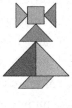

13

Women and STEM

It was January 2013 and I was in Bengaluru speaking at a conference organized by the Association for Computing Machinery (ACM), a US-based non-profit initiative focused on furthering thought leadership and careers in computing. By this time, Avtar had garnered sufficient support for the women's career movement. This meant that more companies, more managers and more leaders were aware of what it meant to employ women and why it was crucial for more women to be employed in the Indian corporate landscape. We had added companies from retail, FMCG, banking, advertising, insurance, e-commerce and publishing to our roster. It also meant that new and fresh challenges, which were either not experienced earlier or, most likely, not articulated, were emerging for us to solve. One such challenge was the one facing women in STEM careers.

Careers in science, technology, engineering and mathematics (popularly known by the acronym STEM) always had a chequered relationship with women. The number of women enrolling in STEM courses has been on the rise since 1990, but the number of women who build sustainable careers in STEM is still pitiably low despite the advent of industries such as IT, telecom, software development, semiconductor manufacturing, data processing, product development, et al. and hence the gap is particularly pronounced in higher-level positions and leadership roles in STEM. The problem in 2013, more than a decade ago, was not just the fact that we had a low number of women in STEM; it was that even discussion of the topic did not have enough takers at a conference. Social issues are always a slow burn. You have to keep stoking the fire over and over in new and inventive ways until it becomes a blazing platform. That was my intent at the ACM conference.

It was a fabulous assemblage of stellar folks, including many women STEM leaders, which is rare. I was sharing the stage with some amazing speakers from IBM, the now-defunct SunGard and Accenture. But our room looked empty and bereft. Women's careers were not 'a thing' at the time and it showed in the couple of dozen people who had come to hear us speak. However, I had prepared a solid deck of slides with powerful data points (primary research and data have always been my arsenal) and was determined to deliver it to the fullest of my energy, notwithstanding the demotivating turnout. I took to the podium to talk about the two major factors explaining the phenomenon of the low participation of women in STEM: the 'Leaky Pipeline' and the 'Vanish Box' (a concept I first came across in a 2011 research paper on gender dynamics in science and technology published in the *Brussels Economic Review*.[1] It refers to women vanishing from science academia and reappearing in fields at the intersection of science and business). As I commenced my speech, I noticed that the first row had a smattering of involved people, among them a bearded gentleman, who paid rapt attention to our discourse.

During the Q&A, he asked pointed and focused questions about my research. He also mentioned that the lack of women in STEM was not just an 'India' problem and referred to the leaky pipeline's presence in US workspaces too. When he began speaking, the students slowly filled up the rows and his short, engaging commentary obtained a huge round of applause. As we stepped off the stage and went across to thank the kindly gentleman for turning the spotlight on our issue, I came to know that we were in the presence of Vint Cerf, the father of the Internet and the originator of the transmission control protocol-internet protocol (TCP-IP). Later that evening, thanks to Vint's thoughts about women in computing, our session got a lot of airtime and also started off the conversation around second careers for women in technology. IBM, Accenture and SunGard signed up to source second-career women and IBM and Accenture also became sponsors of Avtar's Segue Sessions, a skill-building conference that has resulted in over 5000 women embarking on second careers in STEM!

Why is it critical for women to enter STEM? Diversity in STEM leads to increased innovation, which is crucial for us to tackle pressing healthcare and environmental challenges. Another reason to encourage women to take up STEM is that this field offers increased income potential and enhances women's financial independence.

However, gender equality in STEM is still a far-off aspiration. According to the UNESCO Institute of Statistics (UIS), women account for just about 33 per cent of researchers worldwide.[2] This gap can be attributed to a variety of factors, including societal conditioning and pressure to conform to traditional gender roles, limited access to resources and opportunities and a lack of female role models in STEM. The notion that the arts, humanities and social sciences are the 'forte' of women is a stereotype that has been perpetuated in many societies for a long time. We still prefer gifting Barbie dolls to girls and remote-controlled cars to boys, don't we? While there may be historical associations between women and certain academic fields, such as literature, social sciences and the arts, it's important to recognize that talent and passion are not confined to any particular gender. Multiple studies have shown that men and women have equal capabilities when it comes to math and computing.[3, 4]

According to the 2023 Confederation of Indian Industry's (CII) Women in STEM report, women need strong support from their families to take up STEM subjects and pursue STEM careers because career choices, especially in India, are family-driven decisions where the opinions and values of parents carry a lot of weight.[5] Another 2021 study on women's employment in the manufacturing, operations and engineering services sector, conducted by Avtar in partnership with General Electric (GE), which included focus group discussions (FGDs) involving women in these sectors, found that women in STEM can do better when they are extensively supported by their families.[6] This home support becomes more significant because women in STEM face a host of challenges in the workplace.

As women progress in their careers into mid-management, they encounter the leaky pipeline and a significant number of women drop out of STEM fields at these levels. This attrition can be attributed to a combination of reasons: bias, discrimination, work–life balance challenges, limited mentorship opportunities and a lack of supportive policies within organizations, which can lead to feelings of isolation. In the Indian context, though there has been a steady upward rise in the number of women in professional and technical roles, the Global Gender Gap Report by the World Economic Forum spanning several years suggests that this rise does not correspond to equal opportunities for advancement. Women get stuck in the same positions for years. When women in STEM persevere and cross these early barriers at entry level and mid-career, they come up against one of the most critical phenomena that affects a large majority—the imposter syndrome. Imposter syndrome, a common experience among women in STEM, can hinder career progression and self-belief.

In early 2019, I received an email from Rupali, a senior research scientist at a physics lab at a leading university in the US. She had heard about Avtar's contribution in the space of women's workforce participation at a convention and wanted to meet me. She was going to be visiting Chennai soon. I readily agreed as I love meeting people, especially women who create their own success stories despite all odds. I was also curious to find out what made her choose physics and also learn about her contributions to the field. She walked in punctually at the agreed-upon time on a sunny morning in July 2019. A tall woman, Rupali had a cheerful disposition and spoke with an easy flair. We discussed a range of topics—our upbringings, the work that Avtar does, her research in the area of thermodynamics and gender disparity in STEM. She spoke freely about the challenges she faces as one of the few women in her field and shared that she was being evaluated for the coveted position of physics lab head at her university. When I wished her luck, I noticed that she gave me a slightly reluctant smile. For the first time in our entire conversation, I sensed a little discomfort in her. 'I am not sure if I am ready to take on the huge responsibility,' she shared, a little hesitantly. I soon realized that she had come to meet me mainly to open up about her feelings of inadequacy—she needed reassurance and guidance on navigating self-doubt. 'I don't like being in the spotlight because I don't think

I deserve all the praise I get for the work I do. A lot of external factors aligned to help me get to where I am,' she said.

I recognize imposter syndrome all too well because I've frequently grappled with such thoughts myself and I still do from time to time. In March 2023, I shared my experience of feeling like an imposter through a LinkedIn post and the overwhelming response it received from women from all fields shows Rupali and I are certainly not exceptions. But I also believe that imposter thoughts in the right measure can work as an advantage—a not-so-common perspective—and that's what I discussed in the post, which resonated with scores of women.

Why do I think imposter thoughts in moderation aren't all that bad? A person who is experiencing this is likely to make well-thought-out decisions since she questions herself a lot; she is likely to value others' opinions and is receptive to feedback; she does not take her work lightly; she is constantly pushing her boundaries—and these are all great leadership traits!

I spoke to Rupali at length about this ubiquitous problem faced by women leaders mainly because there is a serious dearth of role models for us. While imposter thoughts are not all that bad, the key is to find a way to keep them within reasonable limits.

Here's the Career Doctor's advice for keeping imposter feelings in check:

- Know that you are not alone and that feelings of inadequacy are absolutely normal. A KPMG study finds that 75 per cent of female executives across industries have experienced imposter syndrome in their careers.[7]
- Make a list of all your past achievements and keep it handy.

- Celebrate your achievements.
- Picture success whenever you feel like giving up.
- Connect with other women from different levels, as they can relate to your feelings. Bonding over common challenges can be a powerful way for women to overcome them.
- Remember that imposter thoughts in limited dosages can benefit you and aid your progress.
- Seek professional help if these feelings of self-doubt become overwhelming and begin to hinder your work.

Along with the above steps to tackle self-doubt, what can help women in STEM is making a conscious effort to expose themselves to inspiring stories of women STEM stars. This can help make up for the lack of role models in real life, to an extent. For example, though the name 'Katherine Johnson' may not ring a bell, the minute I mention *Hidden Figures* (the book as well as the movie adaptation), Katherine's inspiring tale of determination, brilliance and breaking down barriers in the world of STEM will likely come to mind. In 1953, Katherine joined the National Advisery Committee for Aeronautics (NACA), which later became the National Aeronautics and Space Administration (NASA). She became part of the West Area Computing Unit, a group of African–American female mathematicians who performed complex calculations by hand, often using slide rules and adding machines. Katherine's breakthrough came during the early days of the Space Race. Her mathematical skills were instrumental in launching the USA's first astronaut, Alan Shepard, into space in 1961. Her trajectory calculations were critical to ensuring Shepard's safe return to Earth. However, Katherine's most significant contributions came during the Apollo programme, where she played a pivotal role in John Glenn's orbital flight in 1962. Her calculations were so accurate that Glenn himself refused to fly unless 'the girl', as he affectionately called Katherine, confirmed the numbers. The Oscar-nominated movie about her life has inspired thousands of girls to aim for the stars, literally! And it clearly shows that media can have a profound positive effect.

Closer home, the Chandrayaan-3 mission had over 100 women in STEM powering it in various capacities, from mission designing and systems engineering to robotics and orbital mechanics. And the media did well to highlight this aspect with extensive interviews and profiles of key contributors. Women such as Kalpana K., Nandini Harinath, Anuradha T.K., Minal Rohit, Moumita Dutta, Tessy Thomas and V.R. Lalithambika have gained widespread recognition on account of this. The Indian Space Research Organisation (ISRO) chairman, S. Somanath, in his interaction with the media, spoke in depth about women's contribution to the mission's success. He said, 'Some of them played a significant role in navigation during the lander's critical descent.' The star women themselves have shared in detail about their contributions, which is something that we absolutely need. Women traditionally shy away from talking about their credentials and achievements and, in the process, fail to seize chances to motivate fellow women. But this time it was a little different. For instance, Ritu Karidhal, popularly referred to as the 'rocket woman' of India, shared on social media, 'Chandrayaan has written India's name on the moon forever. India becomes the first country to reach the south pole of the moon. I and the others played a major role.' An image of sari-clad women scientists from ISRO celebrating the success of the mission went viral across social media, serving as a huge inspiration for girls.

Another much-anticipated project of ISRO's that closely followed the Chandrayaan-3 mission, Aditya-L1, India's first solar mission, was led by a woman too. Nigar Shaji, who joined ISRO in 1987, led the complex assignment for nearly eight years and has been a role model for the other women at ISRO and girls aspiring to have a fulfilling career in STEM.

Pursuing a career in STEM can be incredibly rewarding for women. STEM fields offer exciting opportunities for intellectual growth, innovation and societal impact. By breaking down barriers and shattering stereotypes, women can pave the way for future generations and contribute to a more diverse and inclusive STEM workforce. So, let's make it happen!

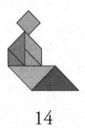

14

Ambition—A Bad
Word in a Woman's Life?

When I grew up in Pondicherry (now known as Puducherry), Anjali and her family were our neighbours. Being a young teenager, Anjali was sufficiently older for me to idolize and marvel, in typical fan-girl style, at her wit, beauty and charisma.

She was the eldest of three children in their family and embodied success and achievement. Sports? She played basketball and kho-kho. The arts? She was a trained dancer and took part in every dance drama that our school produced. She was a girl scout, an National Cadet Corps (NCC) cadet, a prefect at school, a house captain of the 'Daisies' (the other houses were Shamrocks, Hollyhocks and Violets!) and a cultural secretary.

Her pictures—smiling and holding a winner's cup or dressed in Bharatnatyam attire while gracefully receiving a certificate—appeared in our evening tabloid more frequently than the local MLA's photographs. Every teacher vied for the credit of being Anjali's mentor. The headmistress of our school, who perhaps smiled just once a year, reserved that smile solely for Anjali.

Soon, Anjali passed out of school and our paths separated. I moved to Chennai to begin working at Citibank. Over the years, Anjali's name would pop up every now and then and we never failed to talk about how effervescent her early success was. My mom would periodically update me about her: 'Anjali has just completed her BSc.' 'Anjali is getting married.' 'She is dancing at Kamban Kalai Arangam.' 'She had a difficult time with her second pregnancy.'

Until one day, my mom told me that Anjali was divorced and recovering from depression. She added that Anjali would be shifting to Chennai soon after sending her kids to a boarding school in Kodaikanal. 'Why don't you meet her and help her? Anjali's mom wept over the phone yesterday while speaking to me,' said my mother.

While I felt bad that things had taken a difficult turn for the golden girl of our town, I was also excited about meeting Anjali. She'd had a profound influence on me and I wanted to revisit some of those years when I basked in the glow of her companionship. From an academic perspective, I needed to understand why one of the most iconic girls I had known had never risen beyond her first victories.

'I would say that, in my case, I never learned how to manage my ambition,' Anjali got right to the point after we finished our first cups of coffee one warm afternoon at Le Bistro. Her eyes reflected sadness, but I could also sense a certain maturity and calmness in the way Anjali spoke about her adversities. 'A young girl's ambition is a fabulous characteristic. Everyone around you—parents, teachers, neighbours, uncles and aunts—the entire ecosystem appreciates and applauds it. But a woman's ambition is a dirty word,' she said with simple candour.

After getting married, Anjali tried to pursue a career as a professional Bharatanatyam dancer. Frequent fights erupted when her husband's family questioned her need for an identity. They believed it was inappropriate for a married woman to seek recognition and adulation. Deciding to change tracks to a more acceptable pursuit, Anjali set up a beauty salon. Even though the space was different from her career as a dancer, her family still didn't see the case for her to do something on her own when there was no financial pressure. Shutting down the salon, Anjali decided to get into the insurance business as an agent, but that too fizzled out when the demands of meeting people for selling policies were seen as a flagrant conflict of priorities for a woman and mother.

'At school, as I reflect back, everyone accepted my success, since it was a happy, vanilla package of a young girl doing bright things. It was as if success had chosen me and not the other way around, so people were glad to cheer for me,' shared Anjali. But when she hungered for the same success, recognition and adulation after her marriage, it was seen as an ugly, undesirable thing.

Sheryl Sandberg, in a 2014 article for *Cosmopolitan*, speaks of how leadership in women is seen as being bossy, while the same trait in men is encouraged and lauded.[1] The larger societal system seems to be waiting to take over to provide enough reasons why female ambition has to be checked and kept in line. And when competitiveness in girls becomes a pursuit in adulthood and calls for more participation from the family, it becomes a serious problem. Parents enjoy the ambition of their little girls because it reflects well on their own success as creators of successful girl children, but the same parents become deeply uncomfortable when the ambitious woman expects her husband, in-laws or even the parents themselves to make alterations in their lives to accommodate her desire to win.

Indian women have always been kept wrapped in a safe, non-threatening cocoon of the caregiving stereotype. They are not alone in this. Women around the world are expected to 'tone' down their ambition the instant they leave the school campus. There is data from every country on how girls outperform boys in school.[2,3] Life strikes and it's the rare girl who manages to cross it without downgrading her aspirations.

Anjali nodded in agreement but also added, 'Aspiration is merely a desire. You aspire to get a merit card. You aspire to lose weight. You aspire to travel. But ambition is a sustained emotion.' And she is spot on! Ambition defines you. It is the proverbial shifting goal post—a need to differentiate yourself from the next person—a continuous requirement to achieve.

Anjali's description of ambition made me reflect on my own maternal grandmother, Subbulakshmi, who, in the 1930s, was the brightest girl in her family. She was such a good student that when she dropped out of school following puberty, the nuns from the convent school she had been attending visited her home to appeal to her father to let her continue her education. After her marriage, however, her ambition was a cross she had to bear. She was advised to 'be a woman' and stay within the confines of the kitchen. Fortunately for her, when her husband migrated from Madras to Bombay and later to Bangalore to seek out a more prosperous future, she found the freedom to give reign to her own need for an identity.

Whenever I think of her (she was ninety-two when we lost her), I recall how busy and energetic she always was, organizing stuff, helping people and making things happen. She was starkly different from other women of her age. When I once asked her why she was ambitious, she replied, 'The need to excel, to be better than others, to rise to the top, is a feeling that comes from within. You want to be known as someone who accomplishes something, someone who is better.' But she also emphasized that this feeling can't come on its own and that all of us need people who believe in us and who dream for us, to strengthen our confidence.

My grandmother's parents and aunt played a key role in bolstering her self-confidence and instilling motivation and ambition in her very early on. In an era when girls hardly stepped out of their house, my great-grandparents supported their daughter's wish to finish school, even if that meant sending her away to her aunt's home. There, she had the freedom to explore her interests and express her thoughts and ideas. Her aunt (a child widow) impressed upon my grandmom that she was infinitely capable of anything she desired to do. After her marriage, my grandfather valued her individuality and pushed her to take control of her life. It is a matter of phenomenal pride for me that she rose within the small sphere of a primary school educator to become the principal of a prominent school in Bangalore. She also owned and drove the first car in the family in 1969!

A woman's passion and determination to achieve are sparked by her personal motivation, values and interests, which, in turn, are greatly influenced by external factors—primarily the home environment in which she is raised. She blossoms and matures beautifully if her formative years are nurturing and her parents support her immediate interests, encourage her to limitlessly dream of a fulfilling future and motivate her to make her own decisions and take ownership of her dreams. This liberty to dream and aim is critical.

In many cases where ambition seems repressed or vitiated, I have observed that these challenges have arisen from certain experiences in childhood. I urge parents (not just of the girl child, but parents in general) to clearly understand that building ambition can come only from a foundation of acceptance and positivity. In today's age of instant Instagram stardom, I find a lot of parents instilling an imbalanced sense of ambition in their children. This can later manifest as various personality disorders, which require therapy to resolve.

I believe that parents must not:

- 'Push' certain career options on their children just to conform to societal standards. For example, dissuading a girl from pursuing civil engineering despite her interest in the subject because they believe it is a male-dominated field.
- Impose their own aspirations on their kids or try to fulfil their dreams through their kids. For example, a doctor couple forcing their son to pursue medicine or a parent who fervently wished to study law but couldn't push their son or daughter into the legal field.
- Discourage extra-curricular activities because they may hinder their child's academic success.

It's equally important for parents to make sure they are nurturing 'healthy' ambition in their children. By healthy ambition, I mean a constructive and focused sense of purpose defined by a positive mindset and an intrinsic drive to succeed. It involves realistic goal-setting, continuous learning, uplifting others and, most importantly, maintaining ethical integrity without compromise.

My own father played a very important role in shaping my ambition. He always pushed me to work hard, improve my skills and not fear failure. Success was important to him, not just the effort one put in. His favourite blessing (whenever I went to a competition, an exam or even an important meeting later in life) was 'All the best, come first!' Of course, I couldn't stand 'first' all the time! After every competition where I missed the prize or came in second, he would dissect the whole experience, giving me input that was amazingly valuable for the next challenge.

When I was raising my own children, I realized the importance of those words. By saying 'All the best, come first!' my father was telling me that while he appreciated my efforts, the goal was to win. Achievement is essential to building ambition. Not only did my father instil that in my sister and me, but also in many other people whom he mentored. He did not allow us to stay in a state of disappointment for far too long. The next attempt, whether a debate, extempore or essay competition, would have to be lined up fast. His strong values also helped us understand that ambition does not mean pursuing success by any possible means. These learnings have held me in good stead till today.

If you are an ambitious young woman aspiring for success, I have just this to say to you: You are fortunate to have had your ambition honed well by your parents and mentors at a young age. Utilize your ambition and make it a constant in your life. Set clear goals, be proactive and seek out opportunities. Do not fear failure. Don't think you must succeed at any cost; follow your moral compass and never stop learning.

For women like Anjali who have given up their dreams because of a lack of family backing and the resulting feelings of self-doubt and insecurity, let me assure you that it's never too late to change course. As the first step, just reflect on your childhood and early adulthood and the staggering achievements in your kitty—this will remind you of your unique strengths and positive attributes. Set small, realistic goals for yourself and approach the re-entry exercise in an organized manner.

Here's the Career Doctor's list of steps to rekindle your ambition and fulfil your dreams:

1. Explore and identify your current interests and upskill yourself in your areas of interest.
2. Seek support from role models in your field of choice. You will be surprised to know that most people are happy to lend their expertise.
3. Replace negative thoughts with positive self-talk and try to connect with kind and supportive people.
4. Practising self-care is critical.
5. Celebrate your small wins.
6. It's imperative to embrace challenges, even though this is simpler said than accomplished!

15

The Fallacy of Balance

The brilliant blue of the swimming pool was dotted with swimsuits and caps of different hues. Kids happily splashed about and learners moved with focus. It was an unexpectedly pleasant April morning in Chennai. As I entered the pool for my hydrotherapy session, I marvelled at how the buoyancy of the water made such a big difference. I was weightless inside the water and the severe osteoarthritic pain that curtailed my movement on land disappeared. I felt as though I had been gifted new knees. Though I didn't know how to swim and was hesitant at first, my therapist, Sophia, ensured that I experienced the security of balance.

A committed professional, Sophia is proud of her work and ensures that her patients are well cared for. Unlike other therapists, Sophia would not stand at the pool's edge and shout out instructions. She would enter the pool with me and help me perform the calf raises, lunges and side steps. Her calm demeanour and the ease with which she made me practice the moves with non-jarring motions made me hopeful about managing my condition. I admired her capability to teach me ways in which I could balance my body weight to perform the stretches. We would stay at the shallow end of the pool and for a duration of forty minutes, Sophia would build confidence in me to overcome the pain and regain my easy mobility. I soon progressed to performing the exercises with resistance weights around my ankles. The act of removing the ankle bands after the therapy session was both strangely satisfying and metaphoric.

That morning, after a particularly energetic workout and an extra fifteen minutes of walking by myself in the pool, as I entered one of the shower booths, I heard Sophia speaking (on her mobile, I guessed) in the stall next door. She sounded emotional. Emotions tend to accentuate everything and our voices are no exception. The usually composed Sophia was speaking loudly and her anger and sorrow combined into one hard ball of emotion, which ricocheted off the tiny shower stall.

'I don't want to quit, Ma, but I don't have a choice. I don't have work–life balance in this job,' she said, her voice quivering with feeling. Sophia proceeded to elaborate on her challenges— how she was doing six sessions every day and getting back home just in time for her daughter's dinner. 'The way Jenny looks at me at night when I take her from the nanny, that look just kills me,' I heard her say, her voice ragged. I gathered that Sophia was struggling to cope with eight hours of work as well as another eight hours of childcare and house chores and that it was leaving her totally drained. As I further listened, she added with a pinch of annoyance, 'Yes, Ma, I know that I will have to be dependent on Manoj financially. And no, Ma, I can't do virtual sessions. You know I am a hydrotherapist.' Finally, Sophia, who I believe is one of the best in her profession, hung up, saying, 'Sometimes I think I chose the wrong profession.'

Even as I felt bad about eavesdropping on Sophia's deeply personal conversation with her mother, I also felt somewhat guilty.

It was as though patients like me who benefited from Sophia's work were somehow the cause of her problem. More than the challenge of losing my favourite therapist, I was filled with sadness that the world of pain management would lose a really competent specialist. I made an instant mental note to message her—not our usual exchange about the timing of my next session but what she could do to achieve a desirable work–life balance.

However, I have a problem with that term.

Work–life balance is a misnomer. It assumes that work and life inhabit two different spheres. Work here seems to be some kind of punishment, the antidote to which is life. In other words, work and life are perceived as being in conflict with each other. As in the case of a physical balance, where one plate has to come down for the other to go up, work–life balance implies that you can aspire to do justice to only one thing at a time; either work or life and the twain shall never meet.

Let's pause for a moment and look at the history of the term work–life balance. Interestingly, work–life balance did not originate as an issue faced by women. It was created in the mid-1800s by Robert Owen, a socialist manufacturer of textiles, who recommended the split of the twenty-four-hour day into 'eight hours of work, eight hours of recreation and eight hours of sleep'. The theory was built on the fact that work was hard labour, where one toiled in factories and farms or on shopfloors and hence it needed to be balanced out with rest. The view of work being technology-led and not as taxing physically could not have been imagined then.

I first came across the term 'work–life balance' after taking a career break myself over twenty-five years ago. The HR single point of contact (SPOC) in my office classified the cause of my attrition as 'lack of work–life balance'. The words affected me deeply. I was a young mom who had quit her job since I could not convince my supervisor to allow me to work from home and there was no way I could 'outsource' my household chores. Hiring external help for childcare or cooking was largely unheard of back then in middle-class families. After some trial and error, my tasks became manageable and once my older one went off to playschool, I had quite a bit of time on my hands. Naturally, the urge to work on something besides homework began to raise its contentious head. Several discussions with the family ensued. After I had assured them of my continued ownership of responsibilities, I approached a local women's college in Chennai, where they were happy to appoint me as a guest lecturer. Over the next four years, I learned a lot about how women approach their lives and careers. The result was Avtar.

When I set up Avtar in 2000, I began researching 'work–life balance' in earnest. (It's a different story that my own need to create a space where I could work for women's career enablement led to the rise of flexible working for many of my teammates at Avtar! We were among the first organizations in India to provide work-from-home options all the way back in 2002–03. I am delighted to share that they managed their personal lives well while contributing meaningfully to the cause.) By then, I had discovered the phenomenon of Indian women's careers getting aborted midway. Talking to tens, then hundreds and then thousands of women about what made them drop out of the workplace while they really, really wanted that job, I understood the fallacy of balance.

The reason I am uncomfortable with the concept of work–life balance is that it can be draining to constantly strive to strike the perfect equilibrium. In 2012, at Avtar, we began speaking about a more feasible idea—that of 'work–life integration', where you acknowledge that your professional work and personal life are interlinked. You try to find a way to smoothly blend work and family instead of being steadfast in keeping the two realms separate and constantly attempting to dedicate sufficient time for both individually. Practising work–life integration primarily entails flexible work arrangements and making productive use of technology, such as remotely connecting to work, opting for virtual meetings when possible and so on.

Here's a rough sketch of what life looks like for a person who aspires to seamlessly combine work and life: You may kickstart your day early—say around 5 a.m.—and work for a couple of hours, then take a break to get your kids ready for school, leave for the office and resume work, pause once more for lunch and include time for a hobby, attend a quick work meeting in the evening before wrapping up at the office and heading back home to spend time with family, only to reconnect to work late at night after your kids go to bed. At the end of it, you need to feel good. And that is the crux of integrating work and life—it's not about quantity but quality.

At the heart of achieving this effortless fusion of work and life is a solid support structure both at work and home—you cannot do it alone. You need an empathetic boss and considerate colleagues who do not regard flexibility as a mere kind gesture but wholly understand its benefits too. On the personal front, you need reliable pillars of support to shoulder childcare and home responsibilities with you, be it your partner, friend, parent, hired help or your child's daycare centre.

While redefining 'work–life balance' as work–non-work integration allows you to attend to your work as well as family responsibilities throughout the day, it is not free from challenges. It means that you may have long periods where work takes up a lion's share of your time and, conversely, where you are constantly attending to relatives, visiting family or fulfilling personal commitments. It also means accepting parts of personal life flowing into work and vice versa. As a result, you may feel a compulsion to be 'switched on' all the time without a break from work because the boundaries between personal and professional lives are blurred.

For example, Rumi, the editor of a leading news magazine, whom I met at a training session a few months ago, experienced this exact problem. She spoke to me about how the pandemic turned everything upside down in her life. She said that while flexibility greatly enhanced her work–life balance, it was very tough when her home became the destination for everything. It became her workplace, her kids' entertainment zone, her family's restaurant and the mandir for elders. With so much happening around her, it became a struggle for her to focus on her work. She exclaimed, 'My performance dipped to such an extent that I almost quit!'

Unfortunately, when you practise work–life integration, the fuzzy limits between the two can sometimes make you second-guess your decision to pursue a career. One effective way of handling these bouts of self-questioning is by clearly sketching out your work schedule and communicating the same to your family.

Another way to arrive at satisfying work–non-work integration is by identifying your central motive to pursue a career. Are you the primary breadwinner of the family? If so, what kind of support systems and forms of communication help you manage your non-work responsibilities? Is your inclination to work a result of a search for identity? Or is it a natural outcome of your education, leading to self-expression? Or is it a need for economic self-sufficiency? Ask yourself these questions.

Also, consider carefully what your expectations are from your job. Often, work–life integration becomes a problem for women when the returns from the job do not meet the effort we put in or the expectations we have from our job. So, assess if you are receiving what you expect from your job. Reflecting on all of this will help you navigate your apprehensions and vacillations. What's more, the answers could even surprise you—it could turn out that lack of a perceived balance was never the problem for you and that the real problem was perhaps a disappointing remuneration or lack of creative freedom. More often than not, attempting to balance various aspects of life—the things you need to do, must do and like to do—is more in the mind and, in fact, unnecessary. By relentlessly striving to do everything and achieve work–life balance, you are probably attempting to solve a problem that never existed!

Speaking of integrating work and non-work, let's circle back to my hydrotherapist, Sophia. When I reached out to her, she candidly spoke about how constantly being on her toes and ensuring that she is allocating enough time for both work and family is utterly exhausting. She wanted to quit and have some time to unwind. While I completely understood where she was coming from, I knew only too well that the need for relaxation would be short-lived for people like Sophia and that stay-at-home women have their fair share of struggles.

For instance, a few months ago, I met twenty-seven-year-old Satpreet, a stay-at-home mom of two who was looking for a job as a content writer. It was clear to me that she was bored with just doing the household chores. 'There are only so many iterations of efficient re-arrangement of clothes cupboards and kitchen shelves that I can do. And there are only so many YouTube recipes that I can try,' she said with a trace of exasperation. I could see that she was yearning for a work opportunity where she could utilize her writing skills and intellectual capabilities. Not only that, she found the phrase 'work–life balance' cool and exotic and wanted to experience it. 'It's a different kind of "busy". It's the kind of busy that I want,' she said wistfully. I knew what she meant—she wanted to be so busy and occupied with professional work that she would have to find ways to complete the tasks in her personal life because she was tired of them! What a starkly different need compared to Sophia's! So, it is clearly not an ideal world for anyone—be it a working mom or a stay-at-home mom.

When I shared this with Sophia, she seemed to get it and wanted suggestions on how she could manage her work and family better. As you might expect, the first thing I asked her to do was remove the term 'work–life balance' from her dictionary and replace it with 'work–life integration'. And here's the framework I shared with Sophia to achieve work–life integration:

Self-reflective questions	Action
Is your place of work close to your residence?	If your answer is no, try to address this as soon as you can, because only if your commute is quick and easy can you blend work and life. Otherwise, you will continue to pursue work–life balance, mostly in vain, instead of striving for work–life integration.
Why do you work?	Reflect on why you work. Is it because you enjoy it? Is your income crucial for your family? Do you want to be financially independent? Are you keen on putting your skills and learnings to good use? Once you have answers to these, it becomes easier to overcome feelings of weariness, self-reproach or both.

Are you fully leveraging technology?	• Have you explored the option of offering virtual consultations and providing remote guidance? True, remote working is not possible in all professions and, in your case, most patients may prefer in-person sessions. But with the increasing digitization in all spheres, there may be a few people who are willing to explore the virtual mode. So, do not shut out the option. • Have you investigated the idea of offering online hydrotherapy courses to aspiring hydrotherapists? There are various ed-tech platforms that you can explore. • Also, connect with people in your field and brainstorm on how else you can leverage technology to the fullest extent.
Are you openly communicating with your employer and your network of support?	• Be open with your employer about the need for flexibility. And let your boss know when you are available to take on work and when you are not. • Similarly, at home, let your hired help, partner and others in your support network know when you absolutely need to be away for work. Do not hesitate to enlist help from more people if you feel the need.
Can you work part-time?	• If doing six hydrotherapy sessions is a challenge, can you do three instead? That will make it possible for you to spend more time with your daughter. Again, being open with your employer about your needs is key.
Have you explored all possible ways to integrate work and life?	• Think of ways to blend family and work. For example, can you bring your daughter to your workplace in the evening? She can play in the shallow pool while you work nearby.

To sum up, a lack of work–life balance may seem like an insurmountable challenge for women. But by approaching it with a different lens, practising open communication, fully tapping into technology and making slight tweaks to schedules, it can transform into a manageable and inconsequential hurdle. Here's wishing every woman out there the strength and sharpness to overcome this ubiquitous obstacle!

16

Women and Transitions

I am super nervous. I am in Hong Kong and it is my first talk at an international conference on diversity and inclusion. I am wondering how I will connect with an audience that is truly multicultural, multiracial and a mosaic of all things diverse. There are over twenty-seven nationalities, people with differing abilities and a variety of gender identities. I started Avtar in 2000 and it has taken me eight years to get to a global stage. While I am definitely excited, I am also tense. My topic is 'How generational diversity makes a difference while planning career paths for women'. All of a sudden, as I look at my notes, I feel that the findings we painstakingly collated are not powerful enough. I suspect that I am ill-prepared. All kinds of ignominy flash before my eyes. Will I forget my lines? Will my data be completely irrelevant to the audience? Will my session be rated as the worst in the entire conference? Perhaps I should not have agreed to speak. How can Indian research be applicable to such an international, first-world audience? Karthik Ekambaram (senior leader at Avtar), oblivious to the furore in my head, is going over the speaking points with me once again. He has put together the research deck and we are primed for some tough questions. It is 2008 and history is about to be made right during the conference as we would go on to watch the US presidential election results live, where Barack Obama would be elected as the first African–American president of the world's most powerful nation.

As I take the podium, it's a packed room with only standing space. I look at the sea of unfamiliar faces, inscrutable in their expressions and right at the back of the hall is one familiar face. She is Indian, albeit really tall at 5 ft 11. She delivered the opening keynote at the conference and has just walked into the room to check if the session is adequately attended. I am elated that she is here. She is standing at the very end, ready to leave for the next room. Suddenly, I decided that if I'm able to hold her attention and make her stay for the next fifteen minutes, I would have done well for myself. Her bold, black spectacles frame her powerful eyes and even from that distance, I am able to see that she is listening keenly, going along with me as I make my points and giving me the assurance that I am indeed making sense. She laughs at the light joke I make about Woodward's Gripe Water, a legend in Tamil families of the 1960s and seventies, an icon for generational loyalty, and to date, a trustworthy antidote to colic. She nods when I refer to the career cliff of Indian women, from where they drop off, never to be counted among earning members again. The talk ends with thunderous applause and Subha Barry, a successful commodities trader who moved to wealth advisery, then branch management, then multicultural marketing and business development and then to a role in HR as a global head of DEI at Merril Lynch, a master of managing change, walks up to me to offer her congratulations. That moment marks the beginning of our association, which would later translate into India's largest and most emphatic count of the best companies for diversity in India through the Avtar and Seramount 'Best Companies for Women in India' study and 'Most Inclusive Companies Index'.

Whenever I think of change, Subha Barry, CEO of Seramount, is the first name that comes to mind. As a child of the 1960s, Subha experienced change of every kind, from living in five different Indian cities (on both sides of the Vindhyas), going to the US for her post-graduation studies, marrying an American, fighting cancer again and again and making a successful career comeback after losing her job as a result of the sub-prime crisis.

Born in Calcutta to Tamilian parents in 1961, Subha says she had a happy childhood, while at the same time candidly admitting that her paternal grandfather was deeply disappointed when he learned that his son had become a father to a girl and not a boy. Right from her childhood, Subha adapted to change well, studying in seven schools in a span of ten years because of her father's transferrable job and making new friends in each place with ease. After completing her BCom from Ethiraj College, Chennai, and her CA Articleship in Mumbai, Subha pushed boundaries in her very first job at DCM Data Products, where she was the first and only woman sales engineer selling computers to companies.

Firmly believing there should be no difference between opportunities given to boys and girls, Subha says she always wanted to study in the US like her male cousins and become CEO of a top company there. Back in the 1980s, it was culturally unacceptable for girls to move abroad alone, so her parents had other plans. They negotiated with her to get married to a groom of their choice from the US, move there with him and then pursue her studies. Subha says, 'But I felt that using someone as a ticket out of India was simply not right.' However, it wasn't easy to convince her parents and without much choice, Subha acquiesced to their plan and got engaged and her parents let her appear for the Graduate Management Admission Test (GMAT). But when Subha secured admission to Rice University, Houston, for an MBA plus accounting with a scholarship, she decided to break the engagement. Subha recalls, 'It was quite the scandal. I wish I had the courage to refuse the engagement in the first place.'

Subha handled her move to the US admirably and her confidence even back then is evident when she says, 'There was never a time when I felt "less than" my colleagues at college or work. After all, I'd received a scholarship and travelled alone to a country thousands of miles away from home.' She shares that one thing that helped her adjust well to the change was her willingness to make mistakes and view them as a vital part of the learning process. She says, 'I believe some values are non-negotiable, such as kindness, fairness and integrity. But when it comes to other aspects, I'm not worried about making mistakes.'

A couple of years after her move to the US, Subha welcomed another change in her life when she decided to marry Jim Barry, much against her family's wishes. As both of them shared the same fundamental values and beliefs, they embraced each other's cultures with open arms and today, they celebrate both Hindu and Christian festivals with equal cheer. Subha stresses the need for a woman to have a partner who shares the responsibilities of raising children and managing the home to have a fulfilling career. She says, 'Without a supportive spouse, the uphill battle becomes even more challenging!'

Speaking of uphill career battles, Subha has had such a colourful professional journey filled with inconceivable twists and turns! From commodities trader to global HR head, she has handled her career transitions with finesse. 'This is possible when you remain open to new ideas, new opportunities, new possibilities and new ways of thinking about the world around us,' shares Subha.

I am also curious to know if she has ever felt daunted by challenges and unexpected turn of events. She admits she has, but she has used these seemingly insurmountable challenges as opportunities for growth and learning. Subha is a six-time cancer survivor—five times with Hodgkin's lymphoma and once with breast cancer. Yes, you read that right. In 1997, when her children were just eight years and eighteen months old, Subha was first diagnosed with Hodgkin's Lymphoma, a type of cancer that affects the lymphatic system, for which she underwent chemotherapy. But the cancer kept returning again and again, forcing her to fight it six times in about fifteen years.

It was not easy by any means, but Subha credits this life-changing health crisis for her career pivot from a leader in wealth management at Merrill Lynch to heading the multicultural business development unit at the same company. She says, 'When you are not sure of how long you have to live, one begins to think of legacy and impact beyond how much money you make.' Subha shares that cancer led her on a journey of self-discovery and completely changed how she looked at the world and her place in it, and her innate sense of fairness pushed her to take up DEI as her calling. But Subha admits that she had doubts about her drastic career shift and concerns such as reduced income and not having control over the results she would be able to produce. But now, more than a decade later, she says firmly, 'Thank God for my cancer. I'm a better human being because of it!'

Incredible story, isn't it? Now you know why Subha is the first person that comes to mind when I contemplate change and how one must handle it. Few people encounter as much change as Subha has, both personally and professionally. I ask her if there are certain ways of thinking that have helped her adapt to change and she promptly lists a set of practices:

a. Putting yourself in the shoes of others.
b. Believing that people around you have good intentions and if they do something wrong, it isn't on purpose—it's usually out of ignorance.
c. Learning to trust others until they give you a reason to mistrust them.
d. Trusting your own instincts and inner voice more.

Those are valuable tips for any woman, don't you think? I say women, particularly because we often experience more change than men. One of the most common changes that women face is relocation post-marriage. Data from IndiaSpend, a data journalism initiative, reveals that of the people who move after marriage, 97 per cent are women.[1] Other studies have shown that while men generally move for jobs, women mostly move because of marriage. Many women move miles away from home to a place that is vastly different from their native city. The irony is that even today, most parents in India do not encourage their daughters to travel solo or with friends before marriage. But after years of leading extremely sheltered and cocooned lives, these women are magically expected to ace their relocation like pros.

Along with relocation, there are other changes that women encounter after marriage, such as added responsibility on the home front, learning to live with the spouse's family and, of course, motherhood. I am sure most women would have their own stories of transition—some bitter, some sweet and some bittersweet. While there is no ready-made game plan to deal with these transitions, the best way to approach them, as Subha says, is to treat these transitions as opportunities.

I am reminded of the movie *English Vinglish*, where Shashi (played by Sridevi) is a subject of ridicule and embarrassment for her husband and daughter, as she cannot speak English fluently. When her niece invites her to the US to attend her wedding, it is a bittersweet moment for her—she is excited but also filled with self-doubt about how she will manage in an English-speaking country. But instead of being weighed down by these fears, she uses the opportunity to learn English and makes an impactful speech at the wedding, much to the surprise of her family. That's exactly how we must face these transitions.

Here are the Career Doctor's tips to face change without fear:

1. Seek support—you don't have to do it alone. Invest time in building a network of support, be it mentors, friends or family. If your organization has a support system that can help you cope better with the transition, access it. If you find the change too overwhelming, do not hesitate to seek professional help.
2. Take your time to adapt to the new place or situation. Accept that things will not seem rosy on Day 1, Week 1 or even Month 1.
3. Anticipate change. With time, we have come to realize that no one can escape change. When it comes to women, some changes are to be predicted. To boost your preparedness for any change, reflect on the following:

   • What your short-term and long-term changes are
   • How the change will impact your day-to-day tasks
   • The outcome of the changes you foresee

- The opportunities offered by the change
- The enablers that can help you sail through the change
- The challenges

4. Look for avenues to use the change to your advantage. For example, if you are relocating to a different place, you could explore volunteering opportunities in the new place until you fully settle down. Or you could look at online upskilling options if you need to take a career break for personal reasons.

Just remember that change is inevitable. In the process of dealing with change, it is important for you to maintain your authenticity and stay connected to your core values. As Subha Barry says, her favourite change mantra is: 'Be yourself; everyone else is taken!'

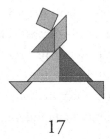

17

When Is It Time for a Career Break?

It is 2004 and a large FMCG company has reached out to us, citing an age-old problem of regretted attrition—where the company loses good performers. We have decided to try something new. Instead of asking currently employed women about their problems at work, we're planning to ask the women who've quit the organization why they did so. It was one of the largest ex-employee feedback surveys conducted at the time, where we reached out to over 700 past employees of the company—both men and women. The question we are trying to answer is this: why do women quit the workplace and is there a right time to do so? As we speak to each of the women who left the FMCG major, we realize that most of them are not working elsewhere— they are homemakers. They were women who had taken a break for a variety of reasons. We have moms who had quit because there was no help at home to take care of their child, women in their forties who were on a sabbatical to attend to their elderly parents or parents-in-law, women who had resigned because managing home and work had left them completely drained, women who had walked out after experiencing neglect, bias and

157

discrimination, and women who had left because they were not interested in pursuing careers—it was a diverse lot indeed. As we read questionnaire after questionnaire, result after result, we found that only a small fraction within the group was wholly enjoying their breaks, while most of them harboured feelings of resentment about their circumstances or had grudgingly made peace with the course of events.

That got me thinking. I wondered if at least a handful of these women could have avoided taking those breaks or planned their breaks better. Mind you, I am not against women (or men) stepping away from work temporarily. I, too, had chosen to take time off to spend quality time with my son, a decision I do not regret by any means. But it does bother me when women leave because of challenges or problems that can be handled or resolved, when they take extended breaks against their will because they think they don't have a choice or when they do not utilize their breaks effectively. When Sruthi Kannan, a business development leader at Cisco, approached me in 2014 to deliver a workshop at the Grace Hopper Celebration of Women in Computing, an annual tech conference for women and non-binary technologists, on how the career break must be handled, my first response was: 'The best way to handle a career break is not to take one!' Of course, I later delivered the workshop to a hall full of very interested women who were extremely keen to know how the break can be managed and the title of the workshop that Sruthi and I came up with was 'Career Breaks Not Heartbreaks Anymore!'

Let's understand what a career break is and when one must consider taking a work hiatus. I do not consider the six-month maternity leave as a career break (even if the leave is stretched by a couple of months), but an extended unpaid maternity leave of a year or more is indeed a career timeout.

For most of us, a career break may be unavoidable. And for some of us, it may not affect our career prospects in any way, thanks to current trends where companies are increasingly hiring second-career women. But there is still a fairly long way to go for us to remain completely unscathed by these breaks. A study conducted by Reed.co.uk in partnership with Research Without Barriers in 2022 states that seven in ten women acknowledge that career breaks have made them less confident.[1] So, it is high time we destigmatize career breaks—not just the organizations; it is up to us women too to normalize our temporary disappearance from the workforce.

Let's also understand that a break can sometimes lead you to a more promising pathway, something I've personally witnessed with a lot of women. In fact, my own career is an example of this. When I took a career break over twenty years ago, it was an era when a gap was perceived as a setback or a red flag on a job application. It worked well for me, though, as it pushed me to start Avtar. Besides, second-career women lead three out of the six capabilities at Avtar. This is a grand testimony to how women on career breaks can make successful comebacks and shine in leadership positions.

Let me also make it clear that a career break does not point to a downfall if it is well thought out. But this is not always the case. In the last twenty-plus years when I have worked extensively with women, I have come across scores of them who have made hasty decisions about going on a break. For example, one of the respondents to the ex-employee feedback survey was Gauri, a financial planner who had impulsively quit after a minor disagreement with her boss. 'I was stressed. I acted recklessly,' she said. It was evident to me that she was regretting her ill-considered decision. An impulsive break or a rage quit is a luxury not everyone can afford, from a financial perspective. Undoubtedly, on bad days, overwhelming feelings can get the better of us, but it is best not to make decisions, especially when it comes to career paths, based on these fleeting moments of exasperation. It is important to note that impulsive career gaps on your resume are hard to explain to your future potential employers. So, let me reiterate: career breaks must always be planned unless there is an emergency.

Unnecessary quitting is no better than impulsive quitting and needs to be avoided too. What do I mean by an unnecessary career break? Imagine these not-entirely-unfamiliar situations. A woman quits her job because:

- Her family wants her to stay at home as it makes it easier for everyone at home.
- She experiences a hostile work environment where her boss and team don't value her contributions.
- She finds herself neither here nor there—unable to give her best at home or work.
- She realizes that her work deserves higher compensation.

Mind you, not for a moment am I suggesting that these aren't valid reasons for a woman to quit work. All I am saying is that there may be other ways to handle these problems and bowing out of the job must be the last option. Openly communicating your challenges and concerns to your manager, HR and leadership, and frankly discussing your goals and aspirations with your family and enlisting their support, could prevent the need for a break, at least in some cases.

Here is a questionnaire that I often use for women contemplating a career break. These are some important points to reflect on before making a decision:

1. **Do you have sufficient financial cushioning?** Make sure your finances are in order by making a detailed assessment of your savings, debt, living expenses, anticipated future expenses and health insurance plans. Ensure that you have an emergency fund that covers at least three months of living expenses.

2. **Are market conditions in your favour?** Evaluate job market conditions. How is your company performing compared to its competitors? Do you find your industry shaky, with limited prospects for individual growth? Are your skills in high demand? Is your field fiercely competitive? Are you likely to get a pay raise and better benefits, including healthcare and retirement perks, when you decide to restart work? Do your research and gather information from job sites, recruitment consultants and industry journals, and make a carefully planned move.

3. **Why do you want a pause in your career?** Analyse your reason for wanting to quit. Is it because of caregiving responsibilities? Is it due to a toxic work culture? Are you feeling burned out? Or is it a combination of multiple reasons? Spelling out the reason will bring clarity to you and help you analyse possible solutions.

4. **Can you avoid the break?** Once you have clearly identified your reason(s) to take a break, explore other options before quitting. For example, if it's to look after your child, consider hiring a nanny or sending your child to daycare. You could also think about working part-time. If you want to quit because of an unsupportive work environment, have meaningful conversations with your manager, team and HR. Write down your ideal scenario and then think of ways to make it happen. If you just need a brief respite from work, do not hesitate to discuss with your HR the option of taking a sabbatical and

returning to the same or a slightly different role after a few months.

5. **Have you timed your break well?** It is important to take your break at the right time so that it has the least negative effect. Once you have made up your mind that you need to take some time off, think about whether you need to take a break right away. Consider if there is any advantage that you, your team or organization can gain if you continue to work a little longer. For example, think about these situations:

- You could be close to getting a promotion—it is usually better to exit on a strong note.
- You could be working on a critical, soon-to-end project and it would be nice to see it through to the end. You could end up elevating your resume and gaining the goodwill of your manager and team. Also, consider serving a slightly longer notice period than the mandatory minimum term, because a longer notification window will help ease the transition for your team.
- You may have a new boss and want to work alongside him or her for a couple more months to build a solid relationship, which can prove useful in the future.
- You could become eligible for certain benefits in your organization, such as gratuity or employee stock options, after a certain tenure.

While an emergency would require you to quit immediately, in other situations, it is important that you consider all possible aspects before drafting that formal resignation email.

6. **Can you maintain your momentum all the way?** A lot of women tend to slow down in their careers way before their

actual breaks. I have met women who completely neglect skill development and networking, try to utilize all their leaves without cause and scale back their career pursuits the moment they start thinking of the possibility of a break, sometimes even earlier. Avoid this at all costs. Sheryl Sandberg discusses this point in depth in her TED talk. She says, 'Don't leave before you leave.'[2] Remember, you need to leave on a high, as it will motivate you to get back to work and help you negotiate a fair and competitive salary. So, stay in the groove until the very last day.

7. **How can you use your break productively?** This is critical. Make sure to spend time developing your professional skills. Your career break could be a portal to opportunities if used thoughtfully. Here are a host of things you can do to make your break count:

- Identify skills that will be of assistance to you and invest time in upskilling yourself.
- Attend workshops and conferences in your field of work or in other fields of work that you are keen on exploring.
- Explore freelancing or volunteering.
- Keep in touch with your professional contacts and actively network both online and offline.
- Do not let your writing and communication skills or your knowledge of current affairs rust. Keep fine-tuning them because they will always hold you in good stead.
- Develop an online portfolio to showcase your work and keep your resume up-to-date.

8. **Do you have a structured return-to-work plan?** Have a rough timeframe for your return to work and chalk out a

plan for your return: Do you want to rejoin your previous employer? Or explore other companies in the same field? Or consider a new line of work? Also, have a clear strategy for job search and tap into diverse channels for job hunting, such as company websites, recruitment agencies, job fairs and online networking platforms.

9. **How do you plan to address the career gap in your resume?** By and large, career breaks are no longer considered taboo because there is a general understanding that women who have gone on breaks are educated, skilled, committed, adaptable and adept at problem-solving. Since March 2022, LinkedIn has allowed its users to include their career breaks in the 'Experience' section. This gives you an opportunity to explain to potential employers the reason for your break and how you utilized it. So, own your break if you can and give it a positive or quirky spin so that your potential employers appreciate the fact that you have acquired a host of skills during the break. This also lets you showcase to your interview panel your sense of humour, commitment and values, all of which are essential aspects they take note of.

There you go. Use this questionnaire every time you deliberate on your career's next steps. Remember, career breaks are not heartbreaks any more if you approach them strategically. So, go ahead and make that break your friend, girl!

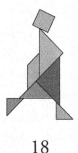

18

Starting Again

It was right in the middle of Durga Pujo 2007 that we landed in Kolkata. The city seemed to be bedecked with feminine energy, very much in sync with our own passion. We were a team of eight of us, crisscrossing the country, travelling to Kolkata, Pune, Jaipur, Ahmedabad, Bengaluru, Hyderabad, Kolhapur and Mumbai, hiring women for part-time work at Future Group's retail outlets. Kolkata was the first stop, even though we wanted to start with Bengaluru (simply because we had opened our second office after Chennai in Bengaluru by then). Kolkata was chosen, I heard, for sentimental reasons—Future Group had started its first Pantaloons store in Kolkata. Sanjay Jog, the then chief human resources officer (CHRO) of Future Group, gave us a simple mandate: 'We need women professionals with some amount of work experience, a positive mindset and who are keen on getting the job.' Educational qualifications came second to trainability. They were part-time jobs (requiring a minimum of four hours of work) at any of the outlets of Future Group, which at the time had formats such as hypermarkets, home improvement, electronics and lifestyle apparel stores.

It was a supremely exciting high point for Avtar—we had convinced one of the country's largest employers at the time to earmark about 30 per cent of all new hires at entry and junior levels as exclusively for women. We had achieved proof of concept, thanks to our other successful assignments, including the one for Standard Chartered the previous year that formally launched us. We were terribly chuffed about the opportunity to hire about 1600 women in all, around 200 women in each city. Between the ten of us (the core team), we did not know the local languages, just a smattering of Hindi, apart from our respective mother tongues (mostly south Indian) but operated with the confidence that whatever the challenges, we would overcome them.

However, Kolkata was a challenge beyond our expectations. We decided that our first job would be to hire a project manager-cum-translator. Kakoli Roy came on board! She was an energetic, committed bundle of speed and determination. We had chosen an auditorium as the venue for the interviews and the team spread themselves through the hall, with the final interview tables set in one corner of the platform. We rigged up a PA system since women were seated right until the end of the hall.

Veena Mukund, Karthik Ekambaram (both senior leaders at Avtar) and I were interviewing women when a former professor visited the venue to see what the hullaballoo was all about. 'You are planning to hire women for jobs?' he asked, a little surprised. 'It's an impossible task. In Kolkata, no one wants to work,' he said. It was barely an hour into the assessment centre and his words fell like doom upon our ears, even though we were conscious of the prevailing viewpoint that Kolkata is not as industry-friendly as the other metros. We all know that the city has gained its celebrated nickname 'City of Joy', largely from its limitless love and zest for art, history, literature and traditions.

The city's women, in particular, are perceived to be passionate about art and literature but not as career-focused compared to women from other cities. However, this experience proved this perception wrong and how!

We knew we had one factor working in our favour: we were seeking second-career women! These are women who had already worked earlier and experienced first-hand the freedom and economic self-sufficiency of working and being employed and therefore would be keen to experience that joy again, we thought. We were right—by the end of the day, we had completed the shortlist of 350 women (from which 200 or more would eventually be hired by Future Group) and we realized that a majority of them were indeed second-career women!

As a second-career woman myself, I know how rewarding it can be. By a second career, I mean transitioning to a different career path after an extended career break. In the previous chapter, we saw how avoiding breaks is possibly one of the best things to do to avoid the heartbreak that follows, but in India, breaks are a very common phenomenon. Women take breaks for a variety of reasons, the most significant of which is motherhood. Avtar's 2019 Viewport study, which focused on women's second careers, shows that nearly 45 per cent of women go on an extended break because of challenges related to motherhood, such as lack of a reliable support system for childcare.[1] Though motherhood is the most common reason for a career break, there are other reasons too. Caregiving for the elderly is another common cause for women in India to give up their jobs. The same Viewport study shows that close to 16 per cent of women in India quit work midway to attend to ageing family members. It also reveals that 15 per cent of women took a break because of marriage-related relocation. Physical and mental health challenges force women to go on long breaks too, with 12 per cent of women surveyed citing it as the cause of their hiatus. About 21 per cent of women report going on a break to pursue a passion or higher education.

Now that we have an idea about why women take extended career breaks, it is fairly clear that most breaks are not exactly women's preferences. They are due to circumstances and/ or societal expectations. Under these conditions, feelings of frustration, victimhood and loneliness are expected and valid. It is not easy to be financially dependent on someone. Nor is it easy to put on hold your aspirations when everyone around you—your partner, ex-colleagues and acquaintances—are forging ahead in their respective careers.

While most women are able to look back on their career breaks with reasonable contentment, during the break itself, women generally report feeling lost and worthless. If you are someone who loved your work, handling the sudden loss of identity and being forced to devote all your time to housework and/or caregiving responsibilities is tough. But know that you are not alone and that you can start over.

However, I will be frank here: restarting after a career break requires effort, even more so if you are venturing into a new career path. You will likely encounter the following challenges:

- Outdated skills (or the need to build a new skillset if you are exploring a second career)
- Lack of confidence
- Tackling stereotypes and bias—a study cited in the Gender Action Portal (GAP), (originally published in the American Journal of Sociology in 2007), states that mothers are considered 12.1 percentage points less committed to their jobs than non-mothers.[2]

- Reduced pay—the same study states that mothers were recommended a 7.9 per cent lower starting salary compared to non-mothers.

On the bright side, career breaks are no longer hushed because there is a reasonable understanding that women who have gone on breaks are educated, skilled, committed, adaptable and adept at problem-solving. So, own your break and give it a positive or quirky spin so that your potential employers appreciate the fact that you have acquired a host of skills while managing your home and kid(s). As mentioned in the previous chapter, LinkedIn now allows its users to include their career breaks in the 'Experience' section. So, explain to your potential employers why you took that break. You can even come up with a quirky title—how about Chief Home Officer or Chief Tantrum Diffuser? The key lies in how you position your break with your employers.

It is also important to utilize your break cleverly. The first step is to reflect on your past career and meditate on whether you want to stay on the same track. Some points to consider:

- Are you genuinely interested in your line of work?
- Does your career allow you to leverage your skills?
- Is the work you do in line with your value system?

If your answer is yes, then you are set! Just make sure you remain acquainted with your ex-colleagues and keep your skills in tune. Enrich your skill base by attending relevant courses and freelancing during your break. Sharon, a senior writer we hired at Avtar in early 2023, joined us after a three-year break in her career. I was impressed by the fact that she had done freelance work throughout her break. She had devoted about two hours a day to work when her baby napped, which helped her keep her writing skills sharp while also offering her a respite from childcare duties. She says, 'Though the income from my freelance projects was minor, the work affirmed my sense of worth.' I could clearly see that Sharon was confident about her skills and able to hit the ground running.

If you did not enjoy the earlier work you did, the maternity break is a perfect time to explore other career avenues. Avtar's Viewport study reveals that 45 per cent of women on career breaks are open to exploring other career options.

There are several examples of successful women who have changed tracks and gone on to shine in their second careers. Take J.K. Rowling, for instance. She worked in various roles, from an administrative assistant and a secretary to an English teacher and a researcher, before taking the world by storm with her iconic Harry Potter series of books. Another great example of a woman who has pivoted not once but multiple times in her career is Michelle Obama. When she was firmly on the path to becoming one of the leading corporate lawyers in the US, she quit to join as an assistant to the mayor of Chicago simply because the opportunity sparked her interest, taking a major pay cut, which, she admits did bother her a little. A major pivot happened again in 2008 when her husband's presidential campaign gathered steam and she had to take a sabbatical from her job at the University of Chicago Medical Center to take care of her daughters. She acknowledges that it was painful to leave a job that she loved, but as we all know, she embraced the role of first lady with amazing vigour.

I cite Michelle Obama's example here mainly to call attention to two points: first, it is okay to take a step back in your career.

When you are exploring a second-career option, don't let the reduced income deter you (if your financial circumstances allow it). Second, it's important to note that sometimes you may not feel a compelling pull towards a job, which is okay too. As long as you don't feel hostile towards it, it is worth giving the role a try before you make up your mind for or against it. If you can, before you zero in on any new field, try volunteering or a short-term internship to better understand your interest in it—like going on a test drive before you purchase a car.

Companies are increasingly embracing 'career returnship' programmes too. Research published in the *Harvard Business Review* states that nearly 40 per cent of Fortune 50 companies have a structured in-house career re-entry programme.[3] As per the 2023 'Best Companies for Women in India' survey conducted by Avtar and Seramount, 83 per cent of the top 100 companies have formal hiring programmes to identify and recruit women on career breaks.[4] Most companies prioritize learnability and willingness to be trained over prior work experience.

How do these programmes work? Most companies hire second-career women for short-term projects and provide them with the training and support they need to perform to their maximum potential. At the end of the project tenure, leading performers are offered full-time jobs and they are provided continued support in the form of mentors, upskilling avenues and networking opportunities. A plethora of possibilities could open for you if you explore these re-entry schemes, which you can access through various diversity recruitment firms such as Avtar.

To sum up, here is a five-step process I often allude to, to help women navigate through their new careers after a long break:

Steps	Explainer/Quick tips
1. Identify your strengths and list them down.	For example, writing, design, quantitative aptitude or people engagement.
2. Mull over what really excites you.	Are you committed to serving the community? Is money a major motivating factor for you? Are you passionate about teaching young children?
3. Reflect on how you can combine your strengths and passion.	If your strength is writing and your passion is educating people about societal problems, then your path is fairly clear—being a social issues reporter sounds like a great fit. Or if your strength is numbers and you are passionate about teaching, math tutoring is a good idea. Connect with your well-wishers or a career counsellor to figure out role options where you can utilize your plusses and pursue your passion.
4. Identify certifications that could truly add value to your resume.	Sometimes, even if you possess all the required skills for a job role, certain certifications may be essential just to clear the screening round. On the plus side, you may end up learning things you didn't know earlier. It's best to be open to learning.
5. Update your resume and your profile on LinkedIn and other top job sites and share them widely.	• Since you are applying as a fresher in practical terms, highlight transferable skills that you can bring to the new role from your earlier experience. For example, if you want to shift from software engineering to data science, your quantitative ability will be a transferable skill; or if you want to move from journalism to marketing, your language aptitude and ability to weave a good story will be valuable transferable skills. • Customize your resume for each role. • Do share your resume with your friends or ex-colleagues for feedback and avail yourself of the services of a recruitment firm. • Job leads can come from unexpected sources. Let all your contacts know that you are open to work.

Taking reference from the world of cricket, a second career is much like the second innings of a cricket game. It is not entirely different from the first inning, but it does involve a slightly different approach. When you start out after an extended break, the possibility of a second career may seem a little far-fetched to you. But trust me, it is doable. I am an example of how fulfilling a second career can be. If I could do it, you can too.

19

The Muscle of Resilience

Yvonne, Sumathi and Pavitra are winners of the Inspiring Second Career Woman Award for 2022. They applied for the prestigious award instituted by Avtar, which celebrates women who have off-ramped their careers and then, as if rising back from the debris of their break, gone on to create successful second vistas for themselves.

Yvonne is a wealth adviser at a prominent national bank. Sumathi works as a programme manager at an IT company, while Pavitra manages inventory for a restaurant chain. All three are in their mid-to-late-thirties, having taken breaks ranging from four to fourteen years. Women re-emerging from an unnerving career break and getting back into the workplace was once a novelty and a rarity, but today, after the immense amount of work done in this space by Avtar and other companies, it is par for the course. As per the 'Best Companies for Women in India' applications, women across India—over 28,000 of them— just in the year 2022–23 have returned to the workforce, after acquiring new skills and preparing themselves for a difficult and different second stint.[1]

What sets apart women like Pavitra, Sumathi and Yvonne is that they've not just resurrected their careers after the proverbial hiatus but also dealt with debilitating life events that upturned their identity and shredded their very existence to bits. Pavitra is a three-time cancer survivor. Her last career break of four years was due to the chemotherapy and radiation treatment that she had to undergo. Yvonne is a 'COVID widow'. Her husband Sam was the sole wage earner in the house and during the second wave of the COVID-19 pandemic, Sam, who was a telecommunications engineer, died, leaving behind Yvonne, their two daughters and her dependent parents-in-law. After an eight-year career break, Yvonne decided to apply for jobs again and landed the banking role. Sumathi fought a bitter custody battle with her husband during the process of their divorce, at the end of which her children were separated from her. The prolonged legal dogfight led to Sumathi developing a heart condition, aggravated by the multiple anxiety attacks that she had along the way. After a fourteen-year career break, which Sumathi had taken to raise her two sons, she decided to find greater meaning in her life and connected with Avtar to find her a job.

Making a successful career comeback is not always about sprucing up your resume, buying a new dress and slapping your game face on. It's not even about the strong-tie networking that career doctors ask you to do or the upskilling that is touted as a panacea to all promotion problems. It is all about building the muscle of resilience to wake up another day and face the very unpleasant life prospects that stare at you. Resilience is a crucial factor for success, innovation and significance, but in order to navigate the volatility, uncertainty, complexity and ambiguity (VUCA) times that are omnipresent, resilience is the only recourse. Even at the risk of stereotyping, it is imperative to state that women's resilience is far more non-negotiable than that of men, especially in a career scenario when thousands of women end up losing their jobs and, thus, their identities whenever a crisis occurs. So, how do women consciously build resilience?

If you've ever attended a training programme on ICP, chances are that you would have crossed paths with Nandini Murali, the vice president of learning and research at Avtar. The author of *Left Behind: Surviving Suicide Loss,* Nandini is a stunning example of how resilience shines in action. But when you ask her about it, she laughs, 'Honestly, I first heard of the term resilience only about fifteen years ago!' With a PhD in gender studies and a double master's graduate in English literature and psychology, Nandini is a practising life coach with a focus on loss and transition. She shares that, in retrospect, she knew what resilience meant because she had seen every member of her family respond with grace, equanimity and strength of character to the disappointments and vicissitudes of life. Today, Nandini is not just a facilitator of sessions on career intentionality or early-career leadership; she is a resilience practitioner and coach, one who brings to the table the conceptual clarity required to enable resilience to be built and nurtured among women. 'Because of my lived reality of engaging with vibrant role models, I organically internalized the essence of resilience. It was elementary and elemental, really!' she mentions.

Life presented Nandini with several gargantuan challenges that incrementally built and honed her resilience. Her struggle with infertility, in a land where overpopulation is the norm, was her first experience with disenfranchised grief. 'When women deal with infertility,' shares Nandini, 'their challenges, both mental and physical, are rarely acknowledged or validated.' Even as Nandini felt a deep sense of loss at the inability to conceive, what made the problem worse was the stigma associated with infertility. The invasive treatments, the physical pain and the emotional highs and lows of hormonal overload wreaked havoc on her. For several years, everything in her life was secondary to her biological clock and body temperature charts.

'How did you deal with this?' I ask and Nandini responds in a flash, 'It is the oxygen of unconditional love and support that fuels the flames of resilience!' Nandini leaned on the support of her husband, late Dr T.R. Murali, her parents and her maternal uncle to handle the agony caused by infertility. She declared herself 'childfree', not childless. She decided that motherhood does not define a woman and that mothering was about nurturing and was completely independent of whether a woman had the ability to reproduce. She chose to reclaim her space and re-discover her voice by beginning a career in academia. However, health challenges continued to plague her. She developed thyroid cancer, which she overcame with characteristic spirit. Multiple spine surgeries conducted on the wrong operation site caused immeasurable pain, but the physical anguish was less than the invalidation she faced when the surgeons said that she was faking her agony. After many misfires, her spine was corrected using a titanium implant.

But her tests for resilience were far from over. Nandini lost her husband, 'bright, bold and brilliant, one of the country's top urologists', to suicide. When I first met Nandini over a Zoom call, two years after the loss of her husband, Nandini's equanimity surfaced as a combination of zen-like peace fused with creative energy. Her decision to pivot into the corporate world, albeit via a social enterprise such as Avtar, was a bold one, considering her earlier experiences were all in the not-for-profit sector. Within months of joining Avtar, Nandini became one of Avtar's most sought-after facilitators, garnering high praise in every session she delivered. Her sessions on Avtar's ICP and pathways to power have been big hits among the audience. What has been equally if not more impactful than these presentations is Nandini's generous sharing of her own lived experience of being a suicide loss survivor, which cuts through the lassitude of every audience and creates profound moments of truth.

'Dealing with the loss of a loved one is always difficult, but losing someone to suicide can add another level of pain to your grief. How did you come to terms with the death of your husband?' I ask her. Before she answers my question, Nandini prefaces her response with a thumb-nail sketch of Dr T.R. Murali, her spouse—his shining academic prowess, his expertise in andrology, paediatric urology and renal transplantation (having successfully performed over 1500 transplants). She describes him as a 'phenomenal clinician and a gifted surgeon'.

'I do not want Dr Murali or anyone who dies of suicide to be defined and remembered by their mode of death,' shares Nandini. On the contrary, she wishes her husband to be remembered for how he lived his life and his stellar professional legacy. 'Similarly, I, too, do not wish to be defined by the suicide of my husband. It is certainly a huge part of my life. However, it does not limit me in any way,' she adds, going on to share that suicide grief is a grief like no other. 'I resonate with the person who evocatively described it as "grief with the volume turned on".'

Until the suicide happened in her own family, Nandini reveals that she naively believed it could happen only to people like film stars, industrialists, celebrities or those who were far from her everyday existence. The death by suicide of her husband shattered 'the otherization of suicide', as she puts it. Healing through a suicide loss is an inward journey, which involves facing one's own naked vulnerability with courage and candour. 'I watched the things I had taken for granted destroyed forever and gradually began the process of rebuilding my life brick by brick,' shares Nandini. She does not condone the social stigma that perpetuates negative attitudes and stereotypes around suicide that people always internalize. This skewed perspective results in people adopting a moral high ground and passing judgements not just on the act of suicide but also on those who died by suicide, suicide-attempt survivors and even survivors of suicide loss.

'What would your advice be to people to build the muscle of resilience after a loss?' I ask. We are seated in my office and Nandini reaches out to open a box of sweets that I always keep on my table. After a few moments of contemplative selection, she chooses a bright purple candy. 'Kintsugi is the ancient Japanese art of fixing pottery with powdered gold,' she states, enjoying the burst of flavour in her mouth. 'Once completed, dazzling flecks of gold glisten in the conspicuous cracks and each "repaired" piece acquires a new identity. In the same way, the cracks and crevices of my life remind me that I may have been broken, but the spirit can never be crushed.'

'What keeps you going?' I ask. I already know the answer to this question, having spent many wonderful moments with Nandini discussing things as varied as English literature, *Ponniyin Selvan*, the Indian woman professional, tender mango pickles and the language of inclusion. She is happy to respond, 'My *dinacharya*, or daily practices, such as prayer, yoga, meditation, the writing that I do, which is a most powerful medium of engaging and expressing, the invaluable time that I spend with Malli, my gorgeous Golden Retriever, and Minnal, my loveable Rajapalayam, and the precious companionship of my parents and sister-in-law.'

The Career Doctor's conversations with real-life resilience ninjas like Nandini Murali and many others offer the following mantras for building resilience:

- **Accept your loss (or any other change):** Your life has changed forever. The loss is inevitable. Your tears, longing, pity or piety—none of it can change the outcome.
- **Pain is inevitable but suffering is optional:** You have no control over the cause, but you can control the outcome by choosing how to respond.
- **Adversity is a matter of chance; the response to it is a choice:** You have no control over what happens to you, but you can choose how to respond.
- **Reclaim your power:** Circumstances have no power over you; you are the author of your destiny.
- **Live in the moment:** Like a trapeze artist, you must know when to hold on and when to let go. Life is a balancing act.
- **Spring clean and declutter your mind:** Let go of the old and make room for the new. You cannot receive until you empty yourself.
- **Choose your focus:** Thoughts have energy. Whatever you focus on, it will manifest itself.
- **Resilience is the norm, not an exception:** Most people not only survive, but they also thrive, bouncing back and moving forward after every challenge. There is something ordinary in the extraordinary.
- **Be a pragmatic optimist:** Know what you can change and have the courage to make those changes. Gain the wisdom to know the difference between what you can change and what you cannot.

- **Draw on your inner resources:** All the resources you need to navigate challenges lie within you. Look within and do a deep dive. You will emerge with pearls of wisdom.

People like Nandini are exemplary in their equipoise. It reflects in the new definition that she gives to the seven colours of the rainbow, VIBGYOR—Vulnerability, Inventiveness, Buoyancy, Grace and Grit, Yielding Oceanic Resourcefulness!

20

Understanding Microaggression

'OMG! You speak English so well.' Shyla is excited to meet Padma, her new colleague.

Padma, a first-generation graduate and the eldest child in her family, has moved to the city from a Tier-3 town. Raised in a financially struggling family, Padma's journey to her dream job has been far from easy, but her parents have wholeheartedly backed her, adhering to a frugal lifestyle to help their daughter follow her dreams. Padma has earned her engineering degree from a college in her town and worked as a math tutor at a local tuition centre for a year. Now, she has shifted to Mumbai to join as a cost engineer at an architectural firm. Although the move intimidates Padma, she is also enthusiastic about her job prospects and appreciative of her parents' unwavering support because they have bravely chosen not to participate in the marriage rat race and are eager to see their daughter succeed.

On her joining day, when Padma hears Shyla's comment, she simply smiles. It is not offensive or insulting, but it makes Padma feel uncomfortable. It reminds her that she is an outsider and makes her wonder if she can match up to the others in the workplace. Shyla is oblivious to the doubts that her 'harmless' comment has triggered in Padma.

This is a classic example of an act of microaggression, which is often subtle, unintentional and passive. The term 'microaggression', coined by American psychiatrist Chester M. Pierce in the 1970s, refers to subtle and inadvertent acts or comments that are often derogatory and directed against disadvantaged individuals.[1] A detailed article on microaggression published in *Cleveland Clinic* discusses Psychologist Dr Derald Wing Sue's classification of microaggression into three formats:[2]

- Microassaults: Intentional offensive behaviour
- Microinsults: Unintentional discriminatory comments or behaviour
- Microinvalidations: Behaviour that undermines the feelings and experiences of the marginalized

Sometimes, microaggression doesn't seem like aggression. Microaggressive comments may seem positive on the outside. For example: 'You play with numbers so well for a woman.' 'You are so fair-complexioned that one cannot guess where you are really from.' 'Considering that you grew up in a small town, you have an amazing sense of style.' The irony is that both the source and the recipient of these comments are ignorant of the fact that these are not 'compliments' but a result of implicit bias, which in turn is a result of conditioning. Non-conscious bias is natural and all of us have it. Though it takes time and effort to change an individual's belief system, it is changeable. If left unaddressed, bias and the resulting microaggressive behaviour can cause harmful consequences for the disadvantaged.

Many people believe that these muted acts of hostility do not cause significant harm. But repeated microaggressions can lead to extreme stress, self-doubt, feelings of isolation and low self-worth, which can hinder the personal and professional growth of the targeted. So, the impact of microaggression is not 'micro' by any means. When I began attending interviews again, after a career break in the 1990s, I would often face statements such as 'for a woman who took a break on account of work–life balance, you are strangely ambitious' and 'it is admirable how you are so irrepressible in spite of being a woman', which would make me wonder if ambition and a never-say-die attitude were such bad traits to have, especially in women. In the face of such comments, I would choose to smile and thank the individual, given that responding to them with a similar sharp comment would only prolong and highlight the veiled put-down. In 2005, when I won a Chevening fellowship to go to the University of Bradford for a three-month-long course on 'Women in Leadership', leaving behind in India my children aged fourteen and nine, I was told by some of my 'well-meaning' relatives, 'You are really bold to leave small children and go on a trip!' Obviously, the 'boldness' comment disguised as appreciation was nothing but a subtle hint that I was furthering my own career selfishly at the expense of my children being left back at home. It didn't matter that they were being looked after by none other than their own father and two sets of grandparents in my absence. During the entirety of the trip and in the days leading up to it, I experienced deep guilt. Severely ingrained biases combined with the leverage that society bestows on people with power result in statements and comments that seem like they originate from a place of concern or praise, but they are actually barbs that hurt deeply. Interestingly, microaggression can even be delivered to companies. In the early days of Avtar, we would be told at business pitches, 'You folks are oddly process-oriented for a social enterprise' and 'the women you are trying to place have already left their jobs once because they couldn't balance work and life. You are really courageous to believe they will not do that a second time!'

A 2022 article in the *Harvard Business Review* by writer and inclusion strategist Ruchika Tulshyan argues that the term 'microaggression' needs to 'retire'.[3] Ruchika writes, 'The term "microaggression" doesn't fully capture the actions' emotional and material effects of how they impact women and people of colour's career progressions.'

Men are also subject to microaggression. For instance, both men and women in their fifties or sixties encounter scepticism when it comes to their technical acumen. Men also come up against comments such as, 'Why are you not retired at your age?' or 'You are too old to pursue this career.' Both single men and women are expected to work overtime because, 'It's not like you have a kid to pick up from school' or 'You can just go back and open up a can of soda and you are done for the day'.

Several studies show that women, especially marginalized women (women from weak socio-economic backgrounds, minority religions and the LGBTQ+ community) bear the brunt of microaggressive behaviour. A Deloitte Global Women at Work 2022 report highlights that almost 60 per cent of women have complained of confronting microaggression; 93 per cent of them believe that reporting such behaviours would only derail their careers; and most of them feel their complaints will go ignored.[4] Several women have shared their painful experiences of being disrespected over the last couple of decades.

Sahana, who applied for a position at Avtar in 2017, shared her encounters with bias during our long chat. 'There have been very few times when I have not been interrupted during meetings, ma'am,' she said. The main reason for Sahana wanting to leave her current employer was her frequent encounters with subtle forms of discrimination. 'People interrupt or ignore me and I am tired of that,' she added. Sahana is not alone. A study conducted by researchers from George Washington University found that 'men interrupted 33 per cent more often when they spoke with women than when they spoke with other men.'[5] A 2020 survey conducted by Catalyst, a non-profit organization that helps build workplaces that are supportive of women, reveals that one in five women say they feel ignored or overlooked during video calls.[6] Other studies have shown that women experience this same feeling during in-person meetings too.

Mansplaining, which refers to the act of a man explaining something to a woman in a condescending manner, is also a common form of microaggression. Alisha, a financial analyst, says, 'I have always been good with numbers. I find it demeaning when my male colleagues try to break down money matters for me.' She goes on to say that most of her male colleagues believed that they were doing her a favour. 'It took me a long time to muster courage and tell them that I do not need their unsolicited explanations,' says an exasperated Alisha.

Sangini, a data scientist, also a numerical genius like Alisha and the only woman in her team, shares that her work-related suggestions are almost always ignored or drowned out. 'But I am unfailingly invited to every team meeting and asked to take down the minutes of the meeting,' she says. Administrative tasks such as note-taking and party planning are often thrust upon women because it is assumed that we enjoy doing these tasks and that we are good at them. This is a form of microaggression too and it stems from bias.

Exclusion is another typical form of microaggression that the marginalized experience. Reva, a marketing specialist and a single mom of a four-year-old, states that she is never invited to work conferences happening outside of her city because her manager and colleagues assume that it will be difficult for her to leave her child behind. 'Let me decide that, please,' exclaims Reva, visibly annoyed. Akshata, a video producer from Kochi who is now based in Mumbai, says, 'I don't speak the local language. So, most of my conversations are strictly work-related. I am never invited to be part of lunch groups or social gatherings.' The feeling of being excluded is painful. Remember the episode in the all-time popular TV series *Friends* where Rachel starts smoking to be part of her manager's inner circle?

Microaggression can take various forms. While it may be relatively easier to 'put up with' certain microaggressive acts, such as listening to unsolicited advice or quietly doing the assigned administrative tasks from time to time, there are some acts of microaggression that leave you deeply rattled. For instance, discriminatory appraisals are profoundly disturbing. Sakina, a senior UX designer by profession who registered with myAvtar in 2022 for a suitable opening, expressed an interest in meeting me. After exchanging pleasantries, she got straight to the point. 'Doctor, all my male peers have been promoted, but my contributions are ignored. They look at only recent performance; they use inconsistent standards and the appraisal process has no transparency at all,' she exclaimed. This gradually led Sakina to question her potential. I could see that she was highly skilled at her work simply from the gamut of job offers she was receiving through the myAvtar portal.

This is what microaggression does to you—it gnaws at your self-confidence. If not recognized promptly, it can lead women to switch roles, fields or give up their careers altogether. What a loss that would be for the team, the organization, the field and the nation.

The first step in tackling microaggression is becoming aware of it and recognizing what it looks like. To broadly sum up, the following actions count as microaggressions:

- Making assumptions about a person's economic status, religion, interests, abilities, etc.
- Ignoring a person's suggestions and contributions.
- Interrupting a person.
- Stealing a person's idea.
- Not inviting a person to be part of social groups and gatherings.
- Offering unsolicited advice on personal matters.
- Asking personal questions about a person's life, family, religion, sexual orientation, etc.
- Using derogatory terms and making belittling jokes or stereotypical comments.
- Talking down to a person and treating them with condescension.
- Assigning office housework to the same person all the time.
- Using different yardsticks to measure performance.
- Ignoring a person's preferred gender pronouns.
- Trivializing a person's challenges.

Now that we have a general idea of situations where microaggressive behaviour is demonstrated, here are the Career Doctor's tips for tackling it:

1. Document incidents of bias that you encounter on a regular basis, as this will help you be prepared for such situations and react in an appropriate manner.

2. Practise assertive communication with your close circle and keep a few responses ready for when you hear biased comments or experience biased behaviour. The key is to be firm without being confrontational. You could choose to respond in one or more of the following ways:

- 'I am sorry, but I don't appreciate the joke.'
- 'That hurts. Could we discuss what prompted you to make that comment?'
- 'Excuse me, can you let me finish speaking?'
- 'I understand that you have a different point of view, but I would like to make my point first.'
- 'Can we be mindful of one another's boundaries?'

3. Make it a point to speak up during huddles and meetings. The best way to avoid being ignored or interrupted is through effective communication: be clear and concise, thoroughly research the topics of discussion and ask astute questions. Speak authoritatively; do not make statements like 'I may be wrong . . .' or 'I'm not sure if what I'm saying is making sense . . .' Use assertive language; say 'I suggest' or 'I know'.

4. Find allies who will stand by you and help amplify your voice. We've already discussed allyship in detail in Chapter 11, 'The Work Family'.

5. Not the least, be open with your manager and HR about your problems and suggest inclusive practices. Do not hesitate to seek clarity about the appraisal process from them.

Tackling microaggression may appear challenging. Reminding ourselves that we are not alone in this fight can help us keep going. Learn to recognize the signs and know that it is not just men who engage in microaggressive behaviour. It can come from anyone, even your juniors. Although it is not entirely in our control to keep microaggressions in check, we can make a significant mark in tackling them. Now is the time to begin.

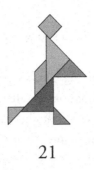

21

How Safe Are You?

Soumya, the HR manager at SmartSoft re-read the resignation letter that thirty-two-year-old Utsa, one of their top developers who had been with the company for over five years, had handed in. 'I am unable to understand this, Utsa,' she said, the incredulity evident in her voice. 'You are one of our cherished employees. You have been growing at a fabulous pace ever since you joined us. You've even been promoted twice, one time more than even me. You won the Chairman's Award three times in a row. You have built an excellent, recession-proof career here. Plum projects are yours for the asking. And now you want to leave?'

'I don't have a choice, Soumya,' replied Utsa with a level of sadness that Soumya had never heard from anyone. When women say they don't have choices, there is usually a choice that they are afraid of, and Soumya knew this. 'It is a toss-up between my career and my marriage. Quitting is my only option to ensure that I remain happy in my married life,' said Utsa. 'But you are pregnant! Don't you want to avail of the six-month maternity leave and all the benefits that SmartSoft offers women?' asked Soumya. 'I promised Dev that I would resign today. I don't want to go back on my word.' Utsa's tone was final as she spoke about her husband, Dev.

Soumya began processing Utsa's separation formalities with a heavy heart, but something bothered her. Soumya thought of the young engineering graduate that she had interviewed five years ago. Utsa had received the highest scores on both the aptitude test and the career intentionality index, a standard test that SmartSoft uses to evaluate all new hires. Her razor-sharp focus and the manner in which she handled challenges were often praised and lauded by her manager. Something didn't add up. Soumya remembered that Kranti, one of Utsa's friends, had mentioned that Utsa was found weeping in the ladies' restroom a few weeks ago. When asked about it, Utsa brushed it off, saying that it was just a pregnancy thing. Soumya dialled Kranti's number.

'Yes, Soumya, your suspicion is correct,' said Kranti. 'I was just about to message you. Something is not right.' Kranti shared that Utsa had become a different person since her marriage one year ago. 'That bubbly energy and joy have just disappeared. Especially after she became pregnant, I find that she is virtually a shadow of her former self,' she remarked. Kranti then referred to Utsa's sudden visits to the company's medical centre of late. She added that once she had found a big bruise on Utsa's forehead and when asked about it, Utsa had said that she had slipped and fallen down in the bathroom. Utsa had also taken to wearing heavy make-up in the last couple of months. 'I think Utsa is undergoing domestic abuse and harassment,' shared Kranti. 'But she does not want to admit it or seek solutions. By quitting, she is only pushing herself into a deeper problem.'

Soumya realized that Utsa's case was more complicated than she assumed and decided to investigate further. The more Soumya investigated, the more clarity she got about Utsa's situation. For instance, she gathered that one reason for Utsa's steadfast decision to quit was because she was finding it difficult to hide her scars any longer. After her pregnancy, Utsa's dependence on her husband had also grown and she was likely feeling a lot more pressure to keep her marriage intact.

There is a reason why women are among the marginalized groups in society. They face social inequities that perpetuate domestic violence and harassment in different environments. Often brushed under the carpet, discussed in whispers or broached upon sporadically, domestic violence has a significant impact on not just the person but also the household, community and society at large. Domestic violence is defined as 'violence committed by someone in the victim's domestic circle'. It includes actions such as hitting, strangling, threatening to resort to violence, non-consensual sex, stalking and destroying personal belongings. These acts of violence can be perpetrated by partners and ex-partners, immediate family members, other relatives and family friends. The term 'domestic violence' is used when there is a close relationship between the offender and the victim. The NFHS-5 has revealed that almost 30 per cent of women in the age group of eighteen to forty-nine have faced spousal violence.[1] Experts believe that the numbers could be higher because, most often, they are not reported.

The solutions to domestic violence can be complex. Victims of domestic violence must reach out for external support, gather evidence of the violence and report the incident to the police as soon as possible. This is easier said than done because women hesitate to reach out for help for various reasons, such as the social stigma surrounding a couple's separation and the general expectation that women must 'adjust' and continue to live with their husbands, whatever the situation may be. Other reasons, such as fear of isolation, feelings of attachment to the spouse despite the violence, child custody issues, lack of financial independence, etc., also add to the humongous complexity of the problem. As a result, women stay in abusive relationships in the hope that things will miraculously improve with time.

Domestic violence may seem like a personal issue, but its impact can be felt on the psychological, physical and social well-being of not just the victim but many closely connected to her. Aruna, a candidate whom Avtar had placed in her first job with a renowned MNC, was a good student throughout her school and college years. She was among the employees that the client would refer to as a 'success story'. Having settled down well in her job, Aruna began dating one of her college mates and married him after a couple of years, despite stiff opposition from her family. Her parents reconciled grudgingly, but when they saw Aruna's husband behave in an unkind and hostile manner, they stayed away. Two kids followed and Aruna started facing the full brunt of domestic violence as her husband, who was often without work, began to beat her, demanding money every day. He would shout at her, call her names and look for excuses to beat not only her but their children too. Embarrassed to stay in the apartment complex where everyone knew about this, Aruna shifted houses and schools several times. Her children experienced the trauma of an unhappy home where violence was the norm. Soon, the harassment started showing up in Aruna's work and her confidence, focus and performance fell drastically. When I met Aruna after nearly a decade, upon a referral by her employer, I was shocked to find that she was a ghost of her former self. It took several weeks of counselling to help Aruna arrive at concrete steps to deal with her situation in a positive manner.

Aruna's story shows that the impact of domestic abuse is not restricted to the employee. It affects the organization too, because an employee who is grappling with abuse at home is simply not in a position to give her best at the workplace. Besides, the risk of abuse or violence isn't restricted to the home environment. The #MeToo movement made it abundantly clear that harassment, violence and abuse are rampant in workplaces. As per the 2021 National Crime Record Bureau (NCRB) data, 17,539 cases of sexual harassment were recorded in the country, of which 418 were from workplace or office premises.[2] The NCRB report also revealed that Assam, Haryana, Maharashtra, Tamil Nadu and West Bengal had recorded the highest number of cases of workplace sexual harassment against women.

Workplace abuse must be handled with a stern hand. For the employee, it results in stress, loss of focus and productivity, reduced job satisfaction and, at times, absenteeism and resignation. For the organization, there are a host of implications, such as poor work culture, higher attrition and, as a result, the loss of diverse talent.

Harassment in the workplace can manifest in many forms, such as forced physical contact, advances or outright demands for sexual favours. Making sexual innuendos, showing pornography and any unwelcome physical or non-physical conduct of sexual nature are categorized as harassment in the workplace. Razia had always been a career-primary individual. It was a dream come true for her when she joined a leading media house as a senior correspondent. The first few months flew by without issues until one of her editors began acting weirdly with her. The initial conversations consisting of praises soon turned into innuendos. When she protested against his demeanour, she was threatened that her assignments would be downgraded and her performance would be rated poorly. A worried Razia raised the issue with her

Internal Complaints Committee (ICC) and demanded action against the editor.

ICCs are an integral part of organizations that take a serious stand against harassment in the workplace. The committee hears complaints by women employees and takes necessary steps as per the Prevention of Sexual Harassment at the Workplace Act, or POSH Act, which came into effect in 2013 for women to seek redressal for harassment in the workplace. It has broadened the scope of the existing laws, such as the Vishakha Guidelines implemented in 1997. POSH mandates companies to conduct training to sensitize the workforce about the issue of sexual harassment and how it has to be dealt with. A POSH-compliant workplace is considered psychologically safe and secure for women.

While sexual harassment at the workplace has begun receiving the due attention that it deserves (at least from the companies that value women), we must understand that abuse need not always involve sexual advances. Women face harassment for other reasons, such as age, caste and religion, apart from attempts to malign and demean them based on their marital status. This was the case with Joyeeta, a mid-career professional in her early forties from Bengaluru. Joyeeta recounts the time when a younger male colleague chose to target her for the appraisal he received from her as his team leader. He often left anonymous notes on her desk, mocking her dressing style and accent. The situation turned worse when some of her colleagues told her they were hearing a lot of gossip about her. She was shocked to find rumours floating around about her marriage and an impending divorce. Joyeeta says, 'They said I was venting my frustration by being nasty to my team members. None of these were true.' She then traced the happenings to her team member and confronted him. Joyeeta says though the person faced action by the management and was asked to leave, the psychological effect lingered for months. 'I felt incompetent, vulnerable and low. Though my husband and family stood by me, I could feel the fear in the air. What if it happens again?'

Far away from Bengaluru, in Delhi, is Riddhi, a young management professional who moved to the capital city from Moradabad, Uttar Pradesh, to complete her MBA. When she landed her first job, her supervisor joked about Riddhi's accent and workwear, and warned her to be prepared for the grind and hard work. All went well the first two months, but soon she found the amount of work almost impossible to manage. When she mentioned this to her supervisor, he replied sharply, 'When you applied for the job and underwent the interview, you knew that the workload would be heavy. If you want a career, then be prepared to work harder than you do now.' But Riddhi noticed that while most of her colleagues got easy tasks for which they were appreciated, the assignments that came to her were often the toughest and most complicated. Receiving very little guidance and support, she was often embarrassed to ask her teammates for input. Over the next few months, she found her working hours increase to almost ten hours per day, leading to her travelling back to the working women's hostel in the wee hours of the morning. After a particularly gruelling week of work, during which she had barely a couple of hours of sleep a night, Riddhi decided to raise the issue again with her supervisor. To her shock, she found that she was placed in a Performance Improvement Plan (PIP), a method whereby poor performers would be given a few months to shape up or ship out. Riddhi spoke to her teammates and understood that her supervisor had flagged off her performance as sub-par. It took her a while to understand that he was deeply biased against her and that she was being targeted for refusing extra work. Unable to take the harassment any longer, Riddhi eventually quit.

Women are at risk of facing harassment and abuse at all points in their careers, irrespective of their seniority. Organizations and leaders are responsible for ensuring a safe and secure workplace for them. Adherence to the provisions in the POSH Act, which include forming a committee and taking steps to look into complaints within the stipulated time, is one part of it. The other aspect is the sensitization of the workforce to what constitutes harassment. Rather than being a tick-in-the-box exercise, leaders should set the tone by showing zero tolerance for harassment of any kind.

Whether Aruna, Razia, Joyeeta or Riddhi, it is true that women remain easy targets. Along with psychological implications, the economic aspirations and independence of women are at risk. Studies have shown that sexual harassment is directly linked to financial stress, as it can cause career interruptions and job changes. A 2017 study titled 'The Economic and Career Effects of Sexual Harassment on Working Women' revealed that harassment between the ages of twenty-nine and thirty increases financial stress in the early thirties.[3] Roughly 35 per cent of this effect can be attributed to the targets' job changes, a common response to severe sexual harassment. Some women quit work to avoid harassers. Others quit because of dissatisfaction or frustration with their employer's response. In both cases, harassment targets often reported that leaving their positions felt like the only way to escape the toxic workplace climate. Dealing with abuse and harassment with an iron fist is paramount. It is equally important for women who survive such harassment to stop seeing themselves as victims and forge ahead, tapping into support systems and redressal mechanisms.

Here's the Career Doctor's advice for both Soumya and Utsa:

Steps for Soumya	Steps for Utsa
• Invite Utsa for an outing and initiate a casual discussion on the extent of harm that domestic abuse and violence can cause for women, children and society in general. Create a safe space for Utsa to talk freely and share her problems with you, but do not force her to open up. • Introduce Utsa to women's support networks that help victims of abuse and share domestic violence helpline numbers and legal resources with her. • Introduce Utsa to the various employee assistance programmes (EAPs) at SmartSoft and encourage her to make use of confidential counselling and mental health support services. • Organize workshops for the entire team on domestic violence, discussing its harmful impact and how one can handle it, and get Utsa to attend them. • Assure Utsa that the organization will provide whatever support they can in their capacity, such as covering immediate emergency expenses and providing physical and emotional support during pregnancy and after.	• First and foremost, know that perpetrators of violence are the ones to be blamed—always. • Reflect on your thoughts and emotions. Think about what is preventing you from speaking up for yourself and why you are unable to step away from the relationship. • Keep emergency helpline numbers handy. This is especially critical considering your pregnancy. • Keep a written record of incidents of violence as well as verbal and emotional abuse. • Have a safety plan in place if or when things go out of hand, which includes identifying places you can go to during emergencies. For example, your parents' place or your colleague's hostel. • Consider living away from your spouse for a while, as it might help both of you gain some perspective. • If opening up to a friend or relative is challenging, meet a counsellor in confidence who can guide you through this crisis. • Initiate an open discussion with your spouse (in a safe and public environment such as a restaurant) on how you feel about the violence and abuse. Jointly reflect on what is causing the violence. There is always an underlying problem. Is it low self-esteem? Is it alcohol abuse? • Explore the option of joint counselling.

Violence of any form, whether domestic or at the workplace, is a very serious issue and each one of us can play a part in mitigating its cruel impact on victims. All it takes is simply highlighting the issue, offering a non-judgemental ear to women suffering from abuse and providing practical help, such as keeping your doors open for them during emergencies. We can also enhance the care ecosystem by providing employment opportunities for women who are survivors of abuse and directing them to the right resources. Volunteering at support centres, sharing your own story of survival and empowering the next generation of men and women by sensitizing them to what violence really is are just some of the ways we can help. Remember, every small step counts!

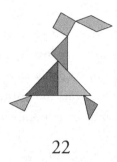

22

Women and Mental Health

It was August of 2005 and I had been summoned to my children's school for a routine meeting. I drove myself to the school, but as I finished parking, I looked around and found that I did not recognize where I had reached. Feeling confused and disoriented, I wondered how I had come to a place of which I had no recollection. Thankfully, I had my trusted Nokia mobile phone with me. I called my husband, Rajesh, and requested that he come and pick me up. Rajesh came to the point where I was waiting. It was indeed my son's school, but I had forgotten that I had to turn into the lane to reach it. I had been experiencing debilitating headaches and attributed the mishap to the migraines. The next week, I entered the school but could not remember how to go to the principal's office. This was the same school that both my children went to—one that I had been going to for the past eleven years. A few days later, when I had been to the supermarket and forgot how to get home, Rajesh decided that a neuro consult was imperative. The doctor examined me and diagnosed my condition as stress-induced hippocampal atrophy. Pathological anxiety and chronic stress had led to the structural degeneration of the hippocampus, which in turn led to neuropsychiatric disorders such as depression and memory loss. I was thirty-seven. Under the advice of medical professionals and well-wishers, I began treatment that lasted for five years and instituted a series of changes to my everyday routine, most importantly, a spiritual practice that I continue to this day.

Deepika Padukone, Oprah Winfrey, Serena Williams, Lady Gaga and J.K. Rowling—what do these women have in common? Well, they've all grappled with mental health issues, but the commonality among these women does not end with that. A more significant element is that all these women have also openly spoken about their struggles with anxiety and depression. *Is that a big deal*, you may ask.

Here are some numbers: A 2023 survey conducted by Mind, a mental health charitable organization in Britain, states that over 36 per cent of people over the age of sixteen never speak about mental health.[1] Another 2018 study involving over 3000 participants conducted by the Live Love Laugh Foundation, a non-profit organization founded by Deepika Padukone, found that 47 per cent of them tend to be judgemental about people perceived as having mental illness and 26 per cent fear people who aren't in their best mental state.[2] The study also explored the various misconceptions that people have about mental illness and found that 47 per cent of the respondents believe that mentally unwell people are retards, 40 per cent think they are mad or stupid, 56 per cent think people with mental illness talk to themselves, 44 per cent believe that they are always violent, 41 per cent feel that when a mentally healthy person spends time with the mentally ill, the former's mental health could deteriorate and 60 per cent feel that mentally ill people need to have their own groups and solve their problems on their own without involving 'mentally healthy' people.

These numbers show that it *is* indeed a big deal when people muster courage and speak up about their mental health issues. Most people with mental health struggles keep mum about it because of the shocking level of stigma and shame associated with it. As the above survey results indicate, people are ignorant about the signs and symptoms of psychological issues. Often, they misconstrue mental health problems as mood swings, a lack of willpower or stress.

This lack of understanding of mental illness affects women more than men because study after study tells us that women are more susceptible to mental disorders and they affect men and women differently.[3, 4] For example, men tend to externalize depression, which results in anger issues or even substance abuse in extreme cases. Women, on the other hand, tend to internalize it and dissociate from people around them.

A gendered mental health study conducted by researchers from the Department of Psychiatry at the Post-Graduate Institute of Medical Education & Research (PGIMER), Chandigarh, in 2015, states that the brains of men and women are wired differently and the way they express their feelings and react to stress differs.[5] The study further states that gender differences are particularly stark when it comes to common mental disorders such as depression and anxiety and that women are more prone to them.

That brings us to the next question: Why are women more vulnerable to mental health issues compared to men? A variety of factors contribute to this: hormonal influences, childbirth and most significantly, patriarchal elements. I have met scores of women whose mental health has taken a beating thanks to patriarchy. The following stories of women show that a male-dominant culture can have a severe and sometimes long-term negative impact on the mental well-being of women.

- Tarani, who has been married for five years, has been experiencing intense worry, sleep disturbances and irrational fears ever since she got married. After a lot of hesitation, she shared this with a friend, who in turn referred her to a psychiatrist. After a couple of sessions, the doctor understood that the fear and anxiety stemmed from the dowry demands from her husband's family during the first couple of years of marriage. Though the demands have reduced, Tarani says there are still implicit demands and that she feels the constant pressure of not meeting their expectations.

- Sylvia, a working mom of two, is solely responsible for preparing meals for her entire family of six, picking up and dropping off her kids at school and all their extracurricular classes and keeping the house spic and span. Her husband, she says, has a long commute to work and a demanding job. So, he gets back by 8 p.m. and prefers to relax. Sylvia's day is so packed that she barely manages to get five hours of sleep. She admits to finding it extremely challenging but hesitates to ask for help. Her in-laws are old and frail, and her husband is 'after all, bringing in the lion's share of money', as she puts it. But lately, she has been grappling with intense fatigue, dizziness, insomnia and lack of concentration, and she knows that she is close to complete burnout.

- Reena, a newly married woman, is experiencing intense feelings of frustration, dissociation and loneliness. I meet her briefly at a temple close to my house, where she's come for some relief. We get talking and she tells me she left her fulfilling job in another city and moved to Chennai at her husband's insistence. She says, 'I was willing to move, but I just wanted to complete the project that I was working on and wait until I found a good opportunity here. Is that too much to ask for?'

- Deepa, an accountant and the mother of a five-year-old, is raring to get back to work after a five-year break. The last five years have been hectic for her as she's almost single-handedly run the home and taken care of the child, so she hasn't kept her skills up-to-date. I ask her why she did not hire any help, to which she replies, 'I wasn't working, so I felt a responsibility to manage everything at home, ma'am.' Now, after unsuccessfully hunting for a suitable job, she has come to meet me. 'The roles I find interesting offer a salary far below what I was earning five years ago. They're also reluctant to allow me any flexibility. I am really starting to doubt whether I can make it in the professional space,' she says agitatedly. I notice that she's very low on self-esteem and experiencing heightened levels of anxiety and loneliness. While I am confident that we can find a fitting role for her over time and with some effort, I can't help but reflect on how deeply various patriarchal elements affect women and their emotional well-being.

While certain factors make women more susceptible to mental illnesses, I believe that we also have unique strengths to fight these mental health challenges.

- **Sharper emotional perception:** It is generally believed that women score better when it comes to emotional awareness and intelligence. Though this is a long-standing debate, we know that women are naturally intuitive, open-minded, sensitive and good at handling conflicts.
- **Strong support networks:** Research shows that women are more empathetic and compassionate compared to men.[6] These qualities make it possible for women to develop strong

support networks. As indicated by the numerous active online mommy support groups, women are naturally inclined to bond over shared struggles.

- **Steely resilience:** Women face more challenges and transitions compared to men right from childhood and we are more used to multi-tasking. So, we are in a much better position to adapt and recover from difficulties.

Now that we understand our unique strengths in facing mental illnesses, here's a framework to help you leverage these advantages and boost your mental health. While I am not a mental health professional, I've witnessed the positive impact of the following steps on women and their psychological balance.

Steps	Description
1. Understand your mental makeup, which is your emotional response to various situations. Your personality, beliefs and values play a role in determining your emotional intelligence or mental makeup.	This involves recognizing your thoughts and emotions and realizing how they influence your actions. • Reflect on how you respond in different situations—happy occasions, challenges, crises, etc. • Make a list of all your positive and negative emotions and map every emotion that you experience to specific situations. • Identify what triggers negative emotions in you. • Identify your core values and beliefs. Reflect on whether you are sometimes forced to compromise your principles and make an exhaustive list of such circumstances. • You could take trusted personality assessments to help you further understand your psyche and temperament. • Write down all your reflections. This is an important step because writing often helps you track your feelings better.

Steps	Description
2. Practice mindfulness, which is nothing but developing complete awareness of your thoughts, emotions and physical responses.	Step 1, 'Understanding your mental makeup', initiates you into mindfulness. In addition, ask yourself the following questions: • When you feel anxious or sad, what are the thoughts that cross your mind? Do you feel like a victim? Do you feel suicidal? Do you feel like a failure? • How does your body physically respond to anxiety and distress? Do you feel your heart race? Do you tear up? • How do you handle fear, anxiety and sadness? Do you endlessly brood over your disappointments? Do you tend to binge-eat when you are sad? Do you talk to someone you trust? Writing down answers to the above questions will help you manage your emotions more effectively. Practise deep breathing and meditation and set aside thirty to forty-five minutes for physical activity every day to enhance your awareness of your emotions and responses. Once you cultivate a more conscious awareness of your emotional self, it will help you: • Explore ways to increase the frequency of events that evoke positive feelings in you. • Look for ways to avoid situations that trigger negative emotions. • Avoid situations that push you to abandon your ideals.
3. Be your own counsellor.	Learn the nuances of cognitive behavioural therapy (CBT), which is an effective intervention for treating mental disorders. The good news is that once you learn the basics of CBT, it can be self-conducted with or without the help of online tools.

Steps	Description
4. Prioritize self-care.	Identify activities that bring you joy and no matter how busy you are, set aside at least twenty minutes daily for an activity you enjoy. If time is a constraint and you feel like skipping self-care, know that it is okay to: • Skip relatively less important tasks, such as folding clothes or preparing snacks. • Delegate chores to others. • Not be perfect in everything you do. Remember, self-care is not selfish.
5. Turn obstacles into opportunities.	• Identify all the challenges that you are facing. • Examine if the obstacle(s) can be avoided. If yes, take steps right away to steer clear of them. • If not, analyse every challenge thoroughly by breaking them into smaller elements and writing down possible silver linings for every hurdle. • Reach out to your contacts to discuss how best to approach these challenges. This is a crucial step; you will be surprised to find that a lot of people are happy to guide and provide support. • Create a plan to make setbacks work to your advantage and always keep the long-term picture in mind. Note that not all challenges have positive sides to them. But it is important that you analyse every problem thoroughly and do your best to turn it to your benefit.
6. Practise positive living routines.	• Spend time in nature. • Connect with your family and friends on a regular basis. Humans are social beings; meeting and interacting with people is like oxygen for us. • Practise gratitude every day. • Make sure your diet is healthy. • Get at least seven hours of sleep every night.

The above framework can positively impact your mental well-being, without doubt. But it is also important to understand that mental illnesses warrant external guidance from a trained counsellor or a psychiatrist, especially if you experience intense distress, find it difficult to perform daily tasks or have suicidal thoughts. The best approach would be to seek professional help right at the initial manifestation of emotional distress signs.

Understand that mental well-being is just as important as physical health and to promote everyone's mental well-being, we need to normalize mental illness. To start with, we could listen to people struggling with mental problems with compassion and without judgement, create safe spaces for women to come together and share their struggles, support mental health campaigns and, most importantly, openly share our personal mental health journey narratives with others.

Remember, everyone—I repeat, everyone—experiences anxiety, fear and distress. So, starting this moment, let's do what we can to normalize mental illness because, in my opinion, this is the foremost step in promoting women's mental health.

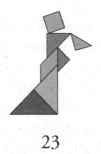

23

The Boss Lady

Sheenam Ohrie is a voracious reader of both fiction and management books and a Hindi movie buff who loves to listen to Mohammed Rafi's songs on repeat. She also enjoys spending hours at the beach, just soaking in the water. Geetha Ramamoorthi is passionate about music, speaking and blogging, and feels privileged to have a family that shares her vision and supports her. Anuradha Sriram, mother to two boys, enjoys books related to scriptures and is closely associated with the Ramakrishna movement. While Sheenam is part of the fintech industry, Geetha is in the space of science, tech and engineering, and Anuradha is into content and e-learning.

It is great engaging with them. We, at Avtar, are fans of each of them and the sentiment is reciprocated in equal measure. They are leaders who have consistently stood up for women's rights. To give you a brief rundown, Anuradha has spearheaded a commendable initiative called WInGs, which is committed to helping the women in her organization rise to their full potential and she has been the chairperson for the Indian Women Network (IWN) in the southern region, an organization that is dedicated to fostering connections among women and strengthening the

entire collective. Sheenam has mentored scores of women in her
three-decade professional journey and is a champion for equal
educational opportunities for girls. Geetha has striven to boost
diversity in her organization and is involved in various social
initiatives to promote women's agency.

Geetha, Sheenam and Anuradha have two things in common:
first, they are all deeply committed advocates for diversity and
gender equality. And second, their designations. Anuradha is
the co-founder and joint managing director of Integra Software
Services; Sheenam is the managing director of Broadridge India;
and Geetha is the managing director of Kellogg Brown & Root.
They are a rare species; each one of them is a crucial part of the
tiny segment of women business leaders in India.

As per a report by the World Economic Forum, only 15
per cent of the CEOs at Fortune 500 companies are female.[1] Like
many things in India where women are concerned, this statistic
too takes a solid beating. A 2021 Deloitte study reveals that the
share of women CEOs in India stood at 4.7 per cent in 2021.[2]
A study conducted among LinkedIn members reveals that the
share of women in leadership positions in education and health
and fitness—fields that are traditionally seen as being dominated
by women—stood at 30 per cent and 24 per cent, respectively.[3]
Women leaders remain scarce across industries and nations. The
scarcity of women in leadership positions is commonly referred to
as the 'leaky pipeline' phenomenon. This metaphorical pipeline
represents the gradual attrition of female talent as they ascend the
corporate ladder. What is causing this? There is no simple answer
to this, as it involves a combination of factors.

1. **Historical baggage:** Throughout history, women have been
   relegated to subservient roles, with power concentrated in the

hands of men. This historical imbalance has created lingering discomfort for women when they wield authority. The legacy of being denied power for centuries has left an indelible mark, making it challenging for women to fully embrace their potential for leadership and influence.

2. **Double-bind dilemma:** Women often find themselves ensnared in a double-bind quandary. When a woman exhibits agentic leadership qualities, such as confidence, assertiveness and ambition, she is seen as too bossy and when she exhibits communal leadership qualities, such as kindness, sympathy and respect, she is seen as too soft and as someone who does not have it in her to be an effective leader. This is the result of deeply ingrained societal expectations and stereotypes—we expect women to be soft, nurturing and empathetic, and leaders to be assertive and ambitious. We are unable to decide whether we want women leaders to exhibit feminine traits or traditional leadership traits. This bind places women in a perpetual state of trying to meet others' expectations, making it difficult for them to find a comfortable equilibrium.

3. **Likeability challenge:** Women leaders who display agentic leadership qualities find themselves less liked by their peers and subordinates, leading them to question their skills and hindering their ability to lead.

4. **Harsh assessment:** Historical practices and beliefs have led us to believe that women are not natural leaders. Hence, we (mind you, both men and women) tend to evaluate women leaders more stringently than male leaders, which puts a lot of pressure on women.

In the several trainings that I have done for women leaders, I have met women who have shared very similar narratives about their difficulties. One conversation stands out in my memory. I met Komal in Lucknow in 2016 at an instructional event. A vice president of a leading private bank, Komal had stellar academic credentials, multiple professional accomplishments to her credit and clear goals for herself and her division. Yet, when she met me for a one-on-one consultation, she said, 'I have almost seventeen years of work experience in this field. Why do I still feel I'm not good enough?' She went on to elaborate that she constantly battles self-doubt, fears failure and often feels that her past successes are largely because of favourable luck. She was struggling to figure out if being too gentle and accommodating was hurting her and had briefly even resorted to using a loud voice and micromanaging her subordinates' work to show her authority, but had not felt comfortable doing that. As our conversation progressed, I also learned that Komal worked hard—too hard for her own good. When I asked her why she felt the need to push herself so much, she replied, 'Because my hard work can help compensate for my other shortcomings.'

I've met other senior women with similar concerns. After all, imposter thoughts are pretty common among women leaders because of the tough yardstick that everyone uses to gauge us, a lack of role models, gender-related norms imposed on us and the pressure to uphold the accepted ideals regarding leadership traits. Komal handled these imposter thoughts by constantly pushing herself to excel, sometimes setting unrealistic targets for herself. When she met me, she was close to complete burnout.

I shared some quick tips with Komal, stressing that she needs to embrace both communal and agentic leadership qualities as per the situation. I gave her examples of women leaders, such as Michelle Obama and Jacinda Ardern, who've been kind and empathetic while also being firm, confident and goal-oriented. To combat her self-doubt, I urged Komal to write down her past achievements. Finally, I wanted her to understand that no one can escape criticism—especially women—because we are always under severe scrutiny and that no matter how much she slogs, there will be people waiting to find fault with whatever she does. Unfortunate, but true. So, I guided her to see that one important thing that she can and must do is stick to her values under all circumstances, embrace her authentic self and use her position to initiate conversations about equity and inclusion to drive gradual change. However, along with these steps, I knew that Komal needed stronger guidance to fully realize her worth and grasp the intricate relationship between women and power.

Which brings me to the concept of power distance. It is nothing but the degree of acceptance in a society or organization that power is indeed distributed unequally. The Dutch psychologist Geert Hofstede is credited with devising this theory after a decade-long study he conducted through IBM, based on which he created a tool to measure the power distance in a setting.[4] The power distance index (PDI) measures the extent to which a country or organization accepts the unequal allocation of power and the results can be high, moderate or low. In a high-power-distance setting, traditional norms and beliefs are deeply ingrained, and the majority accept and encourage this power gap. In a low-power-distance setting, there is a push for equality, flexibility, joint decision-making and attention to inclusivity. It goes without saying that women, especially women at the top, find the high-power-distance context more challenging and there is greater pressure and need for women in such settings to strive to break down this power gap and progress towards equality.

I strongly believe that women's leadership potential can be fully tapped by enabling them to understand these power dynamics and the different kinds of power that they can leverage.

Each type of power offers a unique toolkit, which, when wielded responsibly and effectively, can help women overcome challenges, influence change and navigate the complexities of leadership. At Avtar, we conduct a detailed 'Pathways to Power' training programme for women leaders that engages deeply with the different types of power. I asked Komal to attend the training programme and she readily agreed as she was desperate for solutions. Here, I discuss those various facets of power in brief:

The Seven Types of Power

1. **The power of clarity:** List the words that often come to mind when you think of the term 'Power'. Authority? Dominance? Control? Loud? The concept of power has traditionally been associated with these qualities and hence many people, particularly women, aren't too comfortable with it. So, for women, having a sound understanding of what power is and what it is not becomes a crucial aspect of their leadership journey. At its core, power is not a monolithic force but a multidimensional concept that can manifest in various forms. The power of clarity lies in understanding that power does not make a leader fearful or authoritative and that leadership power can be expressed through collaboration, empathy and authenticity. It's about fostering connections, enabling growth and navigating challenges with firmness and resilience. This clarity is so powerful for women, as illustrated by Sheryl Sandberg, whose thorough understanding of what power means and entails has helped

catapult her to a position of great influence and inspiration for women.

2. **The power of vulnerability:** Vulnerability is a unique strength that fosters genuine connections and trust, and the first step to leveraging this power is to understand that vulnerability is neither a weakness nor a dark emotion. A successful leader recognizes this and acknowledges her own vulnerabilities, which helps create an environment where colleagues feel safe to share, make mistakes, innovate and grow. Vulnerability enhances empathy and relatability, facilitating a supportive ecosystem that propels both personal and professional development. While vulnerability is powerful, it's important to navigate it with wisdom and strike a balance between openness and maintaining professional boundaries. Vulnerability shouldn't be an invitation for exploitation but a conscious choice to share in a way that benefits collective growth. For example, Satya Nadella, in his book, *Hit Refresh: The Quest to Rediscover Microsoft's Soul and Imagine a Better Future for Everyone*,[5] candidly writes about the various trials he's faced, including the challenges that came with raising his son, who was born with special needs, and this forthrightness has helped foster an empathetic and inclusive environment at Microsoft. Many top women leaders, such as Kiran Mazumdar Shaw and Debjani Ghosh, haven't shied away from speaking about their struggles with self-esteem and imposter thoughts, and this has helped people hold meaningful conversations about bias and gender barriers.

3. **The power of courage:** It takes courage to be yourself and to be genuine—that is authenticity. However, authenticity is not merely being yourself. Being authentic also involves making conscious choices that align with your core beliefs and values

and persisting with those choices even upon learning the risks of being real, such as the risks of being hurt or not being liked. An authentic leader is one who honestly expresses emotions, admits mistakes, is transparent, keeps promises and maintains integrity even when there may be pressure to sacrifice one's principles. This courage to be authentic is an important power for any leader. CEO of Apple, Tim Cook, for example, came out as gay for the first time in a 2014 Bloomberg editorial[6]— the courage he's displayed to embrace his true self has helped the cause of LGBTQ+ inclusion in workplaces and normalized homosexuality to a considerable extent.

4. **The power of versatility:** Versatility is the hallmark of a leader. A versatile leader can adapt to different purposes, succeed in different settings, lead diverse teams, navigate varied challenges and adapt to changing circumstances. Versatile leadership becomes critical in situations involving intense stress and during conflicts and difficult conversations, such as performance feedback. The essence of versatile leadership is having a range of approaches or responses for any situation and being able to pivot or effortlessly tweak your leadership style to suit different people and circumstances—a quality that helps a leader evolve and thrive amidst uncertainty. When I think of versatility, one of the first leaders that comes to mind is Elon Musk, who I believe has displayed remarkable adaptability and innovative thinking and has made a mark in not one, but multiple fields—from space technology and renewable energy to AI, machine learning and social networking services.

5. **The power of polarities:** Leadership is not confined to absolutes; it thrives in the delicate balance of polarities. A boss lady understands that navigating seemingly contradictory forces, such as assertiveness and empathy, competing and

collaborating, control and freedom, is essential for holistic leadership and that these opposite traits must co-exist.

A successful leader must embrace qualities of agentic as well as communal leadership. Choosing one leadership style over another is not needed, nor is it the right approach. Communal leadership helps bring out the best in individuals, build cohesiveness and generate new ideas, while agentic leadership drives productivity, facilitates goal attainment and creates a results-focused atmosphere. Leaders need both; either–or thinking simply cannot work here. Skillfully managing and embracing these polarities creates a well-rounded leadership approach that resonates across varying contexts. Michelle Obama, for instance, has illustrated this quality numerous times during and after her stint as first lady. Her commanding speech during the Democratic National Convention in 2016, when she uttered the rousing slogan 'When they go low, we go high' is indelibly carved in our minds, isn't it? But she is also widely known and respected for her kindness and empathetic leadership style.

6. **The power of hustle:** Traditionally, the word 'hustle' has negative connotations and is used to describe stealing, cheating, being too aggressive or pushing too hard. In the modern lexicon, however, the term 'hustling' has evolved to mean pursuing goals relentlessly and striving for progress despite all the obstacles in one's career path. A leader who embodies the hustle mentality is tenacious, focused on the future, resilient, optimistic, restless with the status quo and welcomes risks. Hustle, combined with ethical leadership, inspires dedication and a commitment to excellence throughout the organization. For example, Steve Jobs and Dhirubhai Ambani were great

strategic hustlers and both of them weathered several similar challenges, including health problems, falling out with friends, financial constraints and legal battles. What is also common in their success stories is how they embraced those challenges and uncertainties, took risks and displayed tremendous tenacity in navigating through their challenges. Simply put, they learned to feel comfortable with the uncomfortable and uncomfortable with the comfortable, the number one quality needed for a successful hustler–leader.

7. **The power of inclusive allyship:** An effective leader understands that fostering an environment of inclusivity is critical and supports and advocates for diverse voices, experiences and perspectives by embracing inclusive allyship. The foremost step in fostering allyship is self-awareness and self-initiated learning about biases, your privileges and the challenges that marginalized communities face. A transformative leader also encourages other leaders and high performers to speak up, challenge biases and use inclusive language. Keep in mind that allyship goes beyond mere gestures, statements and social media posts. While these steps are crucial, they must be followed by concrete action.

Apart from being an ally to her employees, a boss lady also recognizes the importance of being an ally to herself. Women often believe in quiet hard work and unprompted or organic recognition and they do not communicate their aspirations either. But an effective woman leader recognizes the importance of highlighting her achievements and articulating her goals to others. And not the least, a successful leader becomes a truly effective ally for herself when she not only builds relationships but also leverages them—another action that women are uncomfortable doing. Leveraging relationships to achieve your goals is an intentional action but not an exploitative one and it is almost always a quid pro quo arrangement. All three boss ladies that we encountered at the beginning of the chapter—Sheenam Ohrie, Anuradha Sriram and Geetha Ramamoorthi—are great examples of effective leaders who have fully leveraged the power of allyship, both for themselves and other women.

I met Komal again shortly after she had completed Avtar's comprehensive training programme on gender and its influence on power. We spoke briefly and she seemed self-assured and optimistic. She thanked me for illuminating her view of the subtilities of power. 'I can't wait to put my power-packed learnings to practice!' she said with a smile. The substantial change in Komal's demeanour greatly reaffirmed my conviction that women need to have a comprehensive understanding of the nuances of power to become veritable boss ladies!

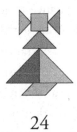

24

Becoming Money Smart

If you ever get a chance to visit South Africa, don't miss it! I was invited by Ralph Fletcher and Claire Garrett of the Top Women Awards to deliver the keynote address at their conference in Johannesburg in August 2019 and I jumped at the opportunity. (It is a matter of infinite joy that the date was 15 August and when I chanted 'Vande Mataram' at the very start of my speech, I had a hall full of multicultural voices repeating the powerful mantra along with me!) South Africa is among those places of verdant, grand beauty that makes one imagine that God was inspired one day to create an entire country by putting together the most gorgeous natural geography. Cape Town is the jewel in its crown. It is on my itinerary and I am thrilled to see the point from which the Mahatma set sail for his motherland and created immortal history. I also see places where slaves were housed and realize the long, uphill battle that was fought to eradicate this most heinous crime. There is deep gratitude for the lives we lead today and for how far humanity has come. Yes, there is a lot more to be changed, but many of the horrors of the past, we hope, will not be revisited.

And if you ever get a chance to go to Cape Town, do not miss a trip to the incredible Adderley Street flower market! When the taxi drops us off near the entrance, I am taken aback at the sheer burst of colour. It's not my first time being stimulated by floral beauty. I was about four when my grandmother took me to the century-old Russell Market in Bengaluru and I watched with open-mouthed fascination exotic flowers like carnations, long-stemmed roses and gladioli. During my frequent visits to Mumbai on work, I would sometimes pass the Dadar Phool Bazaar on my way to the airport, where, as early as 3 a.m., large crates of flowers arrive to be broken down into smaller baskets. In my hometown of Puducherry, we would have the adorable *pookadai* (flower market) with just enough space for one person to walk through, surrounded by tiny stalls filled to the brim with flowers like jasmine, oleander, sweet marjoram and davana.

Adderley Street in Cape Town offers a complete eruption of redolent springtime hues that no camera can do full justice to. A walk through the gorgeous market is like a visit to rainbow land—amid the massive heaps of lilies, iris, chrysanthemums, roses and other splendours whose names I don't know, you will find even more striking women, casually plying their trade and laughing and teasing each other. The story goes that roughly 150 years ago, the first woman flower seller sold her first bouquet and cocked a snook at apartheid. She became a symbol of resistance and even in the times when black people were not allowed to trade or own a business in these places, the Adderley Street market was a departure. Since the 1880s, the flower market has been an essential part of Cape Town's culture.

The most beautiful aspect of Adderley's history, however, is not the flowers; it's the matrilineal tradition of handing over the business from grandmother to mother to daughter. Every one of the 100-plus stalls at Adderley is owned by a woman and she passes it on to a female relative, a practice unbroken for decades. It's a lovely day, 11 August 2019 and I am talking to Gairo, one of the owners at the Adderley Street flower market. 'How long have you been managing the business?' I ask. 'Oh, about two decades and some!' she replies, her face breaking into the most beautiful of smiles. She knows that being a tourist, I will not be buying large bouquets, but still, she engages me in a warm and friendly manner. I tell her about my visit to Russell Market with my grandmother, and she says she first began accompanying her grandmother to the markets when she was barely two years old and we share a laugh. I ask her about the names of some of the flowers that I am seeing for the first time in my life and Gairo points out the agapanthus, the yellow arum lily and the Barberton daisy. I speak about the work I do and our skilling programmes for women and she responds with 'lekker!'—South African slang for 'great!' 'For me, all my skills, I learned from my mother and grandmother. They are my bosses!' she laughs. Then she turns serious as she mentions, 'It is very important for women to know the skill of running a business and making money, yes?'

Gairo's thoughtful comment during a casual conversation reminds me of the omnipotence of money everywhere in the world, especially when it comes to women. At the same time, I can't help but wonder why women and money often seem to exist in different realms. During the innumerable discussions I've had about money with other women—colleagues, relatives and friends—I find that women and money are usually in a complicated relationship. Dr Kate Levinson, in her book, *Emotional Currency: A Woman's Guide to Building a Healthy Relationship with Money*,[1] talks about how women engage differently with money as compared to men. 'Kate Levinson shows how money is both mercilessly public and intimately personal' says Robert Reich, an author and American professor. When a woman has an unclear connection with money, she builds an astonishing range of beliefs about it. Her identity as a career woman, a professional, a mother, a homemaker and a caregiver influences how women relate to and handle money and in many cases, they are not confident about taking control while deciding money matters.

One of my earliest memories of money was when, during Deepawali in 1978, my mother called my sister and me aside and told us that we would not be buying new clothes that year, since we had 'money problems'. We barraged her with innumerable questions on what that meant, until she said, 'You know the cupboard in which we keep the money that Appa earns? Well, that cupboard is somewhat empty. When it fills again, I will get you clothes.' For the next few weeks, I would surreptitiously see the cupboard time and again to know if my mother was 'restocking' it. Much later, I realized that in any business (my father was a pharmaceutical entrepreneur), there would be ups and lows and personal finance needed to be managed with a lot of astuteness to cushion against uncertainties. When I was growing up, it was taboo to speak about money in most homes. The actual presence or absence of it would be gauged by whether one had five dishes at lunch or just two.

Childhood conditioning can significantly impact women's money-making decisions throughout their lives. Here are some more ways it can manifest:

1. **Self-esteem and confidence:** Girls consistently exposed to money-related discussions, encouraged to take risks and pursue ambitious goals may have greater confidence in their money-making decisions.

2. **Money mindset:** The beliefs and attitudes surrounding money that one develops during childhood can impact financial decision-making. For instance, if a girl grew up in an environment where money was scarce or associated with negative emotions, she may have difficulty accumulating wealth or taking risks in her financial pursuits.

3. **Family dynamics:** The financial experiences and management of the family during childhood can also influence a woman's approach to money. For example, if she was raised in an environment where her father made all money-related decisions, she might feel insecure about managing finances and may tend to outsource money management to others, most likely other men.

As there are very few female role models to emulate, most women fall back on what they've seen their father or brother do. Avtar's Viewport research in 2014 on 'The Economic Centeredness of Women' found that only 67 per cent of women took full responsibility for the money they earned.[2] The study also revealed that 49 per cent of women in the twenty- to thirty-year-old age group identified themselves as novices when it came to investing. However, one heartening finding was that 77 per cent of married women stated that their income was important to their families. The study clearly showed that while women are beginning to understand the value of being financially self-sufficient, we have a long way to go for women to achieve complete financial independence.

There is a whole set of impediments to women's access to financial literacy and key among them are gender stereotypes, patriarchal norms, financial education disparities and many institutional barriers. Girl children until the 1970s and even the

1980s would be told that a man's job is to earn money and a woman's job is to look after the home and family. While this began changing with the advent of greater career opportunities, putting money in the hands of women, they still did not get to decide how they would spend it. Over the years, I've interacted with a host of women in various settings about their struggles with handling money and the autonomy they have or choose to exercise in managing their finances. The experiences of these women reflect a broader reality that needs a drastic shift.

Neeta, a single woman, earns about Rs 40,000 per month working as a graphic designer in an ad agency in Mumbai. Yet, when the team decided to take a holiday in Mahabaleshwar, Neeta dropped out, citing money problems. She confided to me that though she earned a reasonably good sum of money, she handed the entire amount to her mother and did not get to decide how it was spent. In turn, Neeta's mother just handed the money to her husband, who then apportioned the money for various expenses. While this is a pretty common occurrence in many homes, the fact that she did not have a say in how her income was spent when she earned a lion's share of the family income irked her deeply. It reinforced her belief that even if she had gotten the freedom to earn money, she could never aspire for the freedom to spend it. The few moments of time when she held the notes from the ATM in her hand before handing them over to her mother was all the pleasure she derived from her month-long effort.

When I first met her, Tamilselvi was earning Rs 12,000 per month as a retail store assistant. After a few months, when I met her again, she mentioned that she had quit her job. When I asked her why, she replied, 'My husband says he will give me the same amount of 12K, ma'am, for taking care of the house.' I appreciate Tamilselvi's husband compensating her for the housework she was doing; however, I'm afraid the ecosystem that organizational employment provides cannot be replicated at home.

Money is not just currency; it is membership in a club of women who are equal to men. From an early age, girls are often conditioned to believe that their primary roles are nurturing, caregiving and supporting others. This conditioning can lead to a mindset that prioritizes needs of others over their own, affecting their confidence and assertiveness in making money-related decisions. Forty-eight-year-old Sherin remembers that she was never taught how a woman can earn, what careers she can pursue and how she could obtain money. Instead, she was given a piggy bank and asked to save. When she landed her first job as an audit assistant in an accounting firm, she was deeply embarrassed to seek the help of her colleagues to open a bank account.

The gravest of all concerns is the lack of intentionality in women about becoming money-smart. Women are stopping themselves from becoming financially savvy. Even the brightest of women, otherwise brilliant at learning things, develop a black box in their minds when it comes to money. Kamna, a web designer running her own business, shares that building her start-up and acquiring customers were, to her, 'more important' than financial matters. Her then-partner, an investment banker, offered to help. In the beginning, Kamna appreciated the support and was glad to be free from worries about the earnings before interest, taxes, depreciation and amortization (EBITDA), salaries and cash flow. As Kamna's business expanded, she began to get into altercations with her partner about how he had invested the money they had earned during boom times. She realized that his investment strategy was a high-risk, high-reward one, which caused great fluctuations in income. Kamna's disconnect with money and her complete ignorance of how her partner made decisions almost brought her to the brink of a massive financial crisis and it took all her bandwidth to pull her company back from it.

Raveena, an IT professional, shares that she would feel overwhelmed by the complexities of investments, budgeting and tax planning. When she began working and earning, her father stepped in to become her financial guru. With every promotion or increment, Raveena began increasingly relying on her father for support regarding her income. This did not mean just taking his advice; it meant that he was a joint holder in her bank account and managed all her transactions, from drawing money to paying taxes. When her father had to relocate abroad to be with her brother, Raveena felt completely lost with regard to her money. From the bank passwords to which accounts he used for which transactions, Raveena felt at sea and had a nervous breakdown.

Being financially independent is not a choice but an essential life skill for any woman, irrespective of her family's financial status. Financial independence is not merely having a steady source of income. It includes independently making financial decisions, clearing personal debt, saving, investing and creating a secure future for yourself and your family. Is it critical to attain financial self-empowerment even if someone reliable is more than happy to manage your finances? The answer is a resounding 'Yes!' and here's why:

- To have unshakeable belief in yourself and radiate self-esteem.
- To have complete freedom in deciding how you want to meaningfully contribute to society and pitching in for causes that matter to you.
- To have full autonomy in pursuing your interests and deciding your purchases with zero guilt.

- To ensure that you can face all kinds of emergencies, such as the loss of a dependable person, layoffs, medical conditions and unexpected expenditures like sudden major house repairs.
- To break gender norms and stereotypes and prove that women are just as adept as men at handling finances.
- To be an inspiration to your daughters and nieces and help them become financially competent.
- To have a secure financial future where you are not dependent on your children or family members for money.

In order to have all of the above, you must invest time and energy in achieving financial empowerment. Trust me, the path to economic self-empowerment may seem intimidating in the initial stages, thanks to our conditioning since childhood, but it is no rocket science.

Here are five key aspects for a woman to become financially savvy:

1. **Budgeting and saving:** Understanding how to create and follow a budget is fundamental to financial literacy. It involves tracking income, expenses and savings to ensure that money is allocated wisely and used efficiently.

2. **Credit and credit scores:** Knowing how credit works, how credit scores are calculated and the impact of credit on borrowing and financial opportunities is essential for responsible financial decision-making.

3. **Debt management:** Being aware of the different types of debt, such as credit cards, loans and mortgages, and understanding how to manage, reduce and pay off debt is crucial for financial health.

4. **Investing:** Once you've strengthened your grasp on budgeting and saving, it is important to learn about additional ways to build wealth and save for retirement. This includes knowledge of savings accounts, retirement accounts, stocks, bonds, mutual funds and other investment vehicles.

5. **Taxes and tax planning:** Being aware of the tax implications of various financial transactions and learning about tax planning strategies can greatly help optimize financial outcomes.

Let's be realistic. Acquiring sufficient knowledge about these financial topics cannot happen overnight; it needs commitment and consistent effort, and you may encounter stumbling blocks. Here, we discuss the common challenges that women face and provide a framework that you can use to overcome the hurdles.

Likely challenges for women	Tips to overcome the barrier
Limited to zero exposure to financial planning and money management	Start with baby steps. There are multiple platforms you can use to educate yourself on essential financial topics: • Books, articles and blogs • Online workshops and beginner courses are available on platforms such as Coursera, Udemy and LinkedIn Learning, and many of them are free. • Financial podcasts and videos • Financial communities exclusively for women, such as physical and online groups for women to share their knowledge, doubts, challenges and hacks with each other. Most top voices in finance today understand that the appeal of the financial domain needs to be enhanced. So, they use various techniques, from humour and games to real-life stories and multimedia tools, to add zest to the topic. The financial sphere is not as drab as it was twenty years ago. It is a lot more fun now!

Lack of time	This is a real challenge. Most women barely have time to relax and when you are exhausted, the last thing you want to do is learn the nuances of finance. I hear you! But we simply can't afford to neglect money planning. So, here are some quick tips: • Set aside just fifteen minutes every day to gain insights on the key financial concepts. • You can also enhance your financial acumen by engaging in regular discussions on money matters with people you trust and whose company you enjoy, such as your spouse, your parents or friends. • Try to pair this knowledge-seeking exercise with another activity that you enjoy. For example, you could listen to a financial podcast while walking in the park. • Pick the right time of the day to enhance your fiscal know-how, as you need to be mentally sharp. • Put your learnings into practice bit by bit. For example, you could start by actively participating in financial decision-making at home.
Elaborate and slightly intimidating process	Approach the process in a step-by-step manner. That will make it less daunting for you. • Maintain a record of your income, expenses and savings, and develop a budget. There are many free budgeting apps that make the process easier with tools like reminders, customized budget plans, expense trackers, etc. • List down your financial priorities: purchasing a house, sending your children abroad for higher education or further studies for yourself. • Now, armed with the clarity of your money situation and spending choices, set short-term and long-term goals. Make the goals specific and spell out the time frame for each goal. For example, a short-term goal could be 'setting aside Rs 10 lakh by 2025 to pursue an MBA from a top B-school'. A long-term financial goal could be 'saving Rs 80 lakh in the next ten years to build my own house'. • When you are clear about your goals, saving and investing in appropriate avenues become easier. Seek expert guidance for this step if needed; it will be a worthwhile investment.

Relatively low income and savings compared to men, which makes future or retirement planning challenging	The gender pay gap and the motherhood penalty are serious issues. Mothers often take career breaks and opt for part-time work after their breaks, which reduces their earning potential. This is certainly not ideal and the situation needs rectification. Given this constraint, how can you build a secure future for yourself? Look for ways to maximize your earnings. • Diversify your investments. Avoid high-risk and high-cost options. • Make good use of discounts, cashback offers, coupons and promo codes. • Avoid unnecessary spending and impulse buys. • Avoid high-interest debt, but if you are in such debt, try to clear it as soon as you can. • Prioritize insurance coverage for health, pregnancy, life and property. • Open a separate retirement savings account and an emergency fund. Automate money transfers to these accounts every month. There are some retirement accounts that come with significant tax-related benefits too.

Our nation can achieve gender equality only if our women have complete autonomy to spend and invest the money they earn. Know that there may be stumbling blocks in your path to complete financial independence. But also know that no hurdle is insurmountable. Get started today!

25

Women's Role in Gender Inclusion

We are huddled into a Tata SUMO vehicle and even with the air conditioning, it's a hot summer day as we drive to a tiny hamlet in Tamil Nadu, about 150 km from the city of Madurai, tucked deep within the innards of the state. It's a choppy ride, as the road, where it exists, is rugged and filled with potholes. It is July 2009 and a few of us from Team Avtar are going on a reconnaissance trip to understand the contours of the assignment we have signed up for. It is one of two listening sessions (the other closer home, in a village about 50 km from Chennai), both in villages where we are meeting women who come together to help and support other women. Our client is Madura Microfinance Limited (currently amalgamated with Credit Grameen Bank), a company that was the brainchild of Dr Thiagarajan, founder of Bank of Madura, whose daughter, the inspiring Dr Tara Thiagarajan, helms the company after his demise. Our project is to identify 500 financial advisers to guide Madura's customers—women from deeply impoverished sections of society—and we need to understand what they expect from such a person.

Dr Tara has invited us to a weekly gathering of one of the self-help groups (SHGs) that's been operational for about two years. We join the circle of women who are seated on the freshly swept floor to discuss the updates of the past week. Madura has been providing loans, credit, insurance, access to savings accounts and money transfers to women running small businesses such as vegetable supply, milk sales or selling processed foods such as pickles or sweets. They are a group of about thirty women who have taken over the reins of their family's economic welfare to ensure that they lead reasonably secure lives, devoid of the uncertainty brought about by the sporadic employment of their menfolk. These women are extremely appreciative of Madura's microfinance because they come from severely underdeveloped parts of the state and have no other access to financial resources than the loan sharks in their village. Each of the women is a member of the SHG (several thousand such SHGs exist in the country), which they have named 'Penn-Shakti' (women power) and they operate a savings-first business model whereby the member's savings are used to fund loans. We are in conversation with them to understand the role played by their co-ordinator and leader in their daily progress and livelihood. While the co-ordinator is a company representative helping them with all paperwork and compliances, the leader is an elected functionary, one who is the moral guiding force of the group.

Avtar: 'How does your leader support you?'

Thenmozhi: 'She is inspiring.'

Surya: 'She helps settle disputes in our group' (laughs).

Suganthi: 'We see what she is doing and we emulate her.'

Yazhini: 'Her life is a lesson.'

Ruby: 'She protects us and ensures that even our family members don't come in the way of our well-being.'

Avtar: 'How does the co-ordinator help you?'

Padma: 'She brings us money' (breaks into a loud laugh, joined by the others).

Prabha: 'She helps fill out all the application forms.'

Vijaya: 'She finds us business contacts.'

Amudha: 'She is trustworthy.'

Avtar: 'Do you believe women need to help other women?'

Santhiya: 'Yes, women should be the biggest supporters of women.'

Christine: 'Women must be united. When women fight, men take advantage.'

Sulochana: 'When women help women, nothing can come in the way.'

Thaamarai: 'Unity should begin at home. Women should never bring down other women'

Buvana: 'Women sometimes tend to view other women as rivals, but this won't help anyone.'

It is not only the women from hinterland villages around the world whose identity is confined to the borders of their homes, who feel this way. The perception that women have a more natural inclination to bring fellow women down and, as such, should band together is one that is prevalent even in steel and chrome buildings housing the most empowered of people. Why do some women tend to view other women as competition and resort to varied tactics to 'win' the race? Let's look at why this happens; it's a combination of reasons.

1. **Female misogyny:** A lot of women have internalized gender biases and stereotypes and expect women to act in a certain way—soft-spoken, submissive, modest, etc.—and believe that the primary responsibility of women lies in childcare. When

such women come across women who don't fit this definition, they sometimes express their displeasure by finding ways to undermine them.

2. **Low self-esteem:** The 'self-esteem' gender gap is significant—women across different ages tend to have lower levels of self-esteem when compared to men because of historical norms, societal expectations and stereotypes. When a woman's self-esteem is low, she turns to tactics that can bring fellow women down so as to paint herself in a better light.

3. **Negativity bias in the media:** Research shows that humans are naturally attracted to negative news and stories.[1] This preference for negativity is reflected in the kind of stories that are produced and the type of content we choose to engage with. So, stories of women fighting with one another, plotting revenge and stabbing another's back take up more air, print and web space than inspiring stories of women providing mutual support and encouragement. This exposure deepens the stereotypes we already hold about women waiting to tear down other women and we are convinced that we can succeed only if we follow the same path.

4. **Scarcity mentality:** When resources and opportunities are scarce for women in a setup, women may feel that there is only so much room for women's growth and recognition. Hence, they try too hard to surge ahead of others and end up stooping to unpleasantness.

5. **Fatigue-induced hostility:** Women leaders often get to the top after immense struggle—the fatigue is real and unmistakable. When it's time for these women leaders to support and mentor the emerging female workforce, it is only natural for the women at the top to feel that the up-and-

coming women need to figure things out on their own, just like they did.

It is high time we broke this widely held perception that women are always looking to bring other women down. We must be part of the change. The power of women coming together is profound, both at the individual and organizational level. I've witnessed this during my interactions with various successful women on various platforms. For example, Vibhuti Lall, director of HR at R1, a leading revenue cycle management company, is a great example of a woman leader who has always striven to uplift other women around her. As a child, she witnessed her father treat everyone, irrespective of their role or designation, the same way. 'That grounded me to treat people fairly,' she says. In her long and inspiring career, Vibhuti has launched several second career initiatives for women and groomed many young women professionals to become powerful leaders. She adds passionately, 'We must support other women without feeling insecure; trust me, there is enough for everyone.'

Another example of a woman who has given top priority to supporting fellow women is Kiran. I met Kiran, the head of business development at a mid-tier IT firm headquartered in Delhi, at the Women of India Leadership Summit in 2018. Kiran shares the story of her climb to the top. 'I didn't have a great start to my career,' she says, frankly. Kiran, who kickstarted her career at a small management firm in 1992, found herself in a predominantly male-dominated environment. As a young mom trying hard to balance home and work, she tried befriending other women in the workplace, most of whom held higher positions than her. 'I desperately wanted reassurance from them. I also needed tips to manage my baby and work,' she shares. But when she reached out to her female colleagues and seniors, she found that most of them engaged with her just out of politeness—that too fleetingly. 'The conversations never went past perfunctory talk. There seemed to be an invisible wall between me and them.' The other women didn't share deep bonds with each other either, a fact that Kiran noticed with relief. 'Women preferred chatting with their male colleagues. To be honest, I felt a little comforted when I realized that I wasn't being singled out.' But it also got Kiran thinking and pushed her to read about this behaviour that quite a few women exhibit, when she came across the term 'Queen Bee Syndrome' for the first time.

Social scientists first used the term 'Queen Bee Syndrome' in the early 1970s to describe a phenomenon where women in senior roles tend to disassociate themselves from subordinate women and refrain from assisting them in advancing their careers. Various reasons are attributed to this, from internalized sexism to the threat of being replaced by other women.

However, Kiran says she felt inclined to question the queen bee theory. 'I wondered if I could help change the narrative, however minutely, because perpetuating this theory is harmful,' she says. Besides, her initial struggle led her to make a conscious effort to ensure that other women felt supported. Kiran began with small steps, such as offering mentorship to entry-level women, celebrating their achievements, sharing tips with young moms on efficient work–home balance and speaking up for equality. Today, as a divisional head, her organization fosters a culture of support and sisterhood, which, Kiran states, has greatly helped boost the organization's productivity. She adds,

'I am where I am today, primarily thanks to my amazing set of female friends at work.'

Like Kiran, a lot of people have raised the issue of whether the Queen Bee Syndrome is a misconception. There are different research studies that support and challenge this viewpoint. For instance, a 2008 study by scientists at the University of Toronto proposed that the Queen Bee Syndrome could be the reason women find working for female bosses more stressful.[2] According to another study by researchers at the University of Arizona in 2018, women experience higher levels of incivility from other women than men.[3]

On the other hand, there is emerging research favouring the perspective that queen bee behaviour is a myth and a harmful stereotype that must be abandoned. A study conducted by researchers at Columbia Business School and the University of Maryland found that when a woman occupies a top position in an organization, it reduces the chances of other women getting a top position by 51 per cent.[4] It doesn't sound encouraging, does it? But the reason they found this to be the case was not due to the woman leader's queen bee behaviour. It was because the organization, which had certain gender diversity goals, gave up promoting women once they had achieved their (meagre) diversity goals. It is critical for us to understand that various factors are at play, so it is unfair and incorrect to single out women's supposed spite for the various problems that women face.

Organizations need to understand that there are numerous benefits when women unite. Women's bonding and solidarity can help increase gender diversity in an organization, boost productivity, employee morale and creativity, improve brand image, attract top talent and reduce attrition. Kiran says, 'In our organization, we recognize and reward women who strive to lift up other women because they are precious to us.'

How does sisterhood positively impact an individual? When you have a solid network of support from fellow women who have likely faced similar struggles and can empathize with you, inspire you and guide you, your confidence and sense of belonging explode! A 2019 study published in the *Harvard Business Review* states that women who have an 'inner circle of close female contacts' are more likely to occupy executive leadership positions compared to women who don't have that tight-knit circle.[5]

At Avtar, we have long understood the power of bringing women together and the crucial role that women can play in gender inclusion. One unquestionable way to harness the power of sisterhood is by prioritizing gender diversity and increasing the strength of women in the organization. 60 per cent of employees at Avtar are women and women make up more than 50 per cent of our leadership. We promote feminine solidarity in multiple ways. For instance, we assign buddies to new joiners. We also have informal chat sessions where women employees come together and share their life updates, challenges, tips, lessons learned—anything under the sun, really. Offering a safe space for women to voice their thoughts and opinions and creating an ecosystem of support for women by women is so important.

So, here's a quick action list for women to lift each other up in the workplace. One sound way to make sure you execute this plan is by setting a goal for yourself. For instance, you could aim to lend assistance to at least one woman a day.

Steps that a leader can take	Steps that an employee can take
• Hire deserving women (not merely to meet diversity goals). • Follow an open-door policy once a week where you are available exclusively for women employees at all levels to discuss their concerns. • Have a suggestion box for women to anonymously submit their challenges and concerns. • Conduct anonymous surveys for women, seeking feedback on their overall experience, particularly covering questions on work culture, physical and emotional safety, and growth opportunities. Include open-ended questions too. Note that it is critical to act on feedback. • Mentor and sponsor subordinate women by providing helpful resources and connecting them to suitable opportunities and leaders. • Advocate for gender equity in every forum—pay parity, unbiased and transparent performance assessment techniques and the provision of enablers such as flexibility and remote work options are some leadership focal points. • Speak up openly when you observe unfairness of any kind, however small the act may appear to be, such as a seemingly harmless instance of mansplaining or gender stereotyping. • Organize informal, exclusive events for women. For example, a lunch or tea party is an ideal setting for women to bond and share tips. • Celebrate women employees' wins in public. • Play an active role in women-centric ERGs.	• Share helpful work-related hacks and resources proactively with fellow women. • Make sure newly hired female employees feel included—be approachable, introduce them to others in the organization, include them in your lunch group and informal outings, share your knowledge about the company, encourage questions and offer guidance. • Be an ally to the disadvantaged women in your organization and speak up for their rights, whether they are newbies, from religious minorities, from the LGBTQ+ community or do not speak the local language. • Organize low-key lunch events exclusively for women where you can all gather to share personal and work-related tips and experiences and discuss gender issues. • Be a part of women-focused ERGs. • Acknowledge and speak about the achievements of women newcomers during team meetings. • Appreciate strong women leaders in group settings, support their ascent to top positions and advocate for their ideas. • Volunteer to help women leaders with tasks related to their interests and skills. This will not only help reduce their workload but will also be an opportunity to prove their worth. • Refrain from spreading gossip about other women. If you have critical feedback about a woman's work or action, discuss it with her directly.

Remember to extend support to women at home and in external settings too. What you can do will depend on your personal situation; for example, offering a listening ear to your mother-in-law, sharing practical tips with your friend on navigating home and work demands, making sure your domestic helpers feel comfortable, offering a lift to your neighbours, giving your bus seat to an older or pregnant woman, etc.

At the end of the project with Madura Microfinance, Dr Tara had this to say: 'We were delighted with the quality of recruits through this exercise. Madura faces the unique challenge of hiring people who are both motivated by a deep desire to serve a social mission and competent in the business aspects of what we do. With this exercise and the process developed with Avtar, we've succeeded on both counts!'

Women often tend to give up on their career aspirations because they assume there are unavoidable derailers in their path to success, such as childcare responsibilities, gender bias at work, unfair pay, etc. I refer to this problem as the 'myth of the derailers' because I firmly believe that every derailment encountered by a woman can only be handled if she is able and willing to accept help from those around her, especially other women.

So here's to the femme force. May each one of you find your girl squad at work and beyond!

26

Building Brand 'You'

The applause was thundering and a hall full of women rose up in a wave to celebrate the rousing thoughts shared by the two brilliant leaders on stage. Both phenomenal role models and powerful articulators, they were bosses who not only inspired loyalty and trust but also steered their respective organizations to tremendous success. The moderator of their keynote panel, who was also the organizer of the conference, was humbled and thrilled to see the speakers stimulate the audience into creating new paths of destiny for themselves. It was 2012 and the event was the 'Segue Sessions' by Avtar, a skill-building, networking conference for over 500 second-career women held in Mumbai. The two chiefs who delivered the powerful addresses were Leena Nair, CHRO of Unilever India, and Sandhya Vasudevan, MD of Deutsche Bank Group. And yours truly was the aforesaid moderator who had the incredible honour of sharing the stage with two powerful leadership brands on this momentous occasion!

My tryst with leadership brands goes back a long way. Before the advent of search engine optimization, search engine marketing (SEM), backlinks and the Internet, one learned about brands by going to a library and picking out books written by the 'father of marketing'—Philip Kotler! One also saw brands engage with customers all around and realized that here was a person, product or message that stayed very powerfully within the psyche of the target audience by being consistently relevant to its consumers. What was the most striking thing about the brand? It had a powerful, recognizable and visual connect. One leadership brand that influenced me deeply as a girl growing up in the 1970s and 1980s was Indira Gandhi.

From the time I was born and for most of my childhood and teenage years, Indira Gandhi was the prime minister of India. But her influence and position in Indian history were strikingly revealed to the young teenager that I was, only on the day she died. It was 31 October 1984, around quarterly exam time, and we were at school. Around 11 a.m., we suddenly heard a loud cacophony and ear-splitting shouts all around. Everyone rushed out of the classes and the proverbially disciplined and well-run school turned into an unrecognizable zone of confusion as students were driven out of the classrooms and into buses and vans as quickly as the administration could manage at a time of a national crisis. But the most unforgettable image etched into my mind was the sight of the strict, stoic nuns of the missionary school, who had transformed into weeping, wailing masses of emotion. Even as the nation (and the world at large) was left shell-shocked at the assassination of one of the most powerful women leaders of the time, I was frozen in the moment when I witnessed our tough-as-nails Mother Superior, our iron headmistress, reduced to sobbing hysteria. Who was this leader who caused such an unprecedented display of sentiment? I became infinitely curious. For the next few days, as mournful santoor music played on Doordarshan, the national television channel, I actually learned about 'Brand Indira'.

Indira Priyadarshini Gandhi, easily the most prominent woman politician and stateswoman India has ever produced, served as the third prime minister of India from 1966 to 1977 and again from 1980 to 1984. Known for her controversial decisions that had sweeping outcomes for the nation, Indira demonstrated the kind of guts to become to India what Margaret Thatcher was to Great Britain—the fiercest, most pugnacious leader her country had ever seen. Indira was also a brand—a woman who loved the spotlight, a powerful, charismatic persona who held the top job of the day, but was also a mother, daughter and wife. Mixing a trench coat and a sari made of Swadeshi cotton, Indira Gandhi displayed the impeccable style of a truly Indian woman who connected effortlessly with the big bosses of the world and who could not be fitted into a box. Hers was a carefully cultivated and strategically crafted personal brand.

Back to Segue Sessions and after the exceptional opening keynotes, we gathered at the foyer for coffee and conversations. Debashri, one of the speakers at the conference, whose talk was scheduled for later that day, walked up to me. 'What a magnificent opening! It gave me goosebumps, Doc!' she said, her eyes sparkling with the energy of someone who had just received a life-changing, historic message. 'Now, I'm super nervous about my own panel,' she confessed. 'I doubt I could ever match up to that.' I told Debashri that each one of us brings something unique to the table and that each one of us is relevant and significant in our own way. We each have our own brand and we also have the choice to shape it to reflect what we want to communicate about ourselves to the world. I also pointed out how sharing her thoughts on what she had just witnessed made her not just a part of the experience but also leveraged the brands of the amazing women leaders she would speak about. Debashri was not convinced. 'I feel like an attention-seeker whenever I post my views on social media, Doc,' she confessed. 'I know that I have a lot to say to the world, but speaking about my achievements makes me feel like I am a show-off.'

Cultivating a strong self-image, which is a major part of branding, is often seen as narcissistic, superficial and a waste of time. But there is no better tool for career growth than branding. Women such as Padmashree Warrier, Roshni Nadar, Anjali Sud, Kiran Mazumdar Shaw, Vanitha Narayanan, Sharmistha Dubey and Aruna Jayanthi are names that instantly blaze a recall of a well-groomed, superbly articulate, self-assured, charismatic woman who is not simply a 'woman' leader but the supreme boss of a global organization, one whose decisions create history. They are brands that signify consistency, value and upward mobility. Both Sandhya and Leena, who spoke at Segue Sessions, are passionate champions of women's causes and both have gone on to carve amazing new futures for themselves since 2012. Leena is CEO of Chanel, while Sandhya is an independent director on several boards, strategic adviser and mentor for start-ups and scale-ups, as well as a committed social venture partner. They are amazing brands too, whose achievements serve as motivation to many. In a country that needs more women in the workplace, more women as managers, more women as VPs, more women on the boards and in leadership positions, branding is a cardinal skill.

Let's consider a few top consumer brands: Apple, Jio, Airtel and Pepsi. What do these brands have in common?

- They all have a clear brand identity, thanks to their unwavering focus on strong brand storytelling.
- They have a clear-cut purpose and well-defined values.

- They embrace a customer-centric approach and nurture a solid emotional connect with their customers by prioritizing their needs and appealing to their ideals.
- They strive for constant innovation.

Every successful brand adopts these facets. At Avtar, we firmly stand for values such as equality, fairness, honesty and compassion. Our purpose is to uphold these values through our work, which pushes us to build equitable and inclusive workplaces where every person feels seen, heard and valued. We have always put our end customers (women and other marginalized people) at the forefront of our goals and plans. As a brand, Avtar has never shied away from strong narrative marketing, which we see as paramount for our organization's success.

All the above dimensions needed for a successful brand apply to individuals too. For example, the story of Taylor Swift is one that I often reflect on when I think of a carefully cultivated personal brand. Many of us are big fans of her mesmerizing songs that often touch upon themes such as empowerment, personal growth and social justice. That is her USP—authentic music on matters of social fairness and self-empowerment that connects deeply with millions of people across the globe.

There are many other personal brands that we can draw inspiration from. For example, Michelle Obama is known for her authenticity, humility, public speaking skills, passion for justice and empowerment of girls. Closer home, take Nirmala Sitaraman. We all know that her signature selling points are empathy, effective communication, confident leadership and her subject expertise. Falguni Nayar, the founder and CEO of Nykaa, who is one of two self-made Indian women billionaires, is famed for her entrepreneurial spirit, innovation and commitment to serving a diverse customer base. These are all women we look up to, don't we? However, their compelling features, which we so deeply admire, did not develop overnight. It took time, effort and focus to build these powerful 'people brands'.

So, how do you build a formidable and inspiring personal brand? The first step is to understand what brand-building means at its core. I often turn to the teachings of Mieko Kamiya to explain the essence of brand crafting.

Mieko Kamiya (1914–79) was a Japanese psychiatrist, author, translator and mother of two. She served as a mentor to Princess Mishiko, the former queen consort of Japan. While researching leprosy patients and the meaning of life, Mieko studied the Japanese concept of *ikigai* (a sense of purpose or reason for living) and later popularized it in her 1996 book *Ikigai-ni-Tsuite* (On the Meaning of Life). A lesser-known book of hers is *Sonzai no Omomi*, a book about creating value. The Japanese lettering for *sonzai* is composed of two characters: *son* (that which grows) and *zai* (that which stays). This, in short, describes what a personal brand really means—one that has elements rooted in consistency and an equal measure of elements that grow and transform. When we apply these two principles of 'son'—one who grows, adapts and sustains—and 'zai'—one who is anchored in her fundamental values—we get the recipe for a powerful personal brand.

So, the core idea of the concept of 'sonzai' involves embracing both authenticity and growth. To incorporate this theory into developing a personal brand, we must understand the three dimensions of personal branding.

- Gravitas (how you act)
- Influence (how you work)
- Communication (how you speak)

Developing each of the above dimensions in the right way is essential for a powerful and positive brand image. Here's the Career Doctor's advice to Debashri on what each dimension means and entails.

Dimensions	Explanation
Gravitas (how you act)	Your executive presence is an important aspect of how you act. A positive executive presence involves: • Displaying confidence • Being authentic • Demonstrating empathy • Being open to change • Having a clear vision • Communicating clearly • Empowering and motivating others • Being resilient and displaying courage in the face of challenges • Upholding your values in every action
Influence (how you work)	Influencing others positively involves the following actions: • **Rationalizing**: Leverage logic, facts, expertise, reasoning and experience to drive home your point. Do not rely on emotions or personal beliefs to influence others. • **Asserting**: Rely on your confidence and authority to influence others. Never resort to manipulation, unnecessary arguments, shaming or other negative methods of persuasion. • **Negotiating**: Be willing to make trade-offs to achieve an agreement and always look for a win–win situation where both parties benefit from an outcome. • **Inspiring**: Use inspiring stories and research to encourage people to work towards a common objective. • **Bridging**: Collaborate, engage and consult with people to reach a consensus.

Communication (how you speak)	Clear and confident communication is a critical aspect of developing a positive brand. Leaders need to be able to get their ideas across. • Establish an effective connection with people you are interacting with by being authentic, showing interest in what they have to say (smiling, nodding, maintaining eye contact), identifying common interests and being respectful. • Prepare and practice before you speak, especially when the audience is sizeable. • Ask various people their opinions about you—this will not only help you gain insights about others' perspectives about you, but it will also help build relationships. Make sure you obtain views from people across levels. • Share powerful stories. Stories always catch people's attention. Share appropriate personal anecdotes too; this will make you relatable to others.

We must also understand that our personal brand is an amalgamation of how we see ourselves and how others see us. It is important that these two aspects align with each other in order to achieve authenticity. Following the above framework will help you avoid any discrepancies. Remember, while the above structure is a broad roadmap for you to build a meaningful legacy for yourself, there is no ONE success formula. Your blueprint for brand-building will depend on your line of work, your work environment, your support structure and more. One ingredient is universal—identifying and developing your USP. So, analyse your personality, passions and strengths and identify what makes you different. Embrace your life story—it is unique to you.

Acknowledgements

I can give you myriad reasons why *Conversations with the Career Doctor* got written, but the simplest would be to say that I wanted to relive the amazing moments of thought exchange with the hundreds of women who have traversed my life. Some I advised, some advised me, and some just lived their life in a way that made me wonder how such grace could exist. In every city in India and around the world that I have had a chance to visit or work in, I have been deeply inspired by how women, holding multiple avatars and with it some incredible skills, have won impossible battles and thrived in ways that are quite ineffable. They are everyday women, like you and me. They are bold, confident, courageous, and lively, and in each, I have found reasons for why they are the best career doctors one could have.

I find it difficult not to admire every woman I get to meet. I am often asked why this is so. What is it about the working Indian woman that inspires such deep emotions in me? Is it perhaps that I see in every woman various aspects of my own thinking? Is it that I observe her actions through ages and stages? Is it that I witness divinity in her various roles? Yes. But there's

251

more. I see the Indian woman not just as a girl, a young woman, a mother, a wife or a professional but also as a grandmother. Yes, grandmother. Because, for me, my greatest inspiration was my maternal grandmother, Subbulakshmi Shankar, who lives within me and guides me to date.

My first memories of her are at her home in Bangalore, in the early 1970s, when as a three- or four-year-old, I would sleepily walk into her kitchen early in the morning and see her bustling about, wearing a crisp saree and a huge hair bun, making fragrant coffee, cooking breakfast and lunch (non-fancy, simple stuff) for the family and packing lunch for herself, as she prepared to go to work as headmistress of a school in Ulsoor. On some days, I would accompany her to school, sitting in the passenger seat and watching her with open-mouthed awe as she drove her Herald. She was the first working woman of her family, who in the mid-1950s, moved to the strange far-away city of 'Bambai' from a sleepy hamlet called Thirumangalam near Madurai. She was my first Career Doctor, the one with whom I have had endless conversations on marriage, work, business, parenting and just living. Till her death in 2015, she maintained a wall of my press cuttings, featuring interviews or articles. Every curious guest in her home would be given a detailed tour, featuring highlights about Avtar and me. Besides teaching me that it was right to aspire for a better life for yourself while still being a great support to every member of your family, she also taught me the need to build a network of women who stand for you, stand by you and help you succeed. Aunty (we used to call her that), I love you and hope that you are proud of this book.

To my mother Shantha Chandrasekar—a complete antithesis of her mom, in the nicest, sweetest, most calming way possible—who has been the most resilient woman I have ever seen. Her amazing discipline, her ability to draw diverse people into her fold and her holding her own between two impossibly strong people in her life—her mother and her husband—Amma, you took the cards dealt to you and made them a winning hand. I feel so proud to be your daughter.

To my father, who believed in the power of women and pushed my sister and me to succeed, while anchoring us in the concept of surrender to the divine will. You are no longer with us in physical form, Appa, but whenever I see intentionality, I see you.

To my husband Rajesh, whose nuanced understanding of me has become my biggest source of strength, my grateful thanks. You have journeyed with me, all these years, offering your reflection, your views and values, but never once insisted that I follow them. I know how much you have changed for me and I deeply respect that. Here's to more decades of mutual allyship!

To my sister Jayapriya—my soulmate, my partner-in-crime and the one I go to for sage advice on some of the quirkiest stuff that life is made of—love you Pilloo. I hope to do those journeys and trips we constantly dream of.

To my son, Akshey, who has been a huge cheerleader of my work and an amazing conversationalist himself, to my daughter-in-law Rajshree, whose awesome intellect and intentionality never cease to inspire me, and my darling granddaughter Adhvaitha, to whom I hope to be even a fraction of the kind of Patti that I myself had.

To my daughter, Shivangi, whose all-consuming focus and positive energy towards anything she sets her mind to, are the stuff of dreams, and to Adithya, my son-in-law, whose world view informs my own and from whom I am learning lots.

To my leadership team at Avtar—Umasanker Kandaswamy, Karthik Ekambaram, Priya Dayabaran, Eswar Bala and Roy Vijaykumar—you are amazing contributors to this book by way of your own experiences and your learnings, which you share with generosity.

To Divya Ramesh, senior manager, project management office at Avtar, whose empathy, brilliant work ethic and uncanny ability to magically comprehend what I am trying to say, and tweak that sentence in some tiny way to elevate it so beautifully—manifold thanks! You are a veritable example of how Indian women—the winners, the champions—succeed by gorgeously integrating work and life and yet, stay true to their passion and definition of their own identity!

To Radhika Marwah of Penguin Random House India for her wonderful partnership throughout the creation of this book and to Aparna Abhijit for her meticulous editing.

To the fabulous industry experts who are also advisers to Avtar—Bhavani Balasubramanian, Lalitha Balakrishnan, Kannan Hariharan, Sriram P., Amita Kasbekar, Tammy Redpath, Keshav Prasad and Bhaskar Prasad—the jury is still out as to who enjoys the others' company more, you or Avtar!

To the set of incredible women leaders at Avtar—Veena Mukund, Anju G. Parvathy, Usha Pillai, Shankari Nandi, Rashmi Ravindran, Lakshmi Vijaykumar, Sridevi Bharadwaj, Nandini Murali, Janani Sampath and Swetha Lakshmi Narayanan who are my extraordinary circle of support and encouragement.

To my amazing team of researchers and content developers—Athira Premarajan, Hima Elizabeth Mathew, Janani Sampath and Sumona Chetia, whose solid secondary research, attention to detail and efficiency in managing tight schedules greatly helped me in my writing process.

To the recruitment team at Avtar that works tirelessly to help scores of Indian woman professionals build enriching and fulfilling careers for themselves.

To the Avtar sales and marketing teams that work with unflagging energy to enhance our reputation and amplify our outreach.

To Vidhya Rajan and Abraham Pradeep, for just all that they do to make life easier for me!

To the women featured in this book—Subha Barry, Jo Keiko Terasawa, Geetha Ramamoorthi, Anuradha Sriram, Sheenam Ohrie, Naila Choudhry, Dr Tara Thiagarajan, Vibhuti Lall, Leena Nair and Sandhya Vasudevan, who readily contributed valuable insights, both directly and through their interviews and quotes, greatly enhancing the value of this book.

To my male allies showcased in the book—C.K. Kumaravel, Raman Ramachandran and Pavan Mocherla, who dedicated time in their hectic schedule to candidly share their experiences and learnings.

And finally, to my Divine Mother, Goddess Abhirami of Thirukkadaiyur, whose manifestation I see in every woman that I come across. It is you, Amma, I know, it is you. Seeking your blessings every day.

Notes

Introduction

1 Sher Verick, 'Women's labour force participation in India: Why is it so low?', ILO, 2014, https://www.ilo.org/wcmsp5/groups/public/---asia/---ro-bangkok/---sro-new_delhi/documents/genericdocument/wcms_342357.pdf.

2 Mitali Nikore, 'Where are India's working women? The fall and fall of India's female labour participation rate', LSE blog, 22 October 2019, https://blogs.lse.ac.uk/southasia/2019/10/22/where-are-indias-working-women-the-fall-and-fall-of-indias-female-labour-participation-rate/.

3 'Girls spend 160 million more hours than boys doing household chores every day', UNICEF, 7 October 2016, https://www.unicef.org/turkiye/en/node/2311#:~:text=NEW%20YORK%2C%207%20October%2C%202016,the%20Girl%20on%2011%20October.

4 'Labour force participation rate, female', World Bank, https://data.worldbank.org/indicator/SL.TLF.CACT.FE.ZS?end=2022&locations=IN&start=1990.

5 Saundarya Rajesh, Karthik Ekambaram, Anju G Parvathy et al., 'Tracking the career trajectories of men and women in India to assess career intentionality', AVTAR, 2015, https://www.avtarinc.com/wp-

content/uploads/2023/04/tracking-the-career-trajectories-of-men-and-women-in-india.pdf.

Chapter 1: Women's Careers—Is That Even a Thing?

1   Annette Dixon, 'Women in India's Economic Growth', World Bank, 16 March 2018, https://www.worldbank.org/en/news/speech/2018/03/17/women-indias-economic-growth.

Chapter 2: Identity of the Indian Woman Professional (IWP)

1   'National Family Health Survey-5', Ministry of Health and Family Welfare, Government of India, 22 September 2021, https://main.mohfw.gov.in/sites/default/files/NFHS-5_Phase-II_0.pdf.

2   Saundarya Rajesh, Karthik Ekambaram, Anju G Parvathy et al., 'Significance of careers to Indian women professionals: A socio-economic study', AVTAR, 2014, https://www.avtarinc.com/significance-of-careers-to-indian-women-professionals-a-socio-economic-study/.

Chapter 3: Pursuing a Career Is Not Selfish, It Is Patriotism

1   Press Trust of India, 'WEF: Gender parity can boost India's GDP by 27%, says IMF Chief, Norway PM', *Business Standard*, 21 January 2018, https://www.business-standard.com/article/economy-policy/wef-gender-parity-can-boost-india-s-gdp-by-27-says-imf-chief-norway-pm-118012100213_1.html.

2   Jonathan Woetzel, Anu Madgavkar, Rajat Gupta, James Manyika, Kweilin, Shishir Gupta and Mekala Krishnan, 'The Power of Parity: Advancing Women's Equality in India', McKinsey Global Institute, 1 November 2015, https://www.mckinsey.com/featured-insights/employment-and-growth/the-power-of-parity-advancing-womens-equality-in-india.

3   Yang Yang, Tanya Y. Tian, Teresa Woodruff, Benjamin F. Jones and Brian Uzzi, 'Gender-Balanced Teams Do Better Work', Kellogg Insight, https://insight.kellogg.northwestern.edu/article/gender-diversity-successful-teams.

4   Vidya Mahambare and Sowmya Dhanaraj, 'Marriage has a significant link in urban India with women's work', *Mint*, 19 February 2023, https://www.livemint.com/opinion/columns/marriage-has-a-significant-link-in-urban-india-with-women-s-work-11676812472445.html.

Chapter 4: The Three Routes to a Successful Career

1   Alex Katsomitros, 'Against the odds: Ursula Burns' extraordinary rise to the top', World of Finance, https://www.worldfinance.com/markets/against-the-odds-ursula-burns-extraordinary-rise-to-the-top.

Chapter 5: Intentional Career Pathing (ICP)©

1   Saundarya Rajesh, Karthik Ekambaram, Anju G Parvathy et al., 'Tracking the Career Trajectories of Men and Women', AVTAR, 2015, https://www.avtarinc.com/tracking-the-career-trajectories-of-men-and-women/.

Chapter 6: Finding Your Ideal Job

1   Saundarya Rajesh, Subha V. Barry, et al., 'Best Companies for Women in India and Most Inclusive Companies Index', AVTAR and Seramount, 2023, https://www.avtarinc.com/wp-content/uploads/2023/11/Avtar-Yearbook-2023-Nov-14.pdf.

Chapter 7: Home or Career—Which Should You Choose?

1   Saundarya Rajesh, *The 99 Day Diversity Challenge* (New Delhi: Sage Publications India, 2018).
2   'National Family Health Survey-5', Ministry of Health and Family Welfare, Government of India, 22 September 2021, https://main.mohfw.gov.in/sites/default/files/NFHS-5_Phase-II_0.pdf.
3   Diva Dhar, 'Indian matchmaking: Are working women penalized in the marriage market?', National Data Innovation Centre, https://ndic.ncaer.org/indian-matchmaking-are-working-women-penalized-in-the-marriage-market/, last accessed 4 January 2024.

4 Dina Gerdeman, 'Kids of Working Moms Grow into Happy Adults', Harvard Business School Working Knowledge, 16 July 2018, https://hbswk.hbs.edu/item/kids-of-working-moms-grow-into-happy-adults.

5 Sylvia Ann Hewlett, Melinda Marshall and Laura Sherbin, 'How Diversity Can Drive Innovation, *Harvard Business Review* (December 2013), https://hbr.org/2013/12/how-diversity-can-drive-innovation.

6 Andreas Schleicher, 'Girls better at cooperating on problems', BBC, 21 November 2017, https://www.bbc.com/news/education-42018274.

7 'Gender equality and poverty are intrinsically linked', UN Women, 2018, https://www.unwomen.org/en/digital-library/publications/2018/12/discussion-paper-gender-equality-and-poverty-are-intrinsically-linked, last accessed 4 January 2024.

8 Kathleen McGinn, Mayra Ruiz Castro, Elizabeth Long Lingo, 'Having a Working Mother Is Good For You, *Harvard Business School Press Release*, 18 May 2015, https://www.hbs.edu/news/releases/Pages/having-working-mother.aspx.

9 Jad Chaaban, Wendy Cunningham, 'Measuring the Economic Gain of Investing in Girls, World Bank, August 2011, https://documents1.worldbank.org/curated/en/730721468326167343/pdf/WPS5753.pdf.

10 NPR, 'Michelle Obama talks parenting, partnership and turning your rage into change', YouTube video, 15 November 2022, https://www.youtube.com/watch?v=H_-iU6AW1c0.

11 Ibid.

12 Sheryl Sandberg, 'Why we have too few women leaders', TED, December 2010, https://www.ted.com/talks/sheryl_sandberg_why_we_have_too_few_women_leaders/transcript?hasSummary=true&language=en.

Chapter 9: Superwoman Syndrome

1 Arlie Russell Hochschild, *The Second Shift* (New Delhi: Penguin Books, 2012).

2 'Men enjoy five hours more leisure time per week than women', Office for National Statistics, UK, 9 January 2018, https://www.ons.gov.uk/peoplepopulationandcommunity/wellbeing/articles/menenjoyfivehoursmoreleisuretimeperweekthanwomen/2018-01-09.

Chapter 10: Housewives and Feminists

1   Kelly Beaver, 'One in three men believe feminism does more harm than good', Ipsos, 4 March 2022, https://www.ipsos.com/en/one-three-men-believe-feminism-does-more-harm-good.

2   Kathy Caprino, 'What Is Feminism, And Why Do So Many Women And Men Hate It?', *Forbes*, 8 March 2017, https://www.forbes.com/sites/kathycaprino/2017/03/08/what-is-feminism-and-why-do-so-many-women-and-men-hate-it/?sh=3717f5eb7e8e.

3   'Women @ Work 2022: A Global Outlook', Deloitte, 2022, https://www.deloitte.com/global/en/issues/work/women-at-work-global-outlook-2022.html, last accessed 4 January 2024.

4   Emine Saner, '"The woman's to-do list is relentless": how to achieve an equal split of household chores', *Guardian*, 15 August 2022, https://www.theguardian.com/money/2022/aug/15/how-to-achieve-an-equal-split-of-household-chores-kate-mangino.

5   Saundarya Rajesh, Karthik Ekambaram, Anju G Parvathy, et al., 'Chore division & dynamics at Indian homes: an exploratory research during covid times', AVTAR, 2021, https://www.avtarinc.com/viewport-2021-chore-division-dynamics-at-indian-homes-an-exploratory-research-during-covid-times/.

6   'Without investment, gender equality will take nearly 300 years: UN Report', United Nations, 7 September 2022, https://news.un.org/en/story/2022/09/1126171.

Chapter 11: The Work Family

1   Saundarya Rajesh, Subha V. Barry, et al., 'Best Companies for Women in India and Most Inclusive Companies Index', AVTAR and Seramount, 2023, https://www.avtarinc.com/wp-content/uploads/2023/11/Avtar-Yearbook-2023-Nov-14.pdf.

Chapter 12: Upskilling: Your Passport to a Recession-Resistant Career

1   Alison Beard, 'IBM's Ginni Rometty on Skill-Building and Success', *Harvard Business Review IdeaCast*, 7 March 2023, https://hbr.

org/podcast/2023/03/ibms-ginni-rometty-on-skill-building-and-success.

Chapter 13: Women and STEM

1   Henry Etzkowitz and Marina Ranga, 'Gender Dynamics in Science and Technology: From the "Leaky Pipeline" to the "Vanish Box"', *Brussels Economic Review* 54 (2011), https://www.researchgate.net/publication/227379745_Gender_Dynamics_in_Science_and_Technology_From_the_Leaky_Pipeline_to_the_Vanish_Box.

2   'UNESCO Science Report 2021: Share of women among total researchers by country, 1996–2018 (%)', UNESCO, 2021, https://www.unesco.org/reports/science/2021/en/dataviz/share-women-researchers-radial.

3   Janet Hyde et al., 'Females are equal to males in math skills, large study shows', ScienceDaily, 13 October 2010, https://www.sciencedaily.com/releases/2010/10/101011223927.htm.

4   Stacy W. Kish, 'Study Finds Girls and Boys Have Equal Math Ability', Carnegie Mellon University, 8 November 2019, https://www.cmu.edu/dietrich/psychology/news/2019/cantlon-math.html.

5   'Report on women in STEM', CII, January 2023, https://www.ciitechnology.in/pdf/report-on-women-in-stem.pdf.

6   'Women's employment in manufacturing, operations, and engineering services sector – an exploratory research by GE and Avtar', AVTAR, 2021, https://www.avtarinc.com/womens-employment-in-manufacturing-operations-and-engineering-services-sector-an-exploratory-research-by-ge-and-avtar/.

7   'KPMG study finds 75% of female executives across industries have experienced imposter syndrome in their careers', KPMG, 7 October 2023, https://info.kpmg.us/news-perspectives/people-culture/kpmg-study-finds-most-female-executives-experience-imposter-syndrome.html.

Chapter 14: Ambition—A Bad Word in a Woman's Life?

1   Sheryl Sandberg, 'Sheryl Sandberg: Let's Stop Calling Strong Women "Bossy"', *Cosmopolitan*, 8 March 2014, https://www.cosmopolitan.com/career/advice/a5891/sheryl-sandberg-ban-bossy/.

2   'Girls outperform boys in academic achievements globally', *Deccan Herald*, 27 January 2015, https://www.deccanherald.com/archives/girls-outperform-boys-academic-achievements-2108653.

3   Kris Holland and PA Media, 'Cambridge study finds girls outperform boys at school', BBC News, 15 January 2024, https://www.bbc.com/news/uk-england-cambridgeshire-67935359.

Chapter 16: Women and Transitions

1   Devanik Saha, '97% of Indians migrating for marriage are female', IndiaSpend, 15 December 2016, https://www.indiaspend.com/97-of-indians-migrating-for-marriage-are-female-36602/#:~:text=That%20observation%20is%20echoed%20in,the%20US%2C%20Germany%20and%20Canada.

Chapter 17: When Is It Time for a Career Break?

1   Mahalia Mayne, 'Career breaks stifling women's confidence at work, study finds', People Management, 20 October 2022, https://www.peoplemanagement.co.uk/article/1802711/career-breaks-stifling-womens-confidence-work-study-finds.

2   Sheryl Sandberg, 'Why we have too few women leaders', TED, December 2010, https://www.ted.com/talks/sheryl_sandberg_why_we_have_too_few_women_leaders/transcript?hasSummary=true&language=en.

Chapter 18: Starting Again

1   Saundarya Rajesh, Karthik Ekambaram, Anju G Parvathy, et al., 'Second careers of women professionals', AVTAR, 2019, https://www.avtarinc.com/second-careers-of-women-professionals/.

2   Shelley Correll, Stephan Benard, In Paik, 'Getting a Job: Is There a Motherhood Penalty?', Gender Action Portal, March 2007, https://gap.hks.harvard.edu/getting-job-there-motherhood-penalty#:~:text=Conversely%2C%20fathers%20were%20allowed%20to,recommended%20starting%20salary%20for%20fathers.

3 Carol Fishman Cohen, 'A New Way to Explain the Pause in Your Career', *Harvard Business Review*, 23 March 2022, https://hbr.org/2022/03/a-new-way-to-explain-the-pause-in-your-career.

4 Saundarya Rajesh, Subha V. Barry, et al., 'Best Companies for Women in India and Most Inclusive Companies Index', AVTAR and Seramount, 2022, https://www.avtarinc.com/wp-content/uploads/2023/11/Avtar-Yearbook-2023-Nov-14.pdf.

Chapter 19: The Muscle of Resilience

1 Saundarya Rajesh, Subha V. Barry, et al., 'Best Companies for Women in India and Most Inclusive Companies Index', AVTAR and Seramount, 2022, https://www.avtarinc.com/wp-content/uploads/2023/11/Avtar-Yearbook-2023-Nov-14.pdf.

Chapter 20: Understanding Microaggression

1 Varghese Punnoose et. al, 'Microaggressions and Strategies to Overcome Prejudice', *Indian Journal of Psychiatry* 64 (3) (2022): S640.

2 Diana Gueits, 'What Are Microaggressions?', *Cleveland Clinic*, 2 February 2022, https://health.clevelandclinic.org/what-are-microaggressions-and-examples/.

3 Ruchika Tulshyan, 'We Need to Retire the Term "Microaggressions"', *Harvard Business Review*, 8 March 2022, https://hbr.org/2022/03/we-need-to-retire-the-term-microaggressions.

4 'Women @ Work Report', Deloitte, 2022, https://www2.deloitte.com/content/dam/Deloitte/in/Documents/about-deloitte/in-about-deloitte-women-at-work-India-noexp.pdf.

5 Leslie Shore, 'Gal Interrupted, Why Men Interrupt Women And How To Avert This In The Workplace', *Forbes*, 3 January 2017, https://www.forbes.com/sites/womensmedia/2017/01/03/gal-interrupted-why-men-interrupt-women-and-how-to-avert-this-in-the-workplace/?sh=6be8056817c3.

6 'Catalyst Workplace Survey Reveals Optimism About Gender Equity During Covid-19, but Skepticism on Commitment of Companies',

Catalyst, 30 June 2020, https://www.catalyst.org/media-release/ workplace-gender-equity-covid-19/#:~:text=1%20in%205%20 women%20has,the%20outbreak%20of%20Covid%2D19.

Chapter 21: How Safe Are You?

1   'National Family Health Survey-5', Ministry of Health and Family Welfare, Government of India, 22 September 2021, https://main. mohfw.gov.in/sites/default/files/NFHS-5_Phase-II_0.pdf.

2   Mansi Jaswal, 'Shikha Mittal: Victim-turned-entrepreneur combats sexual harassment at workplace', Livemint, 8 March 2023, https://www. livemint.com/news/india/shikha-mittal-victim-turned-entrepreneur- combats-sexual-harassment-at-workplace-11678237921220.html.

3   Heather Mclaughlin, Christopher Uggen and Amy Blackstone, 'The Economic and Career Effects of Sexual Harassment on Working Women', *Sage Journals*, 10 May 2017, https://www.ncbi.nlm.nih.gov/ pmc/articles/PMC5644356/#:~:text=Using%20in%2Ddepth%20 interviews%20and,significantly%20alter%20women's%20career%20 attainment.

Chapter 22: Women and Mental Health

1   'Almost 20 million adults never speak about mental health – and it's set to get worse due to the cost-of-living crisis', Mind, 2 February 2023, https://mind.org.uk/news-campaigns/news/almost-20-million-adults- never-speak-about-mental-health-and-it-s-set-to-get-worse-due-to- the-cost-of-living-crisis/.

2   'How India Perceives Mental Health', Live, Love, Laugh Foundation, 2018, https://www.thelivelovelaughfoundation.org/initiatives/ research/how-india-perceives-mental-health.

3   James Ball, 'Women 40% more likely than men to develop mental illness, study finds', *Guardian*, 22 May 2013, https://www.theguardian. com/society/2013/may/22/women-men-mental-illness-study.

4   Inger Sandanger, Jan F. Nygard, Tom Sorensen, Torbjorn Moum, 'Is women's mental health more susceptible than men's to the influence of surrounding stress?', *Social Psychiatry and Psychiatric Epidemiology*

(March 2004), https://link.springer.com/article/10.1007/s00127-004-0728-6.

5   Savita Malhotra, Ruchita Shah, 'Women and mental health in India: An overview', *Indian Journal of Psychiatry* (July 2015), https://www.researchgate.net/publication/281517733_Women_and_mental_health_in_India_An_overview.

6   Jen Christensen, 'All around the world, women are better empathizers than men, study finds', CNN, 27 December 2022, https://edition.cnn.com/2022/12/26/health/empathy-women-men/index.html.

Chapter 23: The Boss Lady

1   Katharina Buchholz, 'How has the number of female CEOs in Fortune 500 companies changed over the last 20 years?', World Economic Forum, 10 March 2022, https://www.weforum.org/agenda/2022/03/ceos-fortune-500-companies-female.

2   'India sees more women in leadership roles but boardroom diversity progressing at a snail's pace', Deloitte, 8 February 2022, https://www2.deloitte.com/in/en/pages/risk/articles/India-sees-more-women-in-leadership-roles-but-boardroom-diversity-progressing-at-a-snails-pace.html.

3   'Share of women in leadership positions in India as of February 2022, by sector', Statista, February 2022, https://www.statista.com/statistics/1320259/india-share-of-females-in-leadership-positions-by-sector/#:~:text=According%20to%20a%20survey%20conducted,estate%20were%20held%20by%20women.

4   Jennifer Zell, Shawn Grimsley, 'Power Distance of Hofstede', Study.com video, 21 November 2023, https://study.com/learn/lesson/what-is-power-distance.html.

5   Satya Nadella, Greg Shaw and Jill Tracie Nichols, *Hit Refresh: The Quest to Rediscover Microsoft's Soul and Imagine a Better Future for Everyone* (Noida: HarperCollins, 2017).

6   Tim Cook, 'Tim Cook Speaks Up', Bloomberg, 31 October 2014, https://www.bloomberg.com/news/articles/2014-10-30/tim-cook-speaks-up#xj4y7vzkg.

Chapter 24: Becoming Money Smart

1   Dr Kate Levinson, *Emotional Currency: A Woman's Guide to Building a Healthy Relationship with Money* (India: Celestial Arts, 2011).
2   Saundarya Rajesh, Karthik Ekambaram, Anju G Parvathy, et al., 'Economic centredness of Indian women professionals', AVTAR, 2014, https://www.avtarinc.com/economic-centeredness-of-indian-women-professionals-2/.

Chapter 25: Women's Role in Gender Inclusion

1   Tom Stafford, 'Psychology: Why bad news dominates the headlines', BBC, 29 July 2014, https://www.bbc.com/future/article/20140728-why-is-all-the-news-bad.
2   Chris Irvine, 'Women find working for female bosses more stressful', *Telegraph*, 23 September 2008, https://www.telegraph.co.uk/news/3064811/Women-find-working-for-female-bosses-more-stressful.html.
3   Allison Gabriel, 'Incivility at Work: Is "Queen Bee Syndrome" Getting Worse?', University of Arizona, 19 February 2018, https://news.arizona.edu/story/incivility-work-queen-bee-syndrome-getting-worse.
4   Cristian L. Dezső, David Gaddis Ross, Jose Uribe, 'A Hidden Quota for Women in Top Management', Robert H. Smith School of Business, 25 March 2015, https://www.rhsmith.umd.edu/news/hidden-quota-women-top-management#:~:text=The%20article%20found%20evidence%20of,about%2050%20percent%2C%20in%20fact.
5   Brian Uzzi, 'Research: Men and Women Need Different Kinds of Networks to Succeed', *Harvard Business Review*, 25 February 2019, https://hbr.org/2019/02/research-men-and-women-need-different-kinds-of-networks-to-succeed.

Scan QR code to access the
Penguin Random House India website